The ASSOCIATED PRESS GUIDE to INTERNET RESEARCH and REPORTING

Also by THE ASSOCIATED PRESS

The Associated Press Stylebook and Briefing on Media Law

The ASSOCIATED PRESS GUIDE to INTERNET RESEARCH and REPORTING

Frank Bass

PERSEUS
PUBLISHING
Cambridge, Massachusetts

Perseus Publishing is a member of the Perseus Books Group.

Perseus Publishing books are available at special discounts for bulk purchases in the U.S. by corporations, institutions, and other organizations. For more information, please contact the Special Markets Department at the Perseus Books Group, 11 Cambridge Center, Cambridge, MA 02142, or call (617) 252-5298.

Library of Congress Control Number: 2001098300
ISBN 0-7382-0533-8

Text design by Jane Raese
Set in 10-point ITC Century Book

1 2 3 4 5 6 7 8 9 10—04 03 02 01

First printing

Find Perseus Publishing on the World Wide Web at
http://www.perseuspublishing.com

CONTENTS

The ASSOCIATED PRESS GUIDE to INTERNET RESEARCH and REPORTING

CHAPTER ONE

Introduction

More than a century ago, Alexander Graham Bell made his fateful call, "Watson, come here! I need you." It marked not just the beginning of a new era in person-to-person communications, but also the beginning of a new era in journalism. Reporters at first were hesitant to exploit the new technology, but the jangling telephone quickly became as much a sound of the newsroom as the clattering teletype or hypertensive editor.

At this dawn of the new century, reporters have access to tools that would have made Watson cringe. Entire encyclopedias are available at a keystroke, thousands of pages of financial documents can be downloaded in a minute, and sources on the other side of the globe can be reached in a matter of milliseconds. The clicking of the computer keyboard has become as much a sound of the newsroom as the jangling telephone . . . or, of course, the hypertensive editor.

Despite the incredible change in tools over the past 100 years, however, the basic rules of reporting still apply:

> Accuracy is foremost; get it right. Fairness. And speed.
> Clear and concise writing.
> And yes, grammar, spelling, and punctuation still count.

Journalism hasn't changed; only the tools have. And while some journalists have maintained a certain sense of denial about the need to master new technology, few journalists long for a return to the old days and the old tools.

When did all these tools become available? Although it probably seems like it happened only yesterday, newsgathering techniques have been evolving over a period of decades. Strictly speaking, journalists entered the computer age in 1952, when television news reporters experimented with computers—CBS used a room-sized UNIVAC—to cover the Eisenhower–Stevenson presidential race.

It was another decade, though, before journalists entered the online age. In the early 1960s, The Associated Press installed its first computers, IBM 1620s, to handle financial news and the stock market report. AP installed its first CRTs (cathode ray tubes or display units), Hendrix model 5200s and 3400s, in 1972. *The New York Times* placed its abstracts on computers in 1971; the *Louisville* (Ky.) *Courier-Journal* and *Detroit Free Press* followed suit shortly after. In 1972, Dialog was created as an online collection of databases, primarily as a research tool for business and academia. The following year, the Mead Corporation started Lexis, a research tool for lawyers. Before the advent of the Lexis service, reporters who wanted to get information out of lawsuits had to do it the old-fashioned way: Go to the courthouse, or worse, the law library. Lexis didn't eliminate those trips entirely, primarily because it was a service geared to a law firm budget, not a newsroom budget. Still, it made it possible for reporters to look at lawsuits across a state or even a region, without having to leave the newsroom.

Reporters, then, could save time, if they had a computer. But most didn't. The nationwide computer boom didn't officially start until 1977, when Apple, Radio Shack, and Commodore all released personal computers. That same year, Bill Gates and Paul Allen created Microsoft Corporation, which would quickly become the world's largest software company. The personal computer age hardly started auspiciously; Radio Shack's planned unveiling of its TRS–80 at a New York Stock Exchange press conference had to be scrapped when news broke that a bomb had exploded only a few blocks away. Some wags said the Commodore offering, the $495 Personal Electronic Transactor (PET), got its name because its marketers assumed that if people were dumb enough to purchase pet rocks, they'd buy a computer with the same name.

Within three years, however, computer use was rapidly spreading beyond the small subculture of computer programmers. CompuServe, an Ohio-based company created in 1969 as a computer time-sharing service, began offering e-mail and technical support to personal computer users. In 1980, it became the first online service to offer real-time chat online with its CB simulator. Computers proliferated rapidly in corporate America in 1979, after Software Arts Inc.'s VisiCalc, the first spreadsheet program, was released. IBM entered the PC business in 1981, which pulled the personal computer into the mainstream. That was followed in 1982 by the introduction of the successful Lotus 1–2–3 spreadsheet. The combination of the business applications, the rapidly expanding online presence, and a hit movie about a teen-age computer programmer who almost unleashes Armageddon by hacking into a Pentagon computer was reflected in increased media attention to the computer. In 1983, the personal computer won acclaim as *Time* magazine's "Person of the Year."

By 1986, 30 million computers were being used in the United States—many of them in newsrooms. Journalists, however, primarily were using them only to write stories. It wasn't until 1988, when the large newspaper chain Knight-Ridder acquired Dialog, that reporters began to use computers to do online research. Suddenly, newsroom researchers had stopped talking about morgues—libraries for old, "dead" news—and were beginning to talk about online resources.

Even so, online research in newsrooms faced an uphill battle. A reporter looking for a specific lawsuit or latest Securities and Exchange Commission filing could spend hundreds of dollars quite easily. Online research had become available, but that didn't always make it affordable, especially for many newsroom budgets.

> *"It's like the world's biggest library—except all the books are on the floor."*
>
> *"It's like a shopping mall after an earthquake."*
>
> **—Descriptions of the Internet**

The Internet

The Internet, ubiquitous in newsrooms today, didn't become an indispensable free research tool for journalists until the late 1990s. Its origins go back nearly four decades, when the former Soviet Union launched an unmanned satellite called Sputnik that was viewed as a threat to U.S. nuclear superiority. In the wake of national concern over Sputnik, the seeds for massive computer networks were sown, especially at the Massachusetts Institute of Technology, where researchers proposed a "galactic network."

The proposal was noticed by the Advanced Research Projects Agency (ARPA, the forerunner of the agency that would later be placed in charge of developing a nationwide space-based missile defense system), which began tinkering with computer networks. One of the major drawbacks to fighting a nuclear war, as the Pentagon saw it, would be the destruction of the military's command-and-control capabilities. Once missiles began flying, it would be extremely difficult for military commanders to communicate with each other and formulate a response to an enemy attack. Presumably, the nation's communications networks would be rendered inoperable by the magnetic aftereffects of nuclear explosions. To retain those command-and-control capabilities, the Pentagon decided, it needed a large computer network that wouldn't be dependent on one or two or even three machines.

Of course, it was a long jump from a network conceived by the military and nurtured by academia to the World Wide Web. It took the Pentagon nearly seven years from the time it noticed the "galactic network" proposal to the time that four "nodes" of the ARPANET, the first wide-area network and precursor to the Internet, were established at Stanford Research Institute, UCLA, the University of California at Santa Barbara, and the University of Utah. Once started, though, the network took on a life of its own. Within three years, e-mail—the first "killer application" of the Internet—had been introduced. Within months of its availability, e-mail accounted for 75 percent of usage among the Internet's 2,000 users. Queen Elizabeth II sent out the first royal e-mail in 1976. Researchers followed the e-mail development shortly with listservs, which allowed users to share e-mails of common interest, and FTP (file transfer protocol) sites, which let users download files.

Restricted to a handful of universities in its infancy, the Internet took off in academia in 1981 with the creation of BITNET, the "Because It's Time NETwork" created at the City University of New York, and the CSNET (Computer Science NETwork) shared by researchers in Delaware, Indiana, Wisconsin, and California. In 1984, researchers introduced the "domain name system," which allowed users to find other computers by name rather than by number. By 1987, there were 10,000 host computers on the Internet; two years later, there were 100,000 host computers on the Internet.

Very few of those host computers, however, could be found in newsrooms. Most editors were still waiting for a cost-efficient method of online research to materialize. Although a new organization, the Missouri Institute for Computer-Assisted Reporting, had been created at the University of Missouri in 1989, it was heavily oriented to reporters who were analyzing government data from tapes rather than online data. And while saving newsroom budgets wasn't exactly what Tim Berners-Lee, a software engineer, had in mind in 1989 with his proposal to create a web, or "mesh," it ultimately had that effect.

Berners-Lee, a trained physicist, was working at the European Particle Physics Laboratory (CERN in the French acronym) and was frustrated by a condition common to newsrooms and other large organizations: As people left the organization, they took information with them. "Often, the information has been recorded, it just cannot be found," he wrote. To remedy that, Berners-Lee proposed a large hypertext database that would link the laboratory's documents.

The idea was approved by CERN, and in 1990, Berners-Lee wrote the "WorlDwidEweb" program, a hypertext editor running on his NeXT computer. That same year, the first commercial Internet Service Provider (ISP) was launched, as well as Prodigy, a joint online venture of Sears & Roebuck, CBS, and IBM. The first remotely operated machine—a toaster—was connected to the Internet in 1990. The next year, the National Science Foundation, which had essentially taken over the "backbone," or infrastructure, of the Internet, lifted the ban on its commercial use. In 1992, the term "surfing the Internet" was coined by Jean Armour Polly, a New York librarian.

Still, the Internet was widely seen as the province of computer programmers—until Mosaic, the first graphical point-and-click interface, was created in 1993 by Mark Andreeson at the National Center for Supercomputing Applications. To say the browser was a success would be an understatement; traffic on the Internet began growing at a 341,634 percent annual rate. Andreeson and his development team left NCSA and released Netscape's Navigator in late 1994. (Microsoft, which was in the process of becoming the world's dominant software company, didn't enter the browser wars until 1995.)

In 1996, one of the last major barriers to widespread use of the Internet in newsrooms fell: America Online, then an 11-year-old company, began offering a flat-rate access fee of $19.95 monthly. Prior to AOL's offer, many newsrooms had been reluctant to make full use of the Internet's potential because of the possibility of outrageous hourly fees. Though the AOL deal caused its network to become overwhelmed by users, it set the standard for other Internet service providers, which began offering flat-fee access as well. There were now approximately 40 million people on the Internet, and the number of Web sites had grown from 130 in June 1993 to 252,000 in June 1996. That number would skyrocket to 22.3 million by October 2000.

While virtually every U.S. newsroom now has access to the Internet in one way or another, the worldwide network is still evolving. Many newsrooms are replacing their old, dial-up modem connections that chugged along at 28.8 kilobytes per second or slower with high-speed cable, DSL, and T–1 lines capable of downloading huge documents in a matter of minutes. Some newsrooms are beginning to give their reporters wireless tools, such as handheld personal digital assistants (PDAs), for filing stories and doing research where there aren't any telephone lines. And others, recognizing that the new tools give their reporters freedom to work outside a standard newsroom, are turning them loose with new bureaus in offices closer to their sources—just never too far from the hypertensive editors.

CHAPTER TWO

Searching the Web

The first rule of Internet searching is fairly simple: Search if you must. Otherwise, guess.

Searching the Internet is hard work that's not always terribly productive. Sometimes, guessing is the better option and, fortunately, guessing is actually easier than it sounds.

Basically, there are two parts of most Internet addresses:

1. Prefix: If it exists—and it usually does—this is almost always www, short for World Wide Web.
2. Domain: This is the really important part. Usually, a domain name is the name of the business, organization, or institution (e.g., IBM, The AP, U.S. Census Bureau, or Harvard) followed by a dot, followed by the hierarchy designation, such as "com" for commercial, "org" for organization, "gov" for government, or "edu" for educational institution.

So let's say we used a search engine to try finding IBM's home page on the Internet. We enter IBM into the box. When we hit Search, we get 1.8 million returns, quite a few more than we really need. So what can you do to narrow it down? Try guessing.

You already know that a Web page URL (the address, short for uniform resource locator) starts with www, then a dot, then the domain name. Since the business name is IBM and it's a commercial entity, we're going to guess that the domain name is ibm.com. So the full address will be www.ibm.com.

Voila! You'll find what you're looking for.

But what if we're looking for something a little less specific—say, information about Propecia, a drug designed to reduce baldness. We could try http://www.propecia.com—and we'd find the manufacturer's description and ad copy. (The http stands for hypertext transfer protocol, used by browsers to connect to Web servers.)

If we want to dig a little deeper than a press release, we'd use an indexer.

Indexers

Probably the best place to start is with an indexer—which lists available categories containing relevant Web pages—such as http://www.yahoo.com (see Fig. 2.1).

On most indexes, there are categories listed to help narrow down a search. In this case, if we scroll down just a little bit, we can see that there's a link for "Health" sites: Click on the Drugs link under Health and we'll find a link to Specific Drugs and Medications. And if we go down far enough, we'll find Propecia.

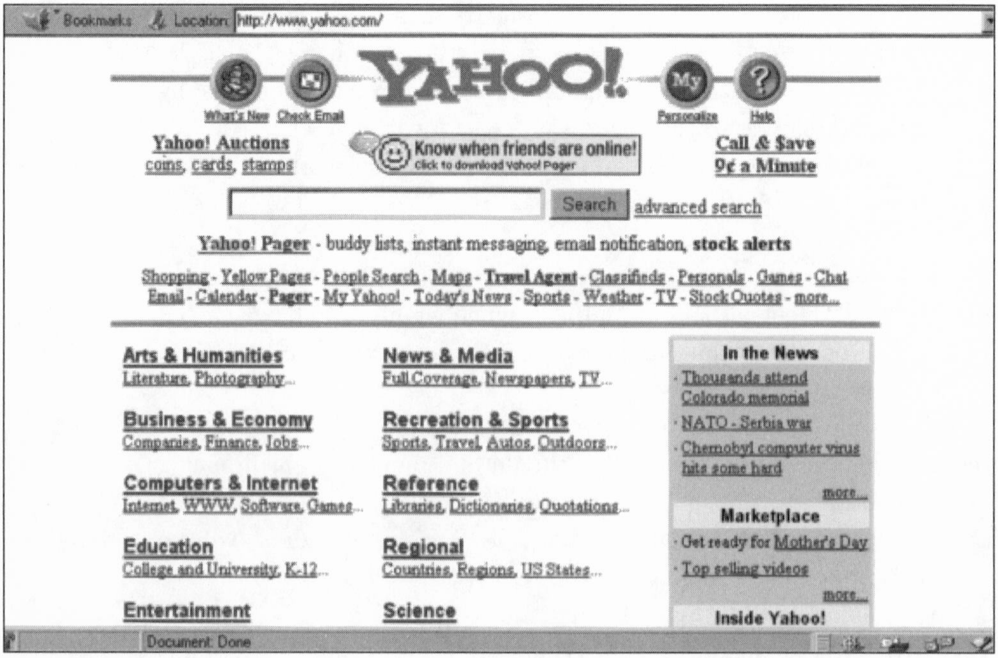

FIGURE 2.1

This gives us more diverse information about the drug. This sort of search is useful, but what if we need more specific information? What if you want to find the range of a Stinger missile? There's got to be a better way than sorting through Yahoo!, which is basically an index. The better approach is to use a search engine.

Search Engines

AltaVista.com and other sites such as HotBot.com and Excite.com are search engines that troll through their own databases to find keywords. A search engine is a program that looks for keywords in documents, sorts them, and returns a list to the user.

Let's go to AltaVista—http://www.altavista.com—and click on the "Advanced" link to the right (see Fig. 2.2).

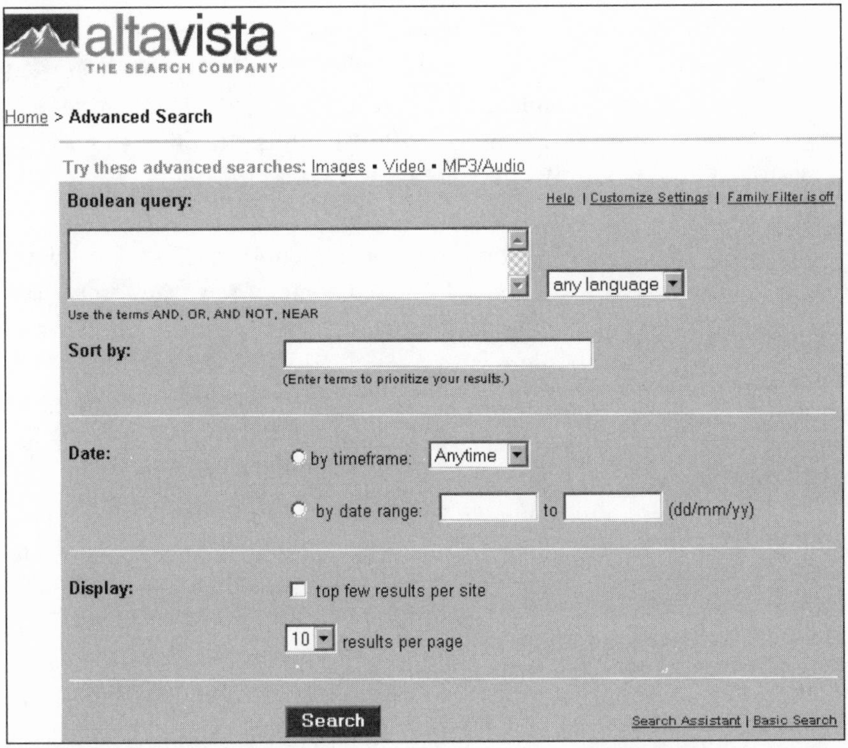

FIGURE 2.2

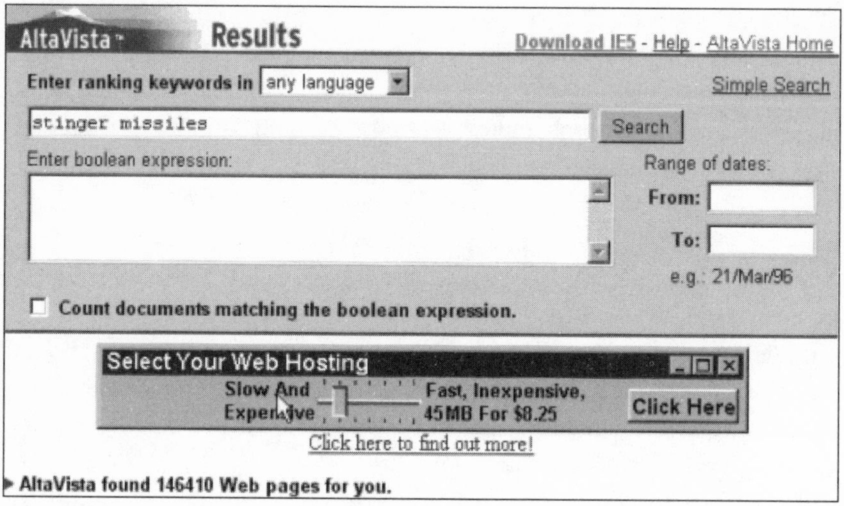

FIGURE 2.3

Now, let's type the words "stinger missiles" in the ranking keywords box and see what happens (see Fig. 2.3).

As you can see, we got 146,410 pages. That's a bit much. One general rule: Try doing an arcane search first. After all, that's the goal—you want to get as few hits as possible. And if you start out with an arcane search, it's a lot easier to go from one hit to 146,410 hits than it is to go from 146,410 hits to one hit. (An "arcane" search refers to complex query language, which uses plus signs and other symbols in the search query.)

But first, let's try narrowing it down using another trick. If you look closely at the search results, you'll see that some of the pages don't have the exact phrase "stinger missiles" in them. They have the word "stinger" and the word "missile," but not as two adjacent words. So let's narrow things down by telling AltaVista to look only for pages that have the exact phrase "stinger missiles" in them. We do that by typing the words in quotation marks in the query box.

This results in a pretty huge improvement—from 146,410 hits to 634. But as a rule of thumb, you're not through searching until you're down to a dozen or fewer hits. So let's use another trick: Boolean logic. Essentially, Boolean logic uses the search terms "and," "or," "not," and "near" to narrow down searches. For example, let's type "stinger" and "not (bee or wasp or hornet)" in the Boolean expression box. We put the Boolean term "or"—technically called an "operator"—in parentheses so that our search eliminates pages with any of the words "bee," "wasp," or "hornet." When we do this search, we narrow our results down to roughly 29,000.

Still, it's a few too many results. Let's go back to using "stinger missile" in quotation marks, but let's try another trick. We can add a domain type to limit our results. Remember, a commercial site is going to end in ".com." So we'll try putting a URL (Web address) limitation to return only commercial pages (see Fig. 2.4).

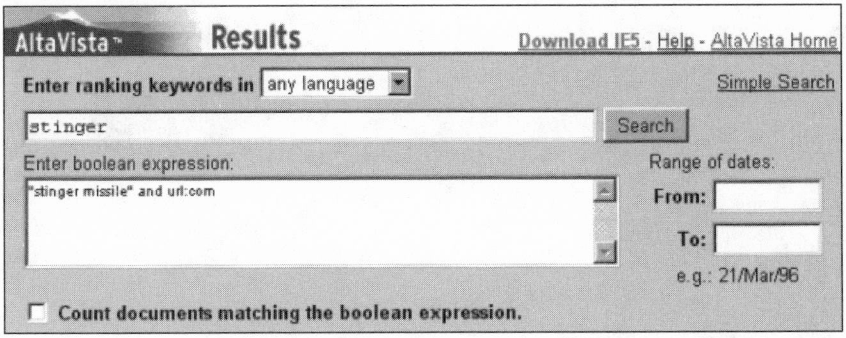

FIGURE 2.4

Now we're getting somewhere, narrowing our results down to 332 possible matches. As shown in Fig. 2.5, we can add another few words and change the ranking keyword to "range" to narrow things down even more.

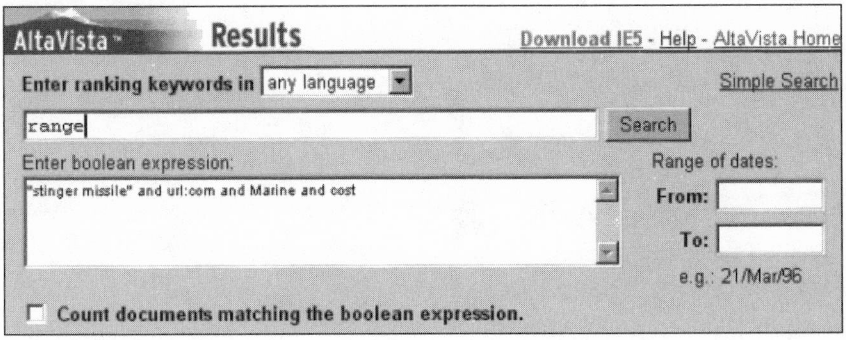

FIGURE 2.5

When we do, we're down to 15 hits (see Fig. 2.6).

In Fig. 2.7 we've added just a few more keywords.

So from our initial search results of 146,410 hits, we've focused in on a single Web page that contains the specific information we were looking for (see Fig. 2.8).

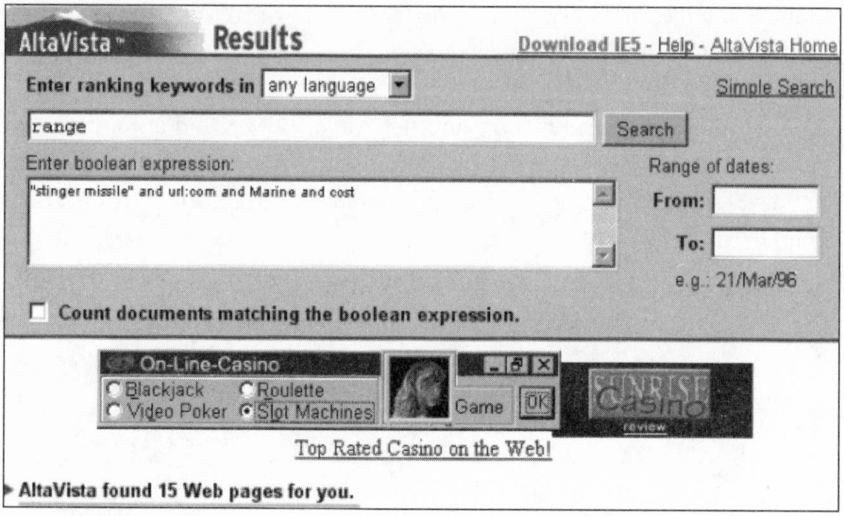

FIGURE 2.6

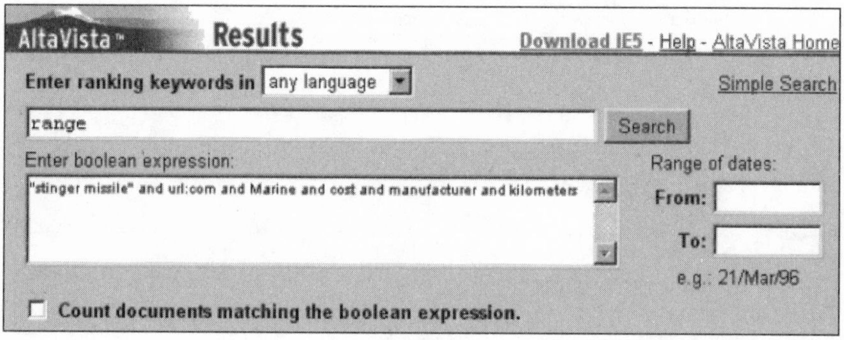

FIGURE 2.7

And when we open up the page, as shown in Fig. 2.9, we find that the range of the Stinger missile is one to eight kilometers.

A few other search tips: AltaVista isn't the only search engine. Perhaps the best search engine on the Internet is found at www.google.com. Google has more than 1 billion pages indexed.

One of the most appealing things about Google is its speed. Because it builds its search engine by pulling pages directly from the Web, it also caches, or stores, these Web pages. So instead of the dreaded "HTTP Error 404—File Not Found" page that reporters get when a page is no longer on the Web, you can click on the "Cached" link at the bottom of each

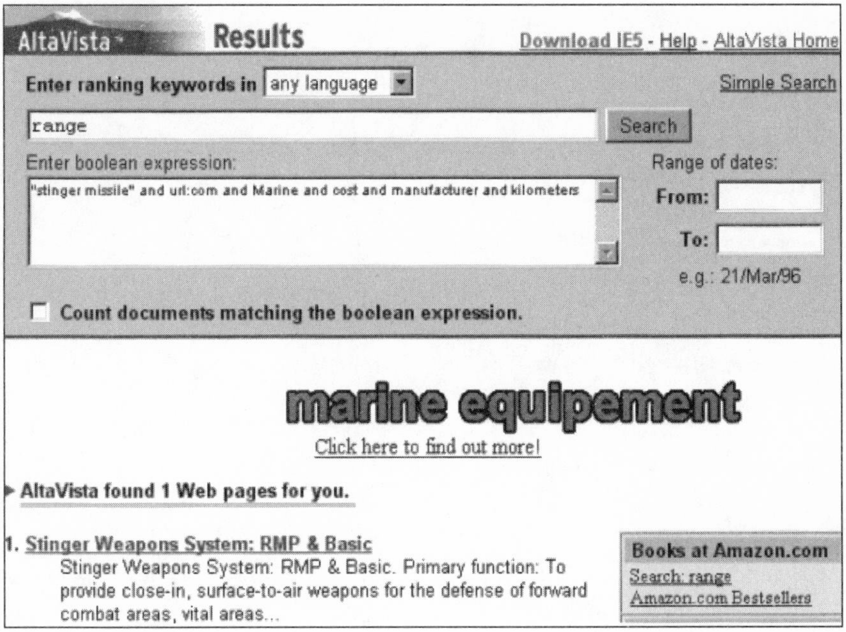
AltaVista
Results
Download IE5 - Help - AltaVista Home
Enter ranking keywords in any language
Simple Search
range
Search
Enter boolean expression:
"stinger missile" and url:com and Marine and cost and manufacturer and kilometers
Range of dates:
From:
To:
e.g.: 21/Mar/96
Count documents matching the boolean expression.
marine equipement
Click here to find out more!
AltaVista found 1 Web pages for you.
1. Stinger Weapons System: RMP & Basic
Stinger Weapons System: RMP & Basic. Primary function: To provide close-in, surface-to-air weapons for the defense of forward combat areas, vital areas...
Books at Amazon.com
Search: range
Amazon.com Bestsellers

FIGURE 2.8

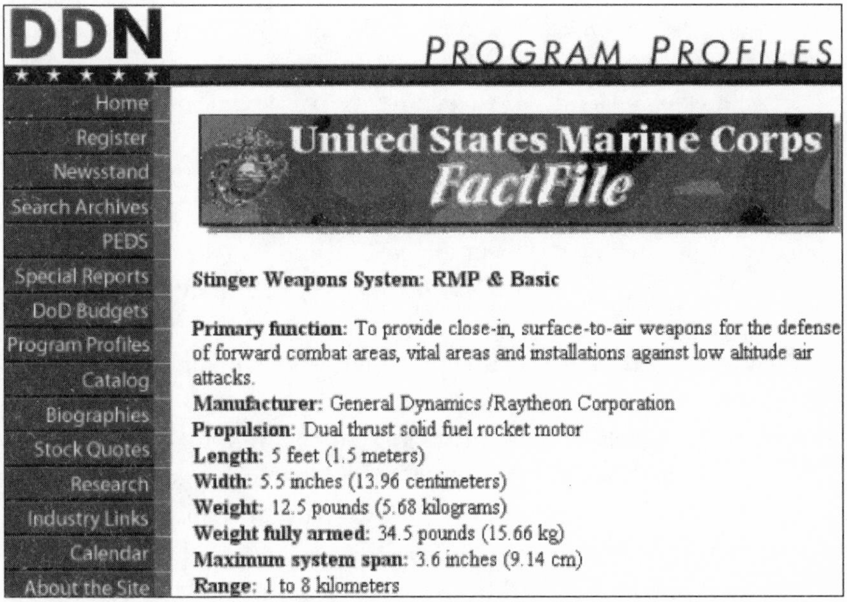
DDN
PROGRAM PROFILES
Home
Register
Newsstand
Search Archives
PEDS
Special Reports
DoD Budgets
Program Profiles
Catalog
Biographies
Stock Quotes
Research
Industry Links
Calendar
About the Site
United States Marine Corps
FactFile
Stinger Weapons System: RMP & Basic
Primary function: To provide close-in, surface-to-air weapons for the defense of forward combat areas, vital areas and installations against low altitude air attacks.
Manufacturer: General Dynamics /Raytheon Corporation
Propulsion: Dual thrust solid fuel rocket motor
Length: 5 feet (1.5 meters)
Width: 5.5 inches (13.96 centimeters)
Weight: 12.5 pounds (5.68 kilograms)
Weight fully armed: 34.5 pounds (15.66 kg)
Maximum system span: 3.6 inches (9.14 cm)
Range: 1 to 8 kilometers

FIGURE 2.9

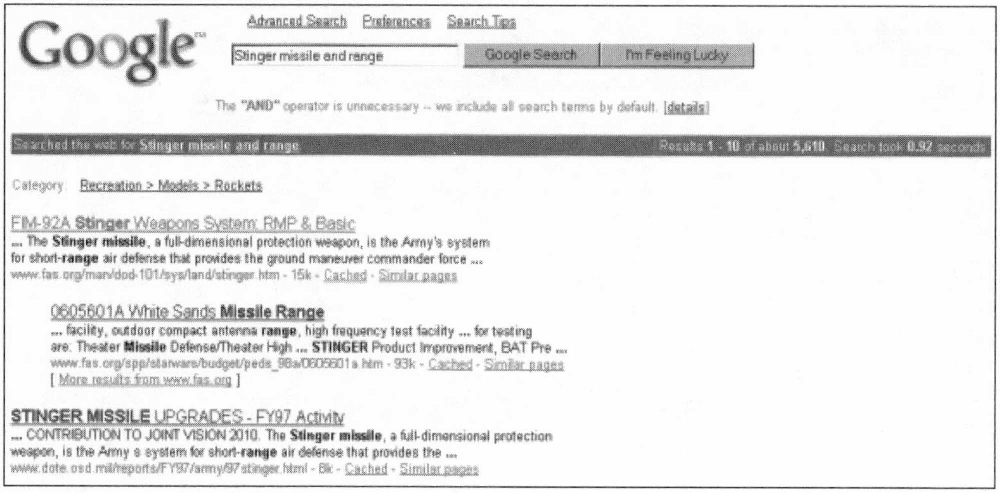

FIGURE 2.10

search result and get an old copy of the Web page. Let's try looking again for the range of a Stinger missile using Google (see Fig. 2.10).

The results page tells you three important things: First, that you got about 5,610 hits from the search. Second, that the page resulting from the search is cached, in case it's unavailable. And finally, that you got exactly what you were looking for. When we click on the very top link, we find a page that mentions the range of the Stinger (see Fig. 2.11).

Often, a Google search won't just return pages with the phrases that were used in the search; it will return pages with links to phrases that were used in the search.

Another comprehensive search engine can be found at www.hotbot.com. Its major drawback is its interface. Still, it does a perfectly good job of finding Web sites. Like AltaVista, HotBot also has an advanced search feature.

A few other Boolean tricks used in both HotBot and AltaVista:

1. If you know where something's located and want to search just that site, use the "host:" command. For example, if you knew that what you wanted was on the U.S. Census Bureau's site but weren't exactly sure just where it was, you could type "host:census.gov," in the Boolean query box and the search engine would just look at that page.

Specifications	
Primary function	To provide close-in, surface-to-air weapons for the defense of forward combat areas, vital areas and installations against low altitude air attacks.
Manufacturer	Prime - Hughes Missile System Company Missile - General Dynamics /Raytheon Corporation
Propulsion	Dual thrust solid fuel rocket motor
Length	5 feet (1.5 meters)
Width	5.5 inches (13.96 centimeters)
Weight	12.5 pounds (5.68 kilograms)
Weight fully armed	34.5 pounds (15.66 kg)
Maximum system span	3.6 inches (9.14 cm)
Range	1 to 8 kilometers
Sight ring	10 mils
Fuzing	Penetration, impact, self destruct
Ceiling	10,000 feet (3.046 kilometers)
Speed	Supersonic in flight

FIGURE 2.11

2. You can use the "link:" command to see who's linked their page to someone else's page.
3. You can also use the "image:" command to find pages for pictures.
4. You can also use an asterisk command as a wildcard. For example, if you know part of a word (but not the exact spelling), you can search using a wildcard. Slobo* Milo*, for instance, will get you information on Slobodan Milosevic.

Meta-Search Engines

We've talked about indexers and we've talked about search engines, but what about meta-search engines? They're basically multiple search engines, to be used when all others fail. Dogpile.com, for example, and Metacrawler use a number of common search engines to return multiple results. In general, meta-search engines should be used only as a last resort. As a rule, they return too many pages to be terribly useful for reporters trying to find specific information.

CHAPTER THREE

The World's Best Library

It's hard to imagine that less than a decade ago, reporters spent an inordinate amount of time trying to track down sources to give them basic information about a state agency, business, or person. Stories were held, deadlines were missed, and errors were made, all for want of good information.

Although the Internet hasn't solved every reporter's deadline problems, it's made the process of finding background information much easier and much quicker. Today, with a computer, some very basic knowledge, and a few mouse clicks, any reporter can use the Internet to get a broad range of reliable information.

The same reporter can use the Internet as a jumping-off point to find stories, talk with people around the planet, keep up with their beat, find out what's on people's minds, or simply ask better questions from sources.

For reporting purposes, there are three major components to the Internet: the World Wide Web, listservs, and newsgroups. In this chapter, we'll look at how reporters benefit from using the Web. At last count, there were more than 1 billion pages on the Web. Anyone who tries to keep a list of all the Web sites useful to reporters will discover quickly enough that there are too many, and that they change too often. Here, we'll just look at some that all reporters should know about.

Another note: Any reporter, given enough time and resources, can find a page on the Web, but it's a lot like calling directory information every time you need to make a telephone call—not terribly efficient. Although bookmarks on Web browsers can help, it's still difficult to transfer them from computer to computer. Often, it helps to just know the Web address (usually called a URL, or uniform resource locator).

Politics and Government

In any newsroom, the biggest number of reporters generally are going to be covering some form of politics or government, whether it's City Hall, the state legislature, a state agency, city department, or just plain politics. Even reporters who don't cover government or politics—those who report on the police, the courts, education, or environmental issues—are affected by politics and government. Sometimes, it seems that the business of most news organizations is politics.

Though former Vice President Al Gore was criticized for having once described himself as the "father of the Internet," the Clinton administration did come up with one of the handiest Web sites for reporting when it developed firstgov.gov—a one-stop shopping center for information on the U.S. government.

FirstGov is the most comprehensive government Web site, but it was hardly the first. Among the pioneers of government on the Web—and still a heavily used site—was THOMAS, the congressional Web site. Using THOMAS (www.thomas.loc.gov), reporters have been able to do research on legislation, hearings, and general legislative workings. (Note that although most sites use a "www" prefix, not all require it. For example, using either "wsj.com" or "www.wsj.com" will take you directly to "public.wsj.com/home.html". Another good jumping-off point for looking at governmental issues is the General Accounting Office (GAO) Web site (www.gao.gov), which serves as a frequent watchdog of state and federal activities. The GAO also offers a handy e-mail notification service for reporters.

Although much of it tends to be political in nature, the White House also maintains a frequently visited Web site. (Be careful to type in the correct URL: www.whitehouse.gov is the official executive branch Web site.)

For reporters who are investigating the sources of political money, there are a lot of options, but the most reliable and easy-to-use Web site is that of the Center for Responsive Politics (www.opensecrets.org), a nonpartisan interest group that specializes in tracking campaign contributions.

Most reporters incorporating government issues into their stories focus on either the executive or legislative branch. But the regulatory process is an often-overlooked aspect of governmental reporting. While Congress passes laws, it's usually up to various governmental agencies to create the regulations that put those laws into effect. For example, Congress or the White House may pass legislation or create an order that limits the amount of emissions from a power plant, but the Federal Register is where the fine print generally is found. The Federal Register (www.nara.gov/fedreg/) also is the place to look for comments on proposed legislative and executive rules from interest groups or the public; thinking reporters can obtain those comments and use them for sources.

The U.S. Census Bureau is also a frequently overlooked source of information on the Web. Although the Census itself is taken only once every decade (and reports from it generally trickle out over a three-year period), the Census Bureau puts out a vast trove of valuable data, ranging from poverty rates in U.S. school districts to annual population estimates to the Consolidated Federal Funds Report, a county-by-county breakdown of how the federal government spends its money. It can be found at www.census.gov.

State and federal government agencies are also establishing Web sites on the Internet. Generally, the best way to find a state's URL is to use the following nomenclature: www.state.(two-letter state postal code abbreviation).us.gov. For example, the state of Alabama's home page would be www.state.al.us.gov.

Reporters covering state government issues also should check www.stateline.org, operated by a branch of the Pew Charitable Trusts. Besides being an extensive resource for seeing what other states are doing, stateline.org is an extremely good place to pick up story ideas.

For reporters working on stories with a more political bent, there's no shortage of good Web resources. Both the Republican and Democratic National Committees have fairly extensive Web sites, at www.rnc.org and www.dnc.org, respectively. The National Conference of State Legislators (www.ncsl.org) is also a good resource for information on state legislative branches. Its executive-branch counterpart is the National Governors Association (www.nga.com).

A growing number of counties, cities, and local agencies are on the Internet as well. If your local government doesn't use the nomenclature

www.city.state.us.gov *or*

www.agency.city.state.us.gov

you should check with local officials (or do a Web search) to confirm the exact URL.

Education

There's no shortage of education sites on the Internet. Like governmental sites, they exist at all levels, from small elementary school districts to the federal government's massive Department of Education. Over the last several years, the Education Department has gone to great pains to make its Web site at www.ed.gov as useful as possible to children, parents, educators, and reporters.

Although it's a part of the U.S. Department of Education and can be found through links on the department's Web pages, the National Center for Education Statistics is a gold mine for reporters looking for background, leads, or sources on education stories (www.nces.ed.gov).

For information on higher education—particularly testing and finances—the College Board does a good job of helping reporters. The Princeton, N.J.–based organization, which administers the SATs and other tests, is located at www.collegeboard.com.

Environment

While just about any reporter can profit from beat-related resources on the Internet, environmental reporters are better off than most. Perhaps it's the Internet's origins as a grassroots computer network; perhaps it's the far-flung nature of the environmental movement. Whatever the reason, the Web offers a wide array of resources for environmental reporters, starting with the U.S. Environmental Protection Agency's home page at www.epa.gov.

The EPA site contains an incredibly rich set of data. Reporters can research toxic emissions in their areas, check on the status of a Superfund cleanup site, or even find out who owns nearby power plants.

The biggest and one of the oldest environmental organizations, the Sierra Club, also maintains a fairly useful site at www.sierraclub.org. Although it's not as data-rich as the EPA site and promotes a strong conservationist point of view, it provides useful background on a number of important environmental issues.

Likewise, the Environmental Defense Fund, another nonprofit environmental organization, takes pro-environment views of the issues. The EDF, however, sponsors one of the more useful Web sites at www.scorecard.org. Reporters can use scorecard.org to find out how their communities rank in terms of hazardous pollutants, emissions, and toxics. This site even allows reporters to use ZIP codes to conduct research on different communities. The League of Conservation Voters (www.lcv.org) is a good, nonpartisan site.

Criminal Justice/Law

Anyone who's ever covered a criminal justice or courts beat knows that judges, lawyers, and police officers are seldom on the cutting edge of technology. One day, perhaps, the majority of reporters will be able to check arrest records and jail bookings from their computers. But that day is a long way off.

Court reporters are in a slightly better position. Though the U.S. Supreme Court refuses to let television cameras broadcast oral arguments, it has a well-organized Web site that's updated fairly frequently. The site, www.supremecourtus.gov, contains not only the usual legal talk for lawyers, but also texts of its opinions and dockets.

After a slow start, the U.S. Justice Department is also catching up with a reporter-friendly Web site. Though the home page itself isn't much to look at, the site at www.usdoj.gov contains useful links to its agencies, including the FBI, Bureau of Justice Statistics, and Immigration and Naturalization Service.

One of the best privately run justice sites on the Web is the Transactional Records Access Clearinghouse (TRAC), created by a former *New York Times* investigative reporter and operated by Syracuse University. Reporters must pay for access to the full site at www.trac.syr.edu, but the free part of it focuses on issues such as IRS audits and Justice Department prosecutions. Indeed, the TRAC site has provided enough reporters with information to anger the Justice Department; the Clearinghouse had to go to court in 1999 to obtain the department's case-tracking system and its master list of federal prosecutions and lawsuits.

One of the most useful sites for finding out information about lawyers is the Martindale-Hubbell directory www.martindale.com/locator/home.html, which was recently acquired by the Lexis-Nexis (www.lexis.com) group. The site allows reporters to type in the name of a lawyer, a legal specialty, or geographical area.

As with other beats, the availability of online criminal justice and legal information at the local level is haphazard. Some police departments have tremendous Web sites and make reports available online; most don't. Some courts have excellent Web sites; most don't.

Transportation

Transportation stories are becoming more of a staple in newspapers and broadcasts than they were 10 years ago. Happily, transportation-related groups and agencies have been keeping pace with the Web's growth, whether it means putting train or airline schedules on the Internet or creating a system of online webcams to divert travelers away from freeway congestion.

The biggest and broadest transportation-related Web site on the Internet, of course, belongs to the U.S. Department of Transportation. The DoT, which is the umbrella organization for agencies such as the Federal Aviation Administration and the National Transportation Safety Board, does a credible job of making information available to reporters at www.dot.gov.

In early 2001, the FAA completed a Web site design that's much more reporter-friendly and includes a more usable search engine for pulling up quick information on crashed airplanes.

The National Transportation Safety Board, which investigates most major accidents in the country, also has an extraordinarily useful Web page.

Business

In the wake of the collapse of the so-called "dot-com economy" of the late 1990s, it might be easier to remember the names of business-related Web sites that shut down, rather than the ones that weathered the storm. There are still some reliable resources out there for business reporters, though, and a good one to start with is EDGAR, the Securities and Exchange Commission's Electronic Data Gathering and Retrieval system (www.sec.gov).

Although a number of companies take financial reports from publicly traded companies and make them available—usually for a fee—on the Web, the SEC site remains the gold standard. The EDGAR system allows reporters to pull up financial reports that can run into the hundreds and even thousands of pages and search them in an instant. Since publicly traded companies are required by law to notify stockholders of any events that might affect their stock prices, smart reporters can find good stories simply by opening a company's 10-Q (quarterly report) on EDGAR and searching for "grand jury" or "fines" or "civil penalties." These things aren't always reported in press releases, but they're invariably found in the very small print of an annual report at the SEC Web site.

The SEC is a good resource for finding information that may be buried in documents. But how about general information, such as annual revenues and stock price fluctuations, that companies aren't as reluctant to publicize? If you can't find the company's Web site by simply guessing—for example, www.ibm.com—two sites offer a trove of business-related information, much of it free.

The first, Hoover's Online, offers free newsletters and limited company research at www.hoovers.com. In contrast to EDGAR, it's an extremely easy-to-use interface, with the only real catch being that much of the research is not free.

Another good for-profit business site is www.wsj.com, operated by the venerable *Wall Street Journal.* Although it's a for-pay site, the subscription rate is surprisingly reasonable. An annual subscription to the *Journal* runs more than $300; a year's subscription to the online *Journal* (which includes all print content, plus research reports) goes for $59, a sum that most newsrooms can afford.

Finally, for reporters on the economics beat who'd like to avoid as much academic or Federal Reserve Board-type jargon as possible, there's www.dismalscience.com. This site, which is sponsored by economy.com, has a wealth of information on economic indicators, some useful calculators, and surprisingly lucid prose about "the dismal science."

Health and Medicine

A recent survey found that more than 50 million Americans were using the Internet to gather health-related information. That, in and of itself, ought to make reporters sit up and take notice of the countless health and medicine Web sites. Although hundreds of sites devoted to medicine appeared in the late 1990s, the ensuing shakeout of unprofitable Web sites caused many to downsize or disappear. By 2001, the primary medical information sites were operated by nonprofit organizations, such as university health care centers or public interest groups. Probably the best of the lot is the National Library of Medicine's MEDLINE (www.nim.nih.gov/medlineplus), an online database of health news, reports, and research articles.

The government's main health care agency, the U.S. Department of Health and Human Services, also maintains a useful Web site at www.hhs.gov. Though some of the content leans to puffery (for example, "Ten Ways to Wish Your Dad a Happy Father's Day!"), the site contains links to major health care entities, such as Medicare and the Health Care Financing Administration.

Sports

Sportswriters have traditionally been among the first in any newsroom to adopt new technologies. Cell phones? Sportswriters were dictating over them years ago. Laptops? Sportswriters have been using variants of them for more than 15 years. The advent of personal computers has made it possible for them to file stories without having to leave the press box, and the Internet is opening up an entirely new set of opportunities for smarter and deeper reporting.

How can sportswriters use the Internet to their advantage? Consider the poor sportswriter who's having to deal with a team he or she has never covered. The first logical stop might be a league Web site, such as the Major League Soccer site. Next, a reporter might want to look at a team site, such as the New England Revolution. And finally, a visit to the team's fan Web page will likely reveal a torrent of information on the fans' latest concerns and debates, as well as good story ideas.

Miscellaneous Sites

Although they're not really connected to any specific beat, four Web sites deserve a special place in every reporter's online Rolodex: The CIA World Factbook, MapQuest, Weather.com, and Investigative Reporters and Editors.

The CIA World Factbook has been around in one online incarnation or another for several years, and it remains the best place to find information about foreign countries. Want to know the inflation rate in Tajikistan? Total highway mileage in Anguilla? Fertility rate in Samoa? The Factbook is the best place for it (www.cia.gov/cia/publications/factbook/).

For reporters who have to hit the road—or even to figure out how many miles apart two towns are—MapQuest at www.mapquest.com is the best reference around. It's got an easy-to-use interface and offers interactive maps as well. Simply click on the "Driving Directions" icon and fill in as much information as you can. Depending on the speed of your Internet connection, you'll get a map with some extremely detailed directions. (Be warned, though, sometimes these directions in seeking the straightest route become ridiculously complex.)

Weather.com is another useful site for reporters on just about any beat. Besides having one of the best forecasts on the Web, this Weather Channel–run site includes alerts on severe weather, historical data, and flight information.

Finally, one of the best journalism-related sites on the Web belongs to Investigative Reporters and Editors (IRE), a nonprofit organization in Columbia, Missouri. IRE's site (www.ire.org) contains a huge database of resources, including tutorials, great investigative stories, and training opportunities.

Web addresses of some of the best sites discussed in this chapter appear in the box on the next page.

FirstGov, www.firstgov.gov
THOMAS, www.thomas.loc.gov
Census Bureau, www.census.gov
Stateline, www.stateline.org
National Center for Education Statistics, www.nces.ed.gov
EPA, www.epa.gov
TRAC, www.trac.syr.edu
FAA, www.faa.gov
IRE, www.ire.org
CIA World Factbook, www.cia.gov/cia/publications/factbook/
Weather Channel, www.weather.com
MapQuest, www.mapquest.com

CHAPTER FOUR

Listservs and Newsgroups

For spot researching, you can't beat the World Wide Web. But sometimes events and information change faster than Web pages. And when they do, owners of Web sites don't always have the time or the inclination for an immediate update. So what do you do? Reach out to the real single-issue obsessives of the Internet—people who populate "listservs" and "Usenet groups," people who spend much of their online time writing messages devoted to cacti . . . or Alice Cooper . . . or Plymouth Barracudas.

Listservs are software programs for setting up and maintaining discussion groups through e-mail. Originally, Listserv was the trademarked name for the software, but it has become so ubiquitous that it is now used as a generic word. (Note that it has no "e" at the end, because program names on older mainframes were limited to eight characters.)

Usenet is a worldwide system of informal discussion areas or newsgroups.

Essentially, listservs and Usenet groups work the same way: People send messages to an e-mail address. The only real difference is in distribution. In a listserv, the message—usually called a "post"—is sent via e-mail to everyone who has subscribed to the list. In a Usenet group, the message—also a "post"—is added to a list of messages that are available for reading, generally at a Web site.

Some people argue that listservs are much easier to manage, since the posts come directly to your e-mail. What you don't want to read, you simply delete from your e-mail inbox. But the archiving and research commands are more esoteric than for Usenet groups. Others argue that Usenet groups are much easier to manage, since they don't take up space in your mailbox or on your hard drive. But you have to navigate to a specific site to read the posts.

Actually, there probably are several listserv and Usenet groups that discuss those very issues; among the computer cognoscenti, the Usenet–listserv debate takes on the aura of a major religion. So we'll leave the debate to them while we figure out how to use discussion groups for our own purposes, namely, to get the news.

Listservs

Since e-mail is rapidly becoming one of the fastest-growing communications media in history, let's start with listservs. First, we need to know what we want. Let's say we're researching a story on crime victims. How do we get to a mailing list devoted to crime victims?

Certainly we could use a search engine—a service that allows a user to find a Web site by typing in the topic—and look for "crime victims" and "listserv" (see Chapter 2 for searching strategies). But there's a much easier way. Go to www.topica.com and see what's available (see Fig. 4.1).

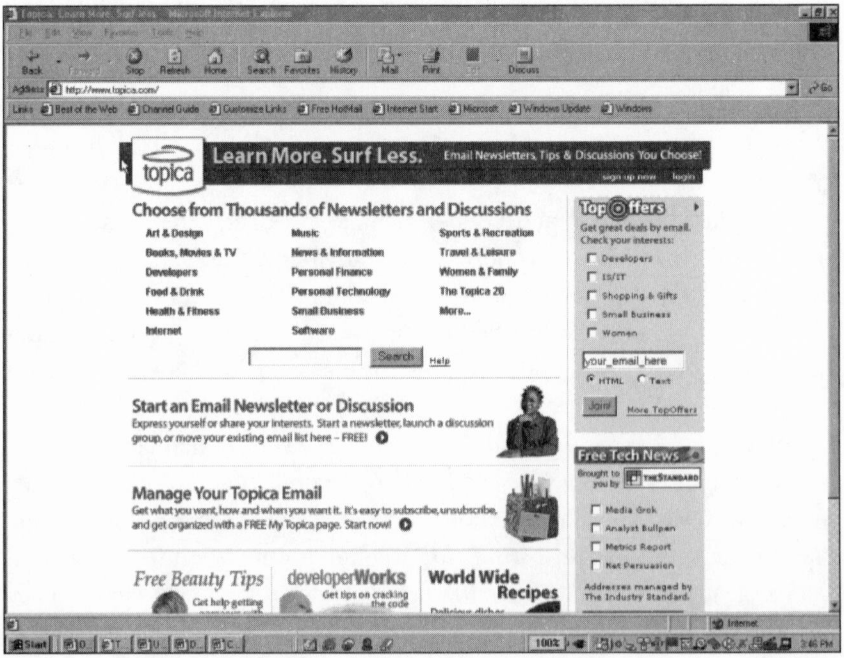

FIGURE 4.1

As you can tell, Topica is organized with both a search engine (similar to HotBot or AltaVista) and an index (like Yahoo!). Just for brevity's sake, let's start with the search engine by typing "crime victims" in the search box and see what we can find. When we get the results page and click on the hyperlink for the "Victim's Rights" link, we can find out a little more about it. If we go to the "victims-assistance-prog" link, we can see it's a mailing list, and there's a button to click that will let us join it. And if you click on the button, you'll come to a screen that asks you for more information. Fill it out, register, and you're subscribed to this listserv.

Of course, not all listservs are kept on Topica. You might find some by just surfing. Among the most useful, for example, are the IRE-L, run by Investigative Reporters and Editors in Columbia, Missouri, and NICAR-L, run by the National Institute for Computer-Assisted Reporting.

Let's try subscribing to IRE-L and see what happens. After we click on the hyperlink to join the list, we're told to send a message to the machine that handles the listserv. We should get an e-mail message back within a few minutes (see Fig. 4.2).

Please respond to listproc@lists.missouri.edu

To: Frank Bass/TheAP
cc: listmaster@nicar.org, listsupport@notes.ire.org
Subject: SUBSCRIBE IRE-L Frank Bass

Dear user,

your request

SUBSCRIBE IRE-L Frank Bass

has been successfully processed.

********** HOW TO POST TO THE LIST **********

Welcome to list IRE-L (IRE-L@lists.missouri.edu). The system has recorded your address as

Frank_Bass@ap.org

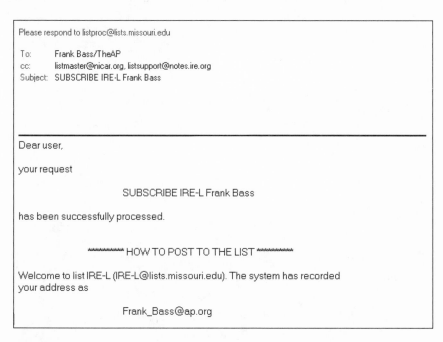

FIGURE 4.2

Now, you're subscribed to the list. And the response from the program that subscribed you to IRE-L comes with a few simple commands that you might want to use. But for a more thorough explanation, it's best to follow the advice of the IRE-L program (see Fig. 4.3).

FIGURE 4.3

```
*********** HOW TO GET MORE HELP ***********

To get more information on how to use this service, please send the following
request to listproc@lists.missouri.edu:

                    HELP
```

When we send out the "help" command, we get a fairly detailed list of commands. Let's try sending a message to the listserv to see how many people are subscribed to IRE-L. We'll send it to listproc@lists.missouri.edu. Had we wanted to post something to the list, we would have sent it to IRE-L@lists.missouri.edu. Be very careful not to confuse the two addresses, or you'll look foolish in front of a lot of your peers. So to start, we'll send a simple command to the listproc, as shown in Fig. 4.4, asking it for the number of recipients.

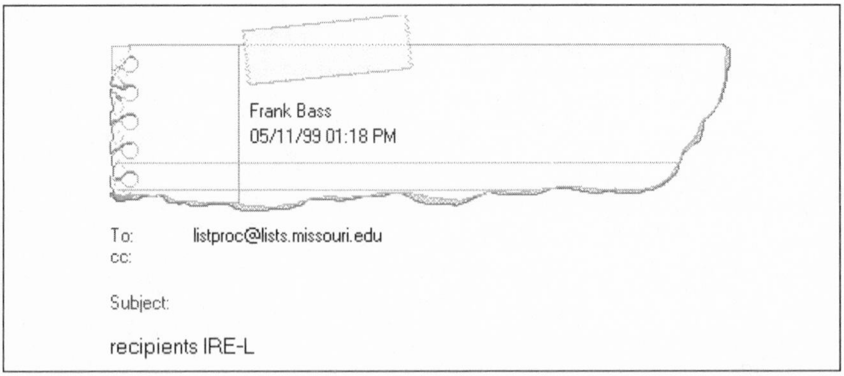

FIGURE 4.4

We should get a quick response like that shown in Fig. 4.5.

It's possible to use listproc commands to get archived material, but it's a lot easier if the listserv owners have a Web-based archive. Both the IRE-L and NICAR-L lists have such archives, and more and more listservs are establishing and maintaining searchable online archives.

Please respond to listproc@lists.missouri.edu

To: Frank Bass/TheAP
cc: listmaster@nicar.org, listsupport@notes.ire.org
Subject: RECIPIENTS IRE-L

***
*** IRE-L@lists.missouri.edu: Discussion of Investigative Reporting Techniques and Training
***
*** Date created: Tue Jul 2 20:48:28 1996

— Here is the current list of non-concealed subscribers:

Total number of subscribers: 1371 (1369 shown here)

FIGURE 4.5

You should also be aware of other journalism-related mailing lists such as those given in the following box.

National Institute for Computer-Assisted Reporting: Subscribe to listproc@lists.missouri.edu, using the command “Subscribe NICAR-L *Your Name*”

Investigative Reporters and Editors: Subscribe to listproc@lists.missouri.edu, using the command ”Subscribe IRE-L *Your Name*”

Society of Professional Journalists: Subscribe to listserv@psuvm.psu.edu, using the command “Subscribe SPJ-L *Your Name*”

CARR-L (Computer-Assisted Reporting): Subscribe to listserv@ulkyvm.louisville.edu, using the command “Subscribe CARR-L *Your Name*”

Foreign Correspondents: Subscribe to majordomo@true.net, using the command “Subscribe Correx-L *Your Name*”

Government Access: Subscribe to majordomo@well.com, using the command “Info GovAccess *Your Name*”

Reporters Committee for Freedom of the Press: Subscribe to rcfp@cais.com, using the command “Subscribe *Your Name*”

A Word A Day: Subscribe to wsmith@wordsmith.org, using the command “Subscribe *Your Name*”

In a related vein, you should be familiar with e-mail alerts, which are automatically sent to subscribers. Basically, they're press releases that are topic-specific. Here are some of the better ones.

U.S. Census Bureau: Probably the best on the Web for reporters looking for local or state-specific angles on federal issues. Go to: www.census.gov/mp/www/subscribe.html

U.S. Environmental Protection Agency: For upcoming reports and studies, press conferences and basic information. Go to: www.epa.gov/epahome/listserv.html

U.S. Department of Education: The URL is: www.ed.gov/MailingLists/

Stocks @ Close: For closing market quotes, including top gainers and losers, go to the NSI Web page (a small design company in Farmingdale, N.Y.): www.nsiweb.com/stocks/

General Accounting Office: The address for its daybook is: www.gao.gov/faq/faq.htm#2.2

FreeEDGAR Watch List: This notifies reporters when companies that they're covering show up in SEC filings: www.freeedgar.com/Search/WatchList.asp

U.S. Department of Agriculture: Go to: www.usda.mannlib.cornell.edu/usda/emailinfo.html

Legal Information Institute: Run by the Cornell University Library, it's been a pioneer in Internet legal research. The URL is: www.law.cornell.edu/focus/bulletins.html

Usenet

But enough about listservs; on to Usenet. Many people consider the difference between the two to be six of one and a half-dozen of the other. Usenet is mostly Web-based; listservs are e-mail-based. You go to Usenets; listservs come to you.

This time, we'll go to groups.google.com, another site operated by Google (which purchased it from deja.com in early 2001). Often, people will substitute "Usenet" for "newsgroup; they're the same thing.

When you get to the site, you'll see a page that looks like Fig. 4.6.

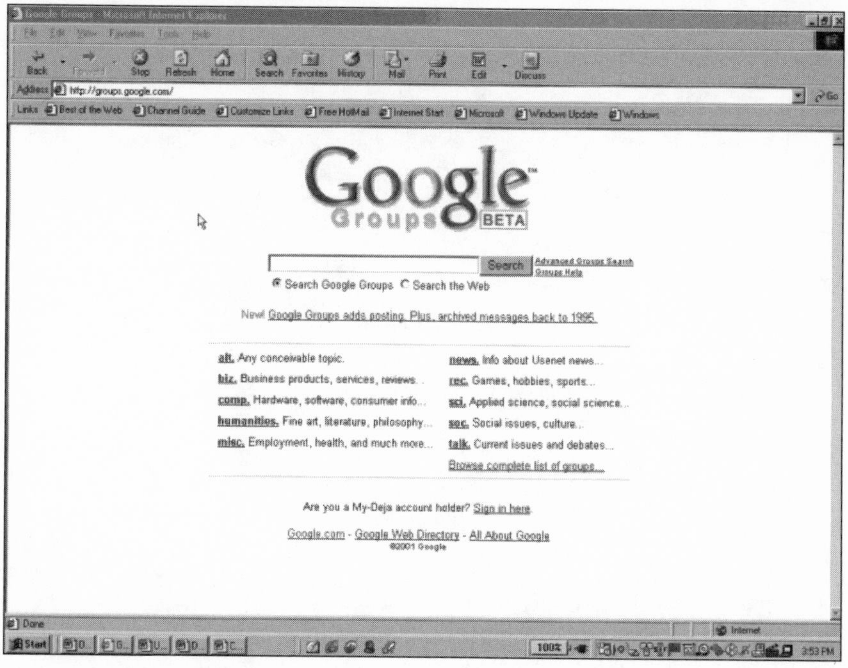

FIGURE 4.6

Again, let's try searching for crime-related newsgroups by typing "crime" in the query box, as shown in Fig. 4.7.

We get over two million hits, which is far too many to be considered a useful search (see Fig. 4.8). This tells us that a more specific query is needed if we hope to narrow the number of hits to those that are directly applicable to our research interest.

Another caveat about newsgroups: They're hierarchically arranged. Usually, the first part of the address is news://, followed by the hierarchy (alt, comp, news, biz, sci, rec), then the name of the group itself.

Most newsgroups are located in the alt hierarchy, which is somewhat disappointing, since it includes such immortal discussion groups as alt.barney.die.die.die, for those people less than enthralled with the purple dinosaur. But for very specific—if somewhat limited—applications, it's possible to use a newsgroup like rec.autos.makers.ford.mustang; such newsgroups can be invaluable. But like all other Internet resources, use caution and use your brain. Check it out carefully. And remember that Web home pages are changing all the time.

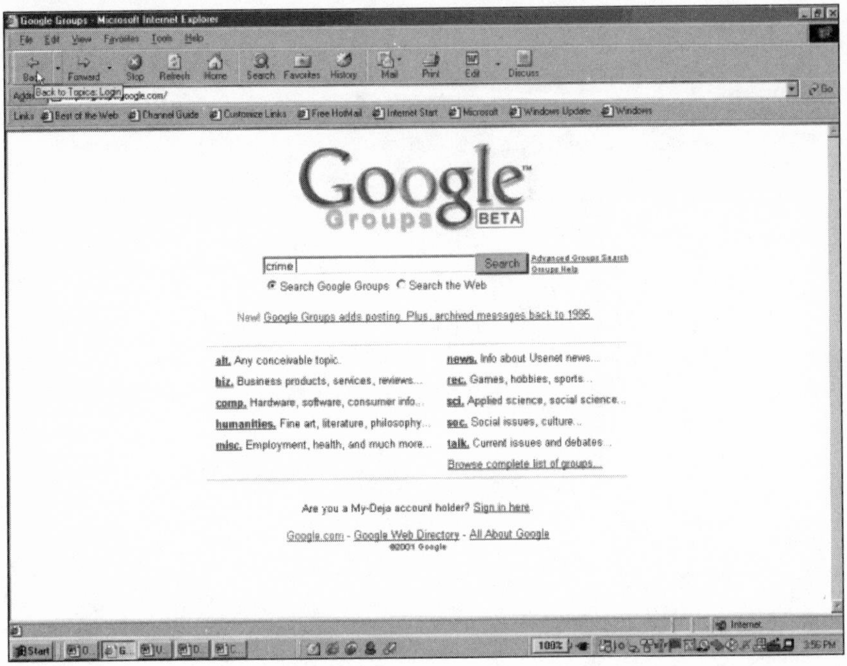

FIGURE 4.7

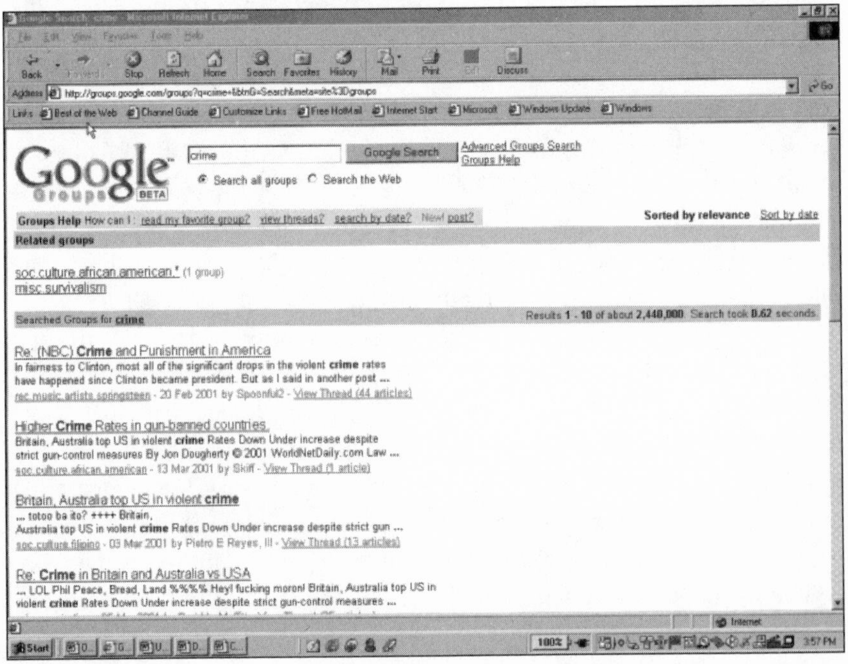

FIGURE 4.8

CHAPTER FIVE

Computer-Assisted Reporting

Computer-assisted reporting—basically just a more specific way for reporters to use the Internet—has been around in one form or another for a half-century. Given the difficulty in defining exactly what computer-assisted reporting is, it's hard to estimate its impact. In many ways, it's still a fledgling technique that depends heavily on the skill of the reporter using the computer.

If you define computer-assisted reporting as the use of computers to analyze data for news stories, its origins lie in the 1952 election, when CBS used a room-sized Remington Rand UNIVAC computer on election night to accurately predict the outcome of the presidential contest between Dwight Eisenhower and Adlai Stevenson. Computers soon became an integral part of election night news broadcasting, with networks hiring specialists to interpret oceans of data.

Though computer-assisted reporting became a staple of election night broadcasts, it wasn't used in newsrooms until the mid-1960s. Phil Meyer, a Detroit reporter, shared a Pulitzer Prize for his 1967 analysis of that city's devastating riots. Meyer used computers to analyze survey data and found that people who had attended college were as likely to have participated in riots as people with no college record.

The following year, Clarence Jones, a Miami reporter, hired University of Miami students to enter Dade County court records for nearly 700 people arrested on vice charges into a database created with COBOL, an early computer programming language. And in 1972, reporter David Burnham used computers to analyze police records for the *New York Times*, finding significant discrepancies among crimes reported and arrests actually made.

Another landmark year for computer-assisted reporting occurred in 1973, with Meyer's publication of *Precision Journalism*, a landmark book that opened the eyes of many reporters to the possibilities of using quantitative analysis in journalism. That same year, two *Philadelphia Inquirer* reporters, Don Barlett and James Steele, painstakingly created a database by taking 42 separate bits of information—on race, sentence, and criminal record—from thousands of court documents and entering the information on punchcards. The punchcards were fed through a mainframe computer, and the 4,000 pages of results served as the basis for a major story on inequities in the court system.

As personal computers began to gain a toehold in American corporations in the early 1980s, reporters began applying quantitative techniques more frequently to news stories. Elliott Jaspin at the *Providence Journal* became curious about the qualifications for school bus drivers after three children were run over by buses in six months. Jaspin took a database of school bus drivers and matched it to a database of traffic violations, taking advantage of one of the most powerful applications of database programs by joining two large sets of information.

By 1989, there was little doubt that computers had entered newsrooms to stay. Although the vast majority of those computers were being used for simple word-processing, reporters continued to push the envelope in using them to analyze data. The National Institute for Computer-Assisted Reporting (NICAR) was created in 1989 and affiliated with the Missouri-based Investigative Reporters and Editors (IRE) shortly thereafter. By the early 1990s, the institute had trained hundreds of reporters at weeklong "boot camps" around the country.

The computers paid off, too. Beginning in the mid-1980s, Pulitzers were awarded every year to newspapers that utilized computer-assisted reporting to frame questions for important social issues. Some of the higher-profile winners included the *Atlanta Journal-Constitution*, which won the 1989 investigative reporting prize for sifting through bank lending records to document racial discrimination in home lending; the *Miami Herald*, which took the 1993 public service award for coverage that showed how lax zoning, inspection, and building codes contributed to Hurricane Andrew's destruction; and the *Associated Press*, which won the 2000 international reporting award for revealing a Korean War massacre of hundreds of civilians.

Smaller newspapers used computers to bring about change as well. The *Alabama Journal* used computers to document the state's high infant mortality rate and won the 1988 Pulitzer for general news reporting; the *Raleigh News & Observer* won for its look at the environmental and health risks in the state's hog industry; and the *Dayton Daily News* won the 1998 national reporting award for its expose of mismanagement in the military health system.

Access to Information

Although computers have proven invaluable in analyzing data for news stories, they've always had an Achilles heel—access to data. As computer-assisted reporting began to gain momentum in the late 1980s and early 1990s, data access issues were primarily confined to hardware. Many government agencies furnished electronic information, but only in multiple databases that were released on bulky nine-tracks or 3490 tape cartridges. Machines that would read those cartridges cost thousands of dollars, and few newsrooms had the budget, inclination, or staff capable of turning them into the basis for a news story.

As government agencies have upgraded their computer equipment over the last decade and Internet use has grown exponentially, data have become easier to obtain in some ways. A great deal of data is freely available on the Internet; much more is obtainable through a simple telephone call to a government source. Yet paradoxically, although more data are available online or on easy-to-read media such as diskettes and CD-ROMs, it seems sometimes that less is available to reporters who request it.

Much of the paradox can be attributed to the explosion of information available on the Internet and ensuing concerns about privacy. Alarmed by reports of "cyberstalkers," Congress passed the 1994 Driver's Privacy Protection Act, cutting off an important source of information for reporters doing basic individual backgrounding. In 2001, the Freedom Forum reported in its annual State of the First Amendment Survey that 71 percent of those surveyed believed it important for the government to hold the media in check—a fairly contradictory interpretation of the First Amendment itself.

Other than proving themselves to be responsible users of government records, reporters have few tools left to pry data from governments; the most significant remains the 1966 federal Freedom of Information Act

(FOIA), which was updated in 1974 during the post-Watergate reform era. Theoretically, the law gives reporters the ability to obtain any records from a federal agency, with nine major exemptions:

1. National security
2. Internal agency personnel rules
3. Information specifically exempted by federal laws
4. Trade secrets
5. Internal agency memoranda and policy discussions
6. Personal privacy
7. Ongoing law enforcement investigations
8. Federally regulated banks
9. Oil and gas well records.

Also exempt are the president and his staff; Congress; the federal courts; private corporations; and federally funded state agencies. In theory, FOIA is a very simple law, requiring only a simple letter of request for information to a federal agency, as in the following example.

To the FOIA Officer:
I am requesting access to an electronic copy of the U.S. Justice Department's case-tracking system for the 2000 fiscal year. This request is being made under 5 U.S.C. §552, the federal Freedom of Information Act.

I agree to pay reasonable duplication fees for processing this request. However, please notify me if the cost of filling this requests exceeds $25.

As a reporter, I am only required to pay for the direct cost of duplication after the first 100 pages. I plan to use this information as the basis for stories of interest to the general public. Therefore, I ask you to waive any fees because release of the information is in the general public interest.

I would appreciate your communicating with me by telephone rather than mail, as this request is of timely value. Please also provide expedited review of this request, which concerns an urgent matter. The public needs to know more about the cases that U.S. attorneys are prosecuting or not prosecuting. I certify that my statements concerning the need for expedited review are true and correct to the best of my knowledge.

I look forward to hearing from you within 20 working days, as the law requires.

Sincerely,

The greatest weakness of FOIA, however, isn't the number of exemptions; it's the refusal of most government agencies to comply with requests. The first barrier is time. By law, the agency has 20 days to respond to an FOIA request. Upon receiving an FOIA request, the vast majority of government agencies will have the same response: They've received the request, and they'll look for documents that are "responsive."

Under 1996 amendments to the act, reporters can ask for "expedited review," which moves their requests closer to the top of the list. The Justice Department specifically has a policy that allows reporters to direct FOIA requests to public information officers for expedited review for a matter of "widespread and exceptional media interest in which there exist possible questions about the government's integrity which affect public confidence." The actual enforcement of the expedited review policy, however, depends heavily on the individual agency.

The 1996 amendments also created a class of requests known as E-FOIA, which allows requestors to specify an electronic format. The amendments, which require agencies to make reasonable efforts to provide records to people in the medium they request, have been modestly successful. The amendments led to the creation of a Government Information Locator Service (www.access.gpo.gov/su/docs/gils/index.html), designed to help the public locate and retrieve electronic information through the Internet. Since its 1997 inception, it has not been uncommon for reporters to find documents through GILS after being turned down by FOIA officers.

Reporters also should keep in mind that each agency is required to keep a log of all FOIA requests. Smart reporters will realize that it's not just journalists making FOIA requests; corporations, attorneys, inventors, and citizens all make them, and make them far more often than journalists. Requesting a copy of an agency's FOIA log can lead to a gold mine of stories that reporters never would have considered. Of course, that's assuming those records are available through FOIA. And what to do if your

FOIA is rejected? If the agency denies your FOIA request, you can always appeal to the head of the agency.

And if an agency denies the appeal, there's always the option of a lawsuit. The Reporters Committee for Freedom of the Press has the following sample complaint you can use.

UNITED STATES DISTRICT COURT
FOR **(the District where you are filing)**
YOUR NAME,
your complete address
your telephone number
Plaintiff,
v.
NAME OF AGENCY WITHHOLDING FILES,
agency address
Defendant
COMPLAINT FOR INJUNCTIVE RELIEF

1. This is an action under the Freedom of Information Act, 5 U.S.C. §552, to order the production of agency records, concerning **(insert very brief description of what you requested)**, which defendant has improperly withheld from plaintiff.

2. This court has jurisdiction over this action pursuant to 5 U.S.C. §552(a)(4)(B).

3. Plaintiff, **(your name)**, is a news reporter **(or researcher, author, historian)** employed by **(name of newspaper, station, university)** and is the requestor of the records which defendant is now withholding. Plaintiff has requested this information for use in a news story **(broadcast, book, etc.)** and prompt release of the information is **(essential to meeting a deadline for publication; important because of the immediate public interest in this information, etc.)**.

4. Defendant **(name of agency)** is an agency of the United States and has possession of the documents that plaintiff seeks.

5. By letter dated **(date)**, plaintiff requested access to **(brief summary of request)**. A copy of this letter is attached as Exhibit 1.

6. By letter dated **(date)**, plaintiff was denied access to the requested information on the grounds that it was exempt from

disclosure under Exemption **(fill in the numbers)**, 5 U.S.C. §§552(b)**(fill in numbers)**. A copy of this letter is attached as Exhibit 2.

7. By letter dated **(date)**, plaintiff appealed the denial of this request. A copy of this letter is attached as Exhibit 3.

8. By letter dated **(date)**, plaintiff's appeal was denied. A copy of this letter is attached as Exhibit 4.

9. Plaintiff has a right of access to the requested information under 5 U.S.C. §552(a)(3), and there is no legal basis for defendant's denial of such access.

WHEREFORE, plaintiff requests this Court:

(1) Order defendant to provide access to the requested documents;

(2) Expedite this proceeding as provided for in 28 U.S.C. §1657;

(3) Award plaintiff costs and reasonable attorneys fees in this action, as provided in 5 U.S.C. §552(a)(4)(E); and

(4) Grant such other and further relief as it may deem just and proper.

Respectfully submitted,

Your signature

Your name

Your address

Dated: **(date)**

As always, though, ask before you file a Freedom of Information Act request. And keep in mind that the federal FOIA isn't much use with state governments; although many state laws are modeled after the federal act, there are differences in all of them. Again, the Reporters Committee maintains an excellent up-to-date collection of state freedom of information laws at www.rcfp.org/tapping/index.cgi.

Access to Data

Although FOIA requests are supposed to be a last resort for obtaining information, they're frequently only the start of an arduous process. Even in the best of situations, translating government data into something that reporters can use can be difficult, mostly because of the wide array of hardware and software used to store and manage the data.

Some government agencies still maintain data on old mainframe computers that are hard to use and harder still to extract data from. By and large, however, most federal agencies are putting records on Windows-compatible computers and can provide data via diskettes, CD-ROMs, or FTP download sites, depending on the reporter's needs.

Software incompatibilities have become a bit more difficult. Although most U.S. newsrooms are using some variant of the Microsoft Office suite (which includes Excel as a spreadsheet program, Word as a word-processor, and Access as a database manager), many are using software that's not always compatible with government data. As a general rule, it's wise to ask for data in a text format, where possible. Generally, text files have one of five endings:

*.txt
*.asc
*.lst
*.prn
*.rtf

Delimited text files, in which fields are separated by a character—generally a space, comma, or tab—also are frequently available. Most comma-delimited files are available in a *.csv format.

Spreadsheet programs generally can import just about any kind of text file. Different spreadsheet programs, however, have different file extensions. Microsoft Excel files, for example, have an *.xls extension. Quattro Pro has a *.wb3 extension, and Lotus 1–2–3 has a *wk3 extension. They don't always work together, either, so it's important to know which program the government agency is using. Likewise, database programs have different extensions. Microsoft Access uses an *.mdb extension, FoxPro and dBASE use *.dbf, and Paradox uses a *.db extension. Even mapping software can get confused; if you've installed ArcView, for example, a saved project has an *.apr extension. But that's also the extension for Lotus Approach 97, another database program.

A word is also in order regarding *pdf, or portable document format files. Although they can be opened with Acrobat, a free piece of software available at www.adobe.com, it takes a little more work to import them into a spreadsheet or database file. Often, reporters will find it quicker to purchase a full version of Acrobat or an extraction program, such as Monarch Redwing, to load them into a spreadsheet or database file.

Most major spreadsheet and database programs can import tables from *.htm or *.html files without a problem, as those are simply Web pages.

Even assuming that the data are obtainable from a government agency and that you do have the software to work with it, reporters need to keep one final thought in mind when working with spreadsheets and databases: There is no such thing as a perfect database or spreadsheet. That's why computer-assisted reporting is the start—and not the end—of the reporting process.

CHAPTER SIX

Spreadsheets

Not all reporters need to use a spreadsheet every day. But all reporters should know how to use one. Whether you're covering a budget, figuring out batting averages, analyzing campaign spending, or trying to nail down federal spending, you need to know how to use a spreadsheet. At its heart, a spreadsheet is just a way of analyzing a list.

Reporters can use spreadsheets for all kinds of chores, but they're most commonly used for four basic things in newsrooms: ranking, sorting, calculating, and filtering.

Let's look at the Consolidated Federal Funds Report (CFFR), an annual county-by-county report issued by the U.S. Census Bureau. If you wanted to find out which counties received the most federal spending in your state, you'd spend a lot of time going through the list of the nation's more than 3,000 counties. If you wanted to rank counties by federal spending, you'd spend a lot more time going through the counties and ranking them. Finally, if you wanted to look at which counties across the nation received the most federal spending on a per-capita basis, you'd spend . . . at least a day and maybe more figuring it out, depending on how fast you were with a calculator.

If you used a spreadsheet with the downloaded CFFR data, however, you could sort counties by total spending in less than 10 seconds. You could filter them by state in about the same time. Finally, you could rank them by per-capita spending in about a minute, depending on how fast you were with a mouse.

Let's look at federal spending for 1999. The first thing you need to know about Excel, which is the most commonly used newsroom spreadsheet—and the building block for everything in computer-assisted reporting—is that it's made up of rows and columns. Rows go across, columns go down.

The intersection of a row and column is called a cell. So in the example shown in Fig. 6.1, the population of Bibb County, Alabama, would be in cell C6.

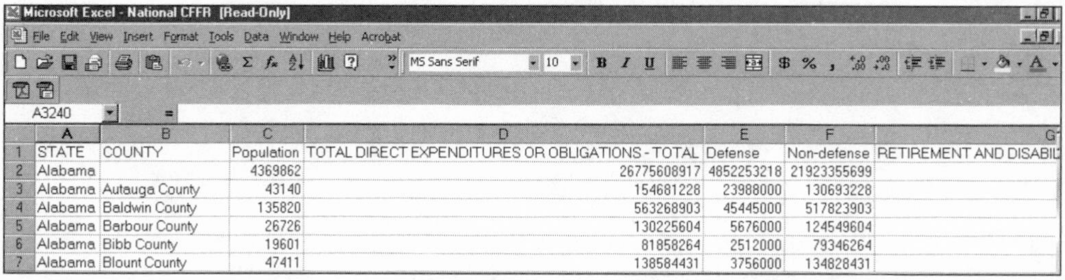

	A	B	C	D	E	F	G
1	STATE	COUNTY	Population	TOTAL DIRECT EXPENDITURES OR OBLIGATIONS - TOTAL	Defense	Non-defense	RETIREMENT AND DISABIL
2	Alabama		4369862	26775608917	4852253218	21923355699	
3	Alabama	Autauga County	43140	154681228	23988000	130693228	
4	Alabama	Baldwin County	135820	563268903	45445000	517823903	
5	Alabama	Barbour County	26726	130225604	5676000	124549604	
6	Alabama	Bibb County	19601	81858264	2512000	79346264	
7	Alabama	Blount County	47411	138584431	3756000	134828431	

FIGURE 6.1

It's important that we know how to define rows and columns. To define (or highlight) a row, click on the row number that you want to define. For example, to click on row 3, simply position the cursor over the 3 and click once. The row should get highlighted (see Fig. 6.2).

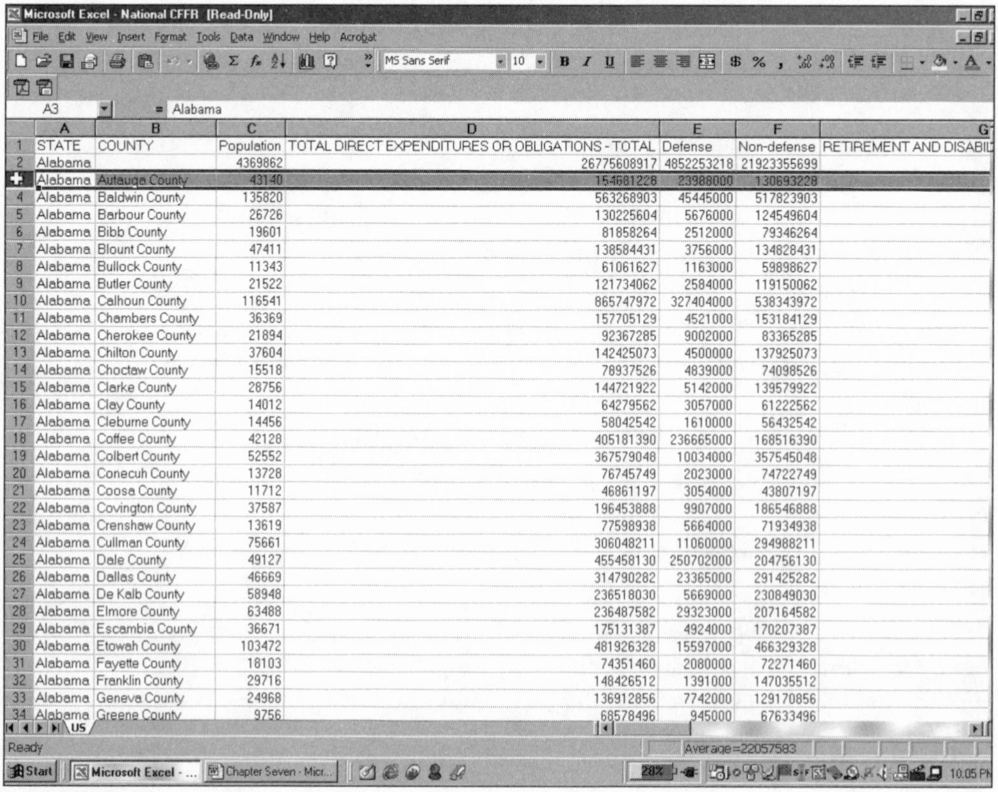

	A	B	C	D	E	F	G
1	STATE	COUNTY	Population	TOTAL DIRECT EXPENDITURES OR OBLIGATIONS - TOTAL	Defense	Non-defense	RETIREMENT AND DISABIL
2	Alabama		4369862	26775608917	4852253218	21923355699	
3	Alabama	Autauga County	43140	154681228	23988000	130693228	
4	Alabama	Baldwin County	135820	563268903	45445000	517823903	
5	Alabama	Barbour County	26726	130225604	5676000	124549604	
6	Alabama	Bibb County	19601	81858264	2512000	79346264	
7	Alabama	Blount County	47411	138584431	3756000	134828431	
8	Alabama	Bullock County	11343	61061627	1163000	59898627	
9	Alabama	Butler County	21522	121734062	2584000	119150062	
10	Alabama	Calhoun County	116541	865747972	327404000	538343972	
11	Alabama	Chambers County	36369	157705129	4521000	153184129	
12	Alabama	Cherokee County	21894	92367285	9002000	83365285	
13	Alabama	Chilton County	37604	142425073	4500000	137925073	
14	Alabama	Choctaw County	15518	78937526	4839000	74098526	
15	Alabama	Clarke County	28756	144721922	5142000	139579922	
16	Alabama	Clay County	14012	64279562	3057000	61222562	
17	Alabama	Cleburne County	14456	58042542	1610000	56432542	
18	Alabama	Coffee County	42128	405181390	236665000	168516390	
19	Alabama	Colbert County	52552	367579048	10034000	357545048	
20	Alabama	Conecuh County	13728	76745749	2023000	74722749	
21	Alabama	Coosa County	11712	46861197	3054000	43807197	
22	Alabama	Covington County	37587	196453888	9907000	186546888	
23	Alabama	Crenshaw County	13619	77598938	5664000	71934938	
24	Alabama	Cullman County	75661	306048211	11060000	294988211	
25	Alabama	Dale County	49127	455458130	250702000	204756130	
26	Alabama	Dallas County	46669	314790282	23365000	291425282	
27	Alabama	De Kalb County	58948	236518030	5669000	230849030	
28	Alabama	Elmore County	63488	236487582	29323000	207164582	
29	Alabama	Escambia County	36671	175131387	4924000	170207387	
30	Alabama	Etowah County	103472	481926328	15597000	466329328	
31	Alabama	Fayette County	18103	74351460	2080000	72271460	
32	Alabama	Franklin County	29716	148426512	1391000	147035512	
33	Alabama	Geneva County	24968	136912856	7742000	129170856	
34	Alabama	Greene County	9756	68578496	945000	67633496	

FIGURE 6.2

Defining a column is done much the same way. To define column C, click on the C at the top of the column, as in Fig. 6.3.

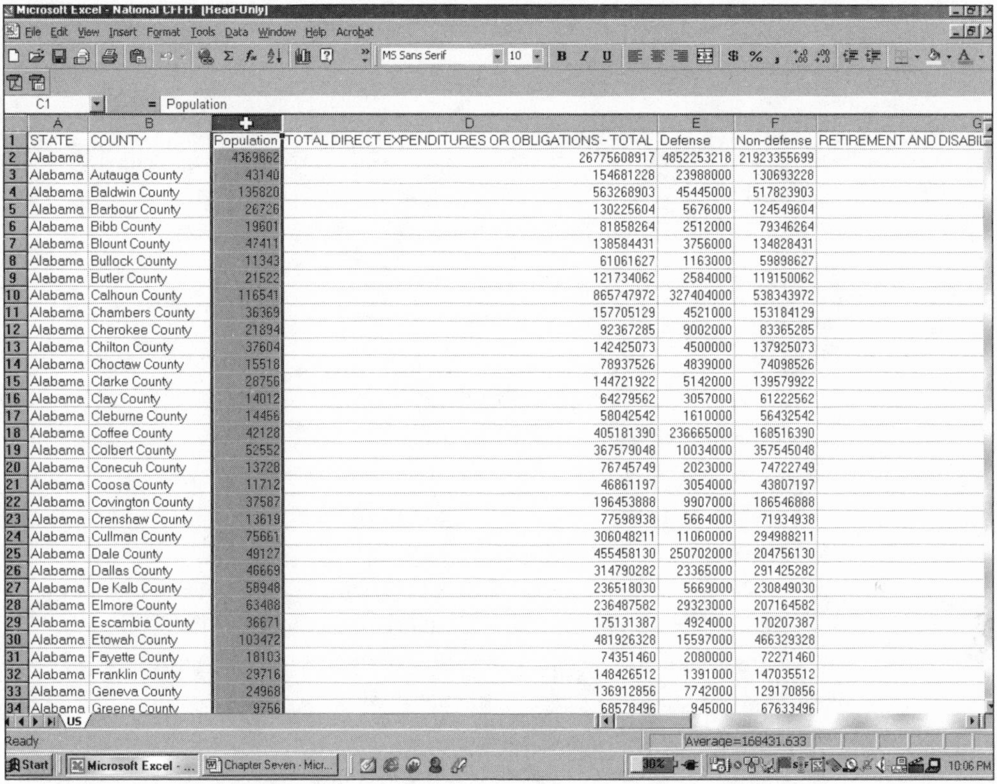

Microsoft Excel - National CFFR [Read-Only]

C1 = Population

	A	B	C	D	E	F	G
1	STATE	COUNTY	Population	TOTAL DIRECT EXPENDITURES OR OBLIGATIONS - TOTAL	Defense	Non-defense	RETIREMENT AND DISABIL
2	Alabama		4369862	26775608917	4852253218	21923355699	
3	Alabama	Autauga County	43140	154681228	23988000	130693228	
4	Alabama	Baldwin County	135820	563268903	45445000	517823903	
5	Alabama	Barbour County	26726	130225604	5676000	124549604	
6	Alabama	Bibb County	19601	81858264	2512000	79346264	
7	Alabama	Blount County	47411	138584431	3756000	134828431	
8	Alabama	Bullock County	11343	61061627	1163000	59898627	
9	Alabama	Butler County	21522	121734062	2584000	119150062	
10	Alabama	Calhoun County	116541	865747972	327404000	538343972	
11	Alabama	Chambers County	36369	157705129	4521000	153184129	
12	Alabama	Cherokee County	21894	92367285	9002000	83365285	
13	Alabama	Chilton County	37604	142425073	4500000	137925073	
14	Alabama	Choctaw County	15518	78937526	4839000	74098526	
15	Alabama	Clarke County	28756	144721922	5142000	139579922	
16	Alabama	Clay County	14012	64279562	3057000	61222562	
17	Alabama	Cleburne County	14456	58042542	1610000	56432542	
18	Alabama	Coffee County	42128	405181390	236665000	168516390	
19	Alabama	Colbert County	52552	367579048	10034000	357545048	
20	Alabama	Conecuh County	13728	76745749	2023000	74722749	
21	Alabama	Coosa County	11712	46861197	3054000	43807197	
22	Alabama	Covington County	37587	196453888	9907000	186546888	
23	Alabama	Crenshaw County	13619	77598938	5664000	71934938	
24	Alabama	Cullman County	75661	306048211	11060000	294988211	
25	Alabama	Dale County	49127	455458130	250702000	204756130	
26	Alabama	Dallas County	46669	314790282	23365000	291425282	
27	Alabama	De Kalb County	58948	236518030	5669000	230849030	
28	Alabama	Elmore County	63488	236487582	29323000	207164582	
29	Alabama	Escambia County	36671	175131387	4924000	170207387	
30	Alabama	Etowah County	103472	481926328	15597000	466329328	
31	Alabama	Fayette County	18103	74351460	2080000	72271460	
32	Alabama	Franklin County	29716	148426512	1391000	147035512	
33	Alabama	Geneva County	24968	136912856	7742000	129170856	
34	Alabama	Greene County	9756	68578496	945000	67633496	

Ready Average=168431.633

FIGURE 6.3

Finally, to define an individual cell, just click on it. For example, to define cell C4, click on it (see Fig. 6.4).

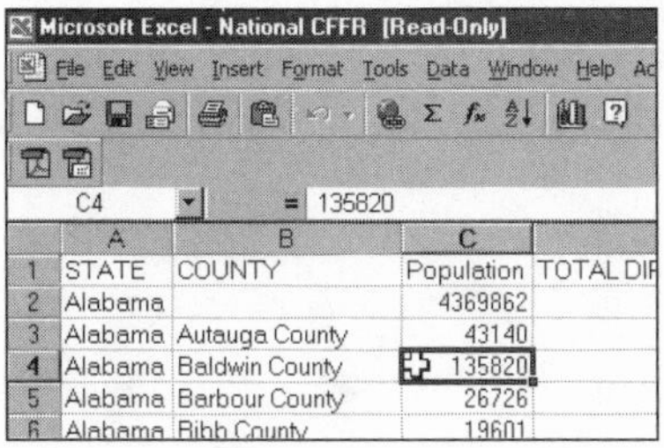

Microsoft Excel - National CFFR [Read-Only]

C4 = 135820

	A	B	C	
1	STATE	COUNTY	Population	TOTAL DIR
2	Alabama		4369862	
3	Alabama	Autauga County	43140	
4	Alabama	Baldwin County	135820	
5	Alabama	Barbour County	26726	
6	Alabama	Bibb County	19601	

FIGURE 6.4

To write something in a cell, simply click on it and begin writing. For example, if we wanted to write "No County" in Cell B2, we'd simply click on it and type "No County". If you look right above columns B and C in Fig. 6.5, you'll see that the text entry is located there. Now, define cell C1. See how it changes?

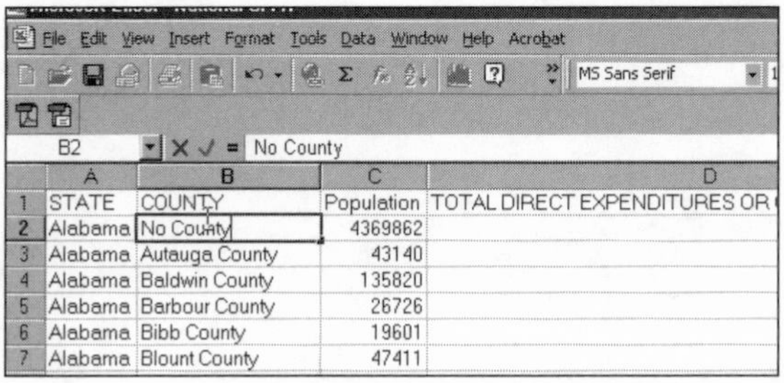

FIGURE 6.5

Next, we'll look at the right-click button, probably one of the most useful features in Excel. Right-clicking anywhere over a spreadsheet gives you access to a number of features. You can use the right-click to cut and paste, copy and paste, format cells (define the size, border, color, width, and height), insert rows or columns, and clear cells, rows, or columns. If you right-click, you should see the dialog box shown in Fig. 6.6.

Let's say we wanted to insert a row at the top. We'd define the row where we wanted to put the inserted row—say, row 1—and right-click, then click on "Insert" (see Fig. 6.7).

The result—a new, blank row above what is now row 2—is illustrated in Fig. 6.8. The same principle (just at a different angle) would be used to insert a column.

Sometimes, you'll find that you've made a mistake and done something you really didn't want to do. Although it's not on the right-click dialog box, you can undo the damage by going to the "Edit" menu and clicking on "Undo." Generally, you can undo things that you've done, going all the way back to the point where you last saved the spreadsheet.

Under the "Edit" menu you'll notice you can do searching and replacing. If you go over to the "Format" menu, you'll see one particularly handy item: the "Column" option. Often when you're working with Excel, your columns won't be entirely visible. There may be 45 characters, but you may only see 10 of them. To fix that, define the entire spreadsheet by clicking on the gray box above row 1 and to the left of column A. The en-

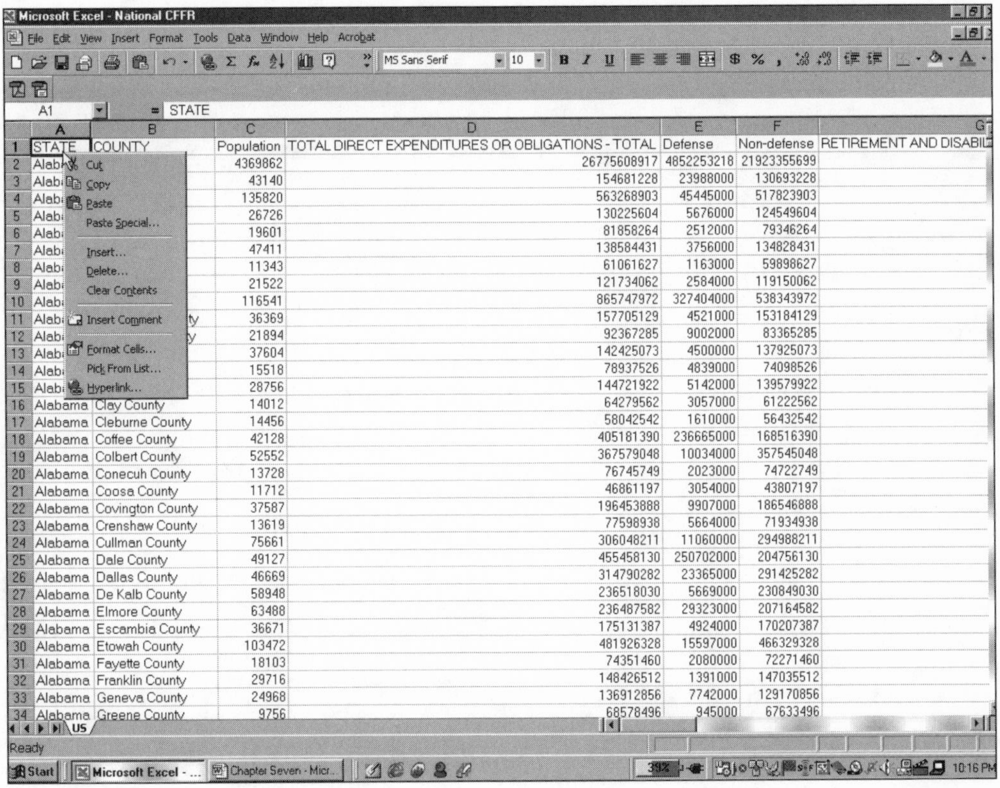

Microsoft Excel - National CFFR
File Edit View Insert Format Tools Data Window Help Acrobat
MS Sans Serif
10
A1
= STATE
STATE COUNTY Population TOTAL DIRECT EXPENDITURES OR OBLIGATIONS - TOTAL Defense Non-defense RETIREMENT AND DISABIL
Cut
Copy
Paste
Paste Special...
Insert...
Delete...
Clear Contents
Insert Comment
Format Cells...
Pick From List...
Hyperlink...
2 Alab 4369862 26775608917 4852253218 21923355699
3 Alab 43140 154681228 23988000 130693228
4 Alab 135820 563268903 45445000 517823903
5 Alab 26726 130225604 5676000 124549604
6 Alab 19601 81858264 2512000 79346264
7 Alab 47411 138584431 3756000 134828431
8 Alab 11343 61061627 1163000 59898627
9 Alab 21522 121734062 2584000 119150062
10 Alab 116541 865747972 327404000 538343972
11 Alab ty 36369 157705129 4521000 153184129
12 Alab y 21894 92367285 9002000 83365285
13 Alab 37604 142425073 4500000 137925073
14 Alab 15518 78937526 4839000 74098526
15 Alab 28756 144721922 5142000 139579922
16 Alabama Clay County 14012 64279562 3057000 61222562
17 Alabama Cleburne County 14456 58042542 1610000 56432542
18 Alabama Coffee County 42128 405181390 236665000 168516390
19 Alabama Colbert County 52552 367579048 10034000 357545048
20 Alabama Conecuh County 13728 76745749 2023000 74722749
21 Alabama Coosa County 11712 46861197 3054000 43807197
22 Alabama Covington County 37587 196453888 9907000 186546888
23 Alabama Crenshaw County 13619 77598938 5664000 71934938
24 Alabama Cullman County 75661 306048211 11060000 294988211
25 Alabama Dale County 49127 455458130 250702000 204756130
26 Alabama Dallas County 46669 314790282 23365000 291425282
27 Alabama De Kalb County 58948 236518030 5669000 230849030
28 Alabama Elmore County 63488 236487582 29323000 207164582
29 Alabama Escambia County 36671 175131387 4924000 170207387
30 Alabama Etowah County 103472 481926328 15597000 466329328
31 Alabama Fayette County 18103 74351460 2080000 72271460
32 Alabama Franklin County 29716 148426512 1391000 147035512
33 Alabama Geneva County 24968 136912856 7742000 129170856
34 Alabama Greene County 9756 68578496 945000 67633496
US
Ready
Start
Microsoft Excel - ...
Chapter Seven - Micr...
10:16 PM

FIGURE 6.6

tire spreadsheet should get highlighted. Then, go to "Format," then "Columns," then "Autofit." All the cells should widen out so that the text is readable.

One other nice option on the right-click menu is "Hide." Let's say we want to see more of the columns to the right of column E, and we don't care about column D. We can hide it. Simply define it, then right-click, then select "Hide." Column D goes away, with a thick line to denote that it's been hidden. To un-hide the column, click on the columns to either side—in this case, columns C and E—right-click, and click on "Unhide."

Another way to see columns without having to scroll over to the right is to use the "Freeze Panes" option under the "Window" menu. Let's say we wanted to look at column AJ, "Guaranteed Loans," and we wanted to see the county name next to it. We'd first define column C to "freeze" the pane, as shown in Fig. 6.9.

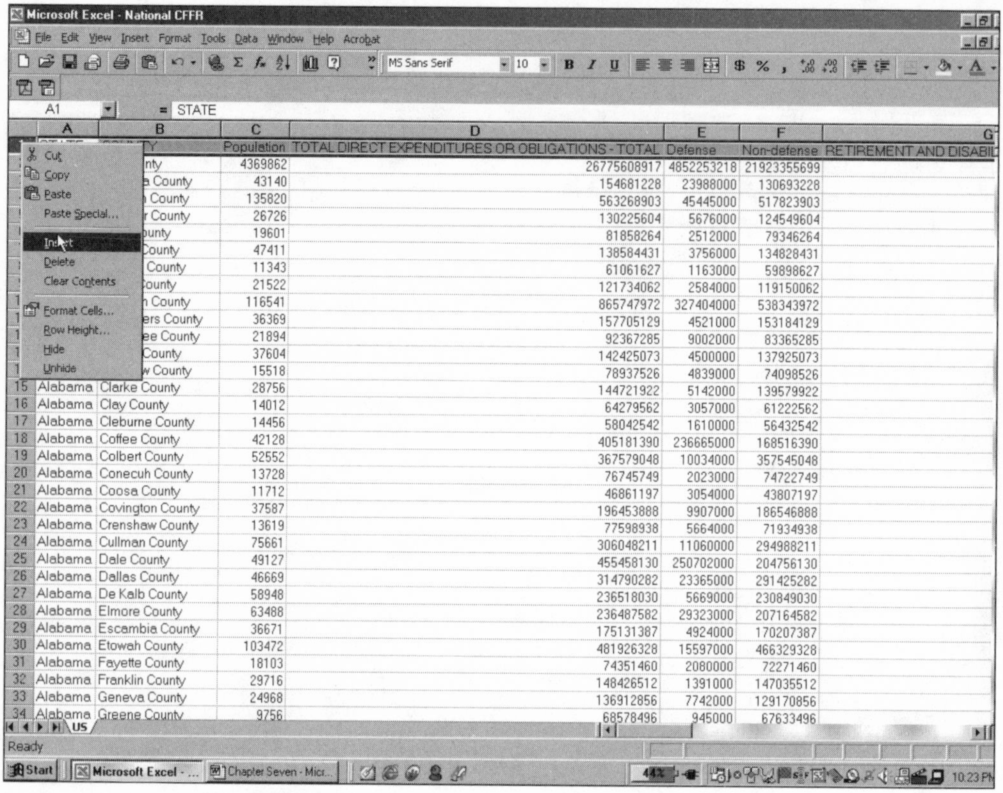

FIGURE 6.7

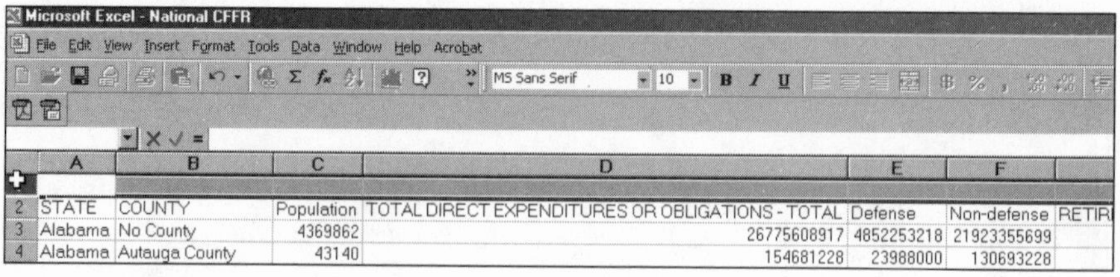

FIGURE 6.8

Next, we scroll over until column AJ is adjacent to column B (see Fig. 6.10).

To unfreeze the panes, just go to the "Window" menu and click on "Unfreeze Panes."(Note: You can also do the same thing horizontally, in case you want to look at the bottom rows in a spreadsheet.)

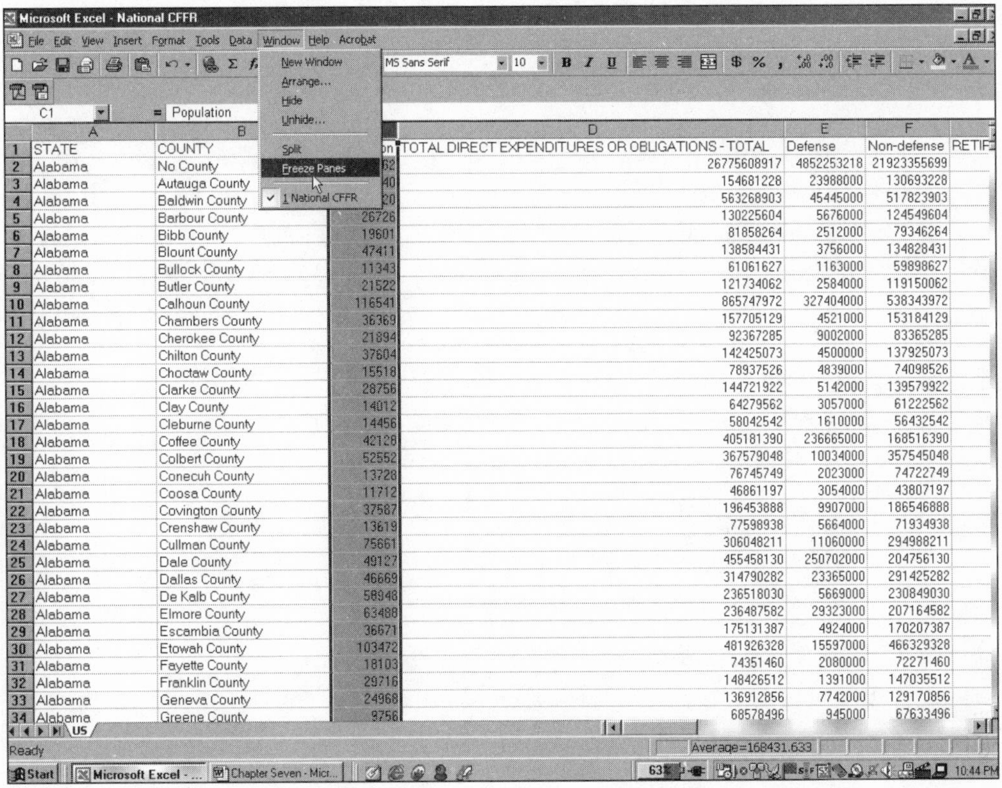

FIGURE 6.9

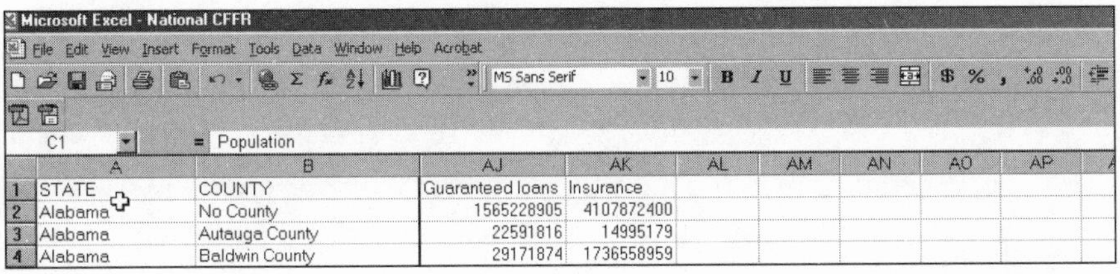

FIGURE 6.10

Now that you're somewhat acquainted with Excel, it's time to get to work. The first thing that you might want to find out from the Consolidated Federal Funds Report is simple: Which county received the most in federal funds, as defined in column D? You could scroll through the 3,000 or so records; chances are pretty good it's a big city, and that narrows it down considerably. Instead, though, we'll use the most commonly used spreadsheet function for a newsroom—sorting.

To perform a sort on a spreadsheet, first define the whole spreadsheet. This isn't always necessary, but it's a good safety precaution. If you don't define the entire spreadsheet, it's possible that you might sort only the rows in the selected column. If you were sorting a spreadsheet of the population of major U.S. cities, for example, and only sorted the population column, you could end up reporting that Anchorage had more than 8 million people. So to avoid that, define the whole spreadsheet by clicking on the gray box above row 1 and to the left of column A.

Next, go to the "Data" menu at the top of the screen and click on "Sort." We should get a dialog box like that shown in Fig. 6.11.

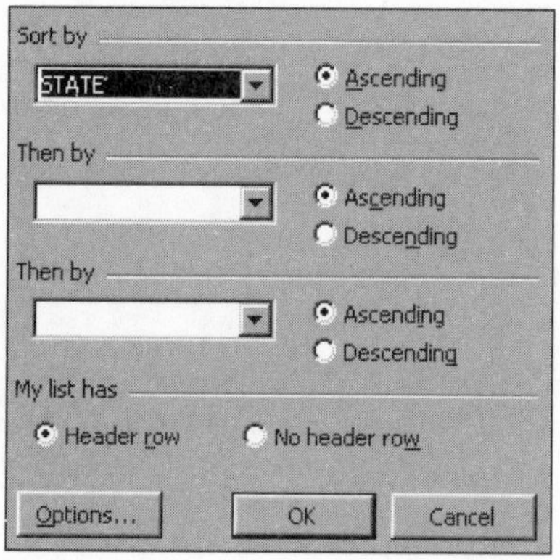

FIGURE 6.11

Three things are worth mentioning here. First, above the three buttons in the dialog box are a couple of radio buttons, for lists having a header row or no header row. Frequently, the headers won't be apparent to Excel, and the "No header row" button will be selected. You'll have to check "Header row" if in fact you have one.

Second, Excel allows you to sort in either ascending or descending order. Ascending is A to Z, or 0 to whatever. Descending is Z to A, or whatever to 0. When sorting numbers, most reporters will want to use a descending sort; when sorting alphabetical characters, most will use an ascending sort.

Finally, you can use the pull-down menus to select a column header to sort on. We don't care about the state, since that's already been alphabetized. We do, however, want to find out which county is getting the most federal funds, so use the pull-down menu to select column D, or "Total Direct Expenditures or Obligations—Total."

Next, click on "Descending" since we want to go from the county with the most funds to the one with the least, then click on "OK" and get the results.

The results are fairly predictable. The Census Bureau treats the five-county New York City area as one county, so it'll come out on top; then Los Angeles, then Washington, D.C., then Chicago. Statewise, California, New York, Texas, Florida, and Pennsylvania get the most federal funds, in that order.

This isn't exactly surprising. Of course money goes where the most people work. But looking at the spreadsheet, we can also see that we have a column for population. What if we could figure out how many federal dollars are spent *per person* in each U.S. county? We can. The first thing we'll need to do is to insert a new column after the "Population" column. We'll call it "Per Capita Spending" (see Fig. 6.12).

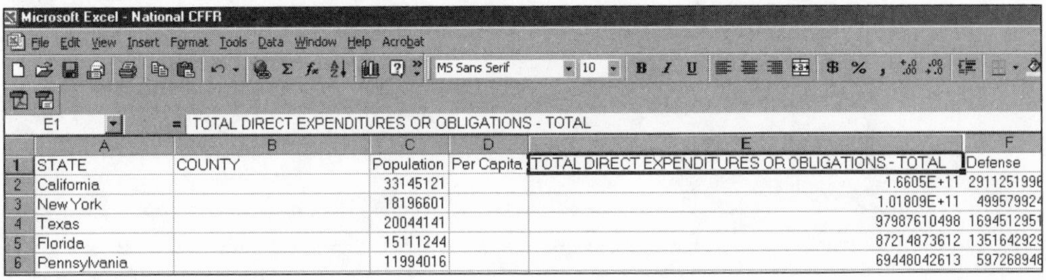

FIGURE 6.12

Note that you may not have enough column space to see all of the header. That's OK; it's there. If you want to see the entire column, just move your cursor until it turns into something that the computer-assisted reporting community calls "a double-headed pointed thingy," and double-click. The column should change to a more usable width.

Next, we start with the essential first step in any formula—the "=" sign. Nine times out of ten, if a formula in Excel doesn't work, it's because you forgot to start it properly. So we'll type an "=" sign into cell D2. We know that we'll need data from two columns to figure out a per-person spending amount by county. The first, of course, will be the population, located in column C. The second will be total spending, which is now located in column E. To figure out total spending per person, then, we'll divide total spending by population. So our formula will be column E divided by column C. Unfortunately, Excel won't let you just divide those two columns. You have to start with the first cell—E2/C2—and copy the formula all the way down (see Fig. 6.13).

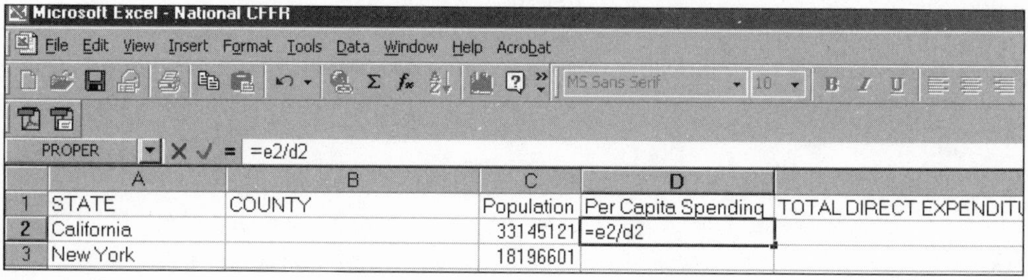

FIGURE 6.13

Fortunately, there's a quick way to copy the formula. Move your cursor to the lower right-hand corner of cell D2, until it resembles a black cross as shown in Fig. 6.14.

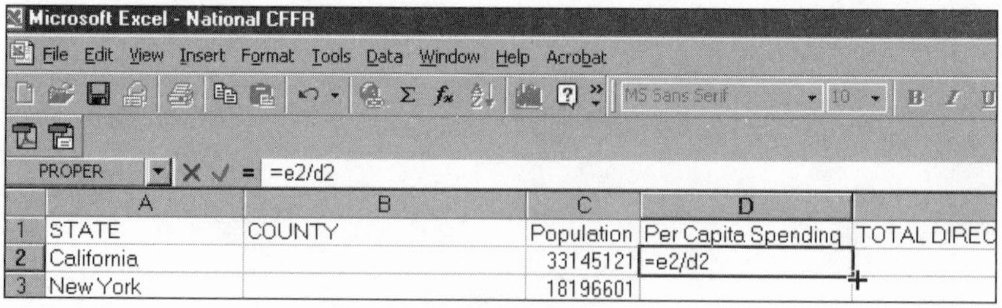

FIGURE 6.14

If you double-click, the resulting per-capita spending figures (using the formula) will be pasted all the way down to the last cell (see Fig. 6.15).

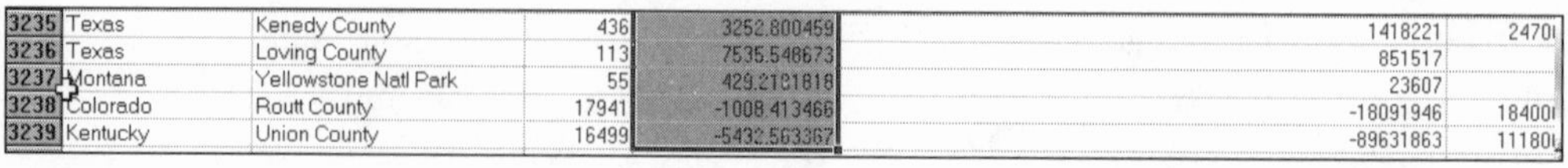

FIGURE 6.15

(Note the negative numbers; when you see these kinds of things happening, you need to check with the source of the data for inaccuracies.)

One other important thing: If you click on a cell—any cell in column D—you'll see in the formula bar at the top that Excel actually sees the formula, not the number. For example, click on cell D3230 (see Fig. 6.16).

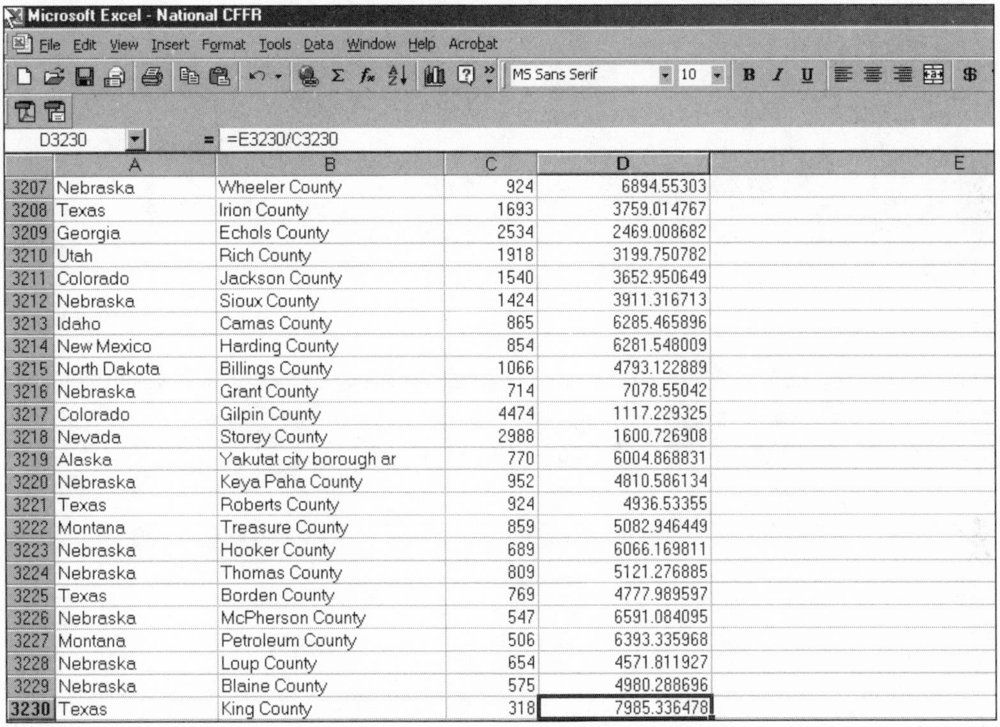
Microsoft Excel - National CFFR

File Edit View Insert Format Tools Data Window Help Acrobat

D3230 = =E3230/C3230

	A	B	C	D	E
3207	Nebraska	Wheeler County	924	6894.55303	
3208	Texas	Irion County	1693	3759.014767	
3209	Georgia	Echols County	2534	2469.008682	
3210	Utah	Rich County	1918	3199.750782	
3211	Colorado	Jackson County	1540	3652.950649	
3212	Nebraska	Sioux County	1424	3911.316713	
3213	Idaho	Camas County	865	6285.465896	
3214	New Mexico	Harding County	854	6281.548009	
3215	North Dakota	Billings County	1066	4793.122889	
3216	Nebraska	Grant County	714	7078.55042	
3217	Colorado	Gilpin County	4474	1117.229325	
3218	Nevada	Storey County	2988	1600.726908	
3219	Alaska	Yakutat city borough ar	770	6004.868831	
3220	Nebraska	Keya Paha County	952	4810.586134	
3221	Texas	Roberts County	924	4936.53355	
3222	Montana	Treasure County	859	5082.946449	
3223	Nebraska	Hooker County	689	6066.169811	
3224	Nebraska	Thomas County	809	5121.276885	
3225	Texas	Borden County	769	4777.989597	
3226	Nebraska	McPherson County	547	6591.084095	
3227	Montana	Petroleum County	506	6393.335968	
3228	Nebraska	Loup County	654	4571.811927	
3229	Nebraska	Blaine County	575	4980.288696	
3230	Texas	King County	318	7985.336478	

FIGURE 6.16

If we were reasonably certain that the numbers in columns C and E weren't going to change, we could make Excel see the numbers—instead of the formula—by defining column D, right-clicking, copying, and then selecting the "Paste Special" option. When we do, we'd see the dialog box shown in Fig. 6.17.

If we select the "Values" button and click on "OK," Excel will now show the numbers in the formula bar rather than the formula (see Fig. 6.18).

But back to the business at hand: Which county receives the most federal funds on a per-person basis? We define the spreadsheet, click on

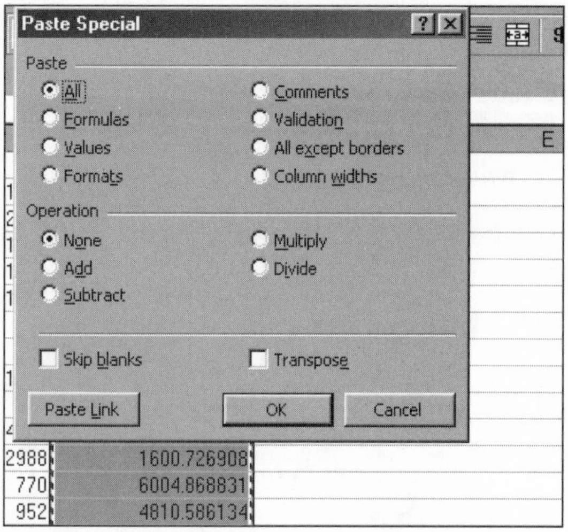

FIGURE 6.17

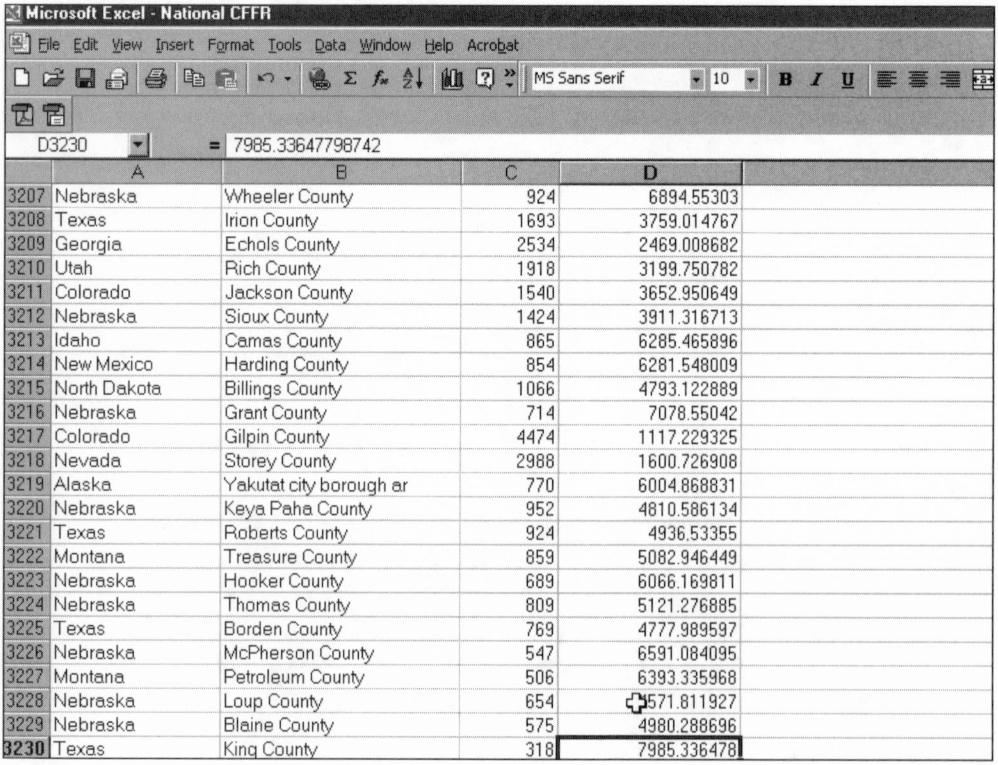

	A	B	C	D
3207	Nebraska	Wheeler County	924	6894.55303
3208	Texas	Irion County	1693	3759.014767
3209	Georgia	Echols County	2534	2469.008682
3210	Utah	Rich County	1918	3199.750782
3211	Colorado	Jackson County	1540	3652.950649
3212	Nebraska	Sioux County	1424	3911.316713
3213	Idaho	Camas County	865	6285.465896
3214	New Mexico	Harding County	854	6281.548009
3215	North Dakota	Billings County	1066	4793.122889
3216	Nebraska	Grant County	714	7078.55042
3217	Colorado	Gilpin County	4474	1117.229325
3218	Nevada	Storey County	2988	1600.726908
3219	Alaska	Yakutat city borough ar	770	6004.868831
3220	Nebraska	Keya Paha County	952	4810.586134
3221	Texas	Roberts County	924	4936.53355
3222	Montana	Treasure County	859	5082.946449
3223	Nebraska	Hooker County	689	6066.169811
3224	Nebraska	Thomas County	809	5121.276885
3225	Texas	Borden County	769	4777.989597
3226	Nebraska	McPherson County	547	6591.084095
3227	Montana	Petroleum County	506	6393.335968
3228	Nebraska	Loup County	654	[illegible]571.811927
3229	Nebraska	Blaine County	575	4980.288696
3230	Texas	King County	318	7985.336478

FIGURE 6.18

"Data," then "Sort," by "Per Capita Spending," in descending order, and get the results in Fig. 6.19.

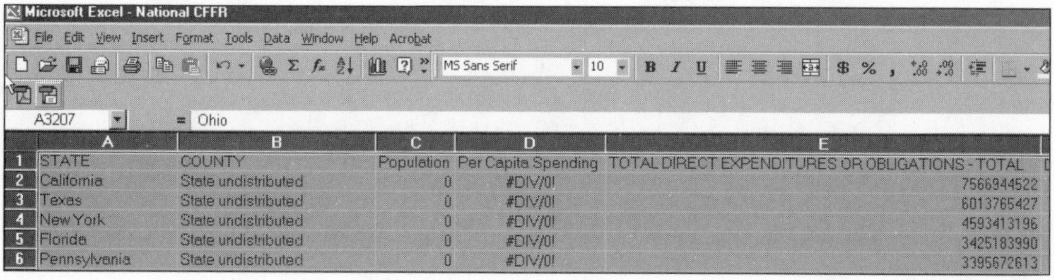

FIGURE 6.19

This isn't much help. Since we're dividing something by 0, Excel won't be able to calculate the formula, hence the "#DIV/0!" warning. But when we scroll down a bit, we'll find that Fairfax County, Virginia, is at the top of the list.

Next, what if we wanted to look at counties within a given state? We could, of course, sort by state name, and then copy-and-paste the counties into a separate spreadsheet, then sort by per-capita spending . . . but that's a bit cumbersome. Instead, we'll use the filtering tool in Excel. If we wanted to look at per-capita spending for Virginia alone, we would define the whole spreadsheet, go to "Data," then "Filter," then "AutoFilter." If we look closely, we can see there are now pull-down tabs across the first row. If we go to the pull-down tab in cell A1, we find more options (see Fig. 6.20).

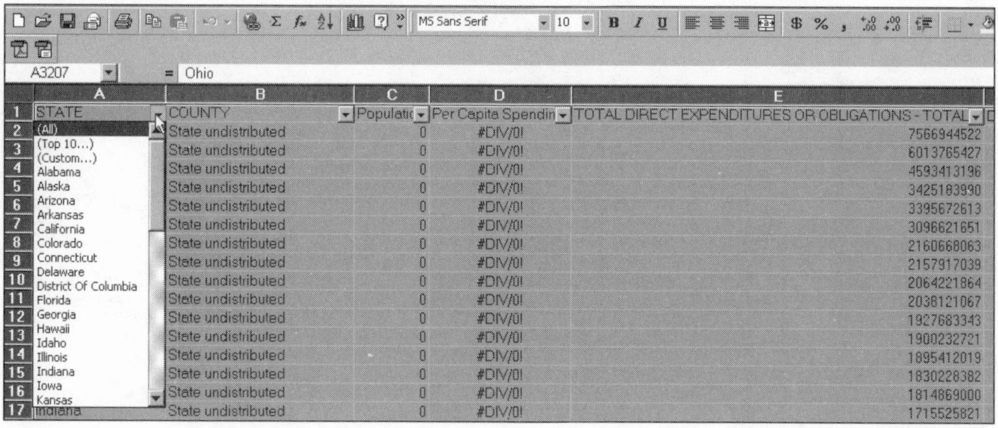

FIGURE 6.20

When we select "Virginia" from the pull-down menu, the spreadsheet becomes considerably smaller. At the bottom of the spreadsheet, we can also see how many records were found (see Fig. 6.21).

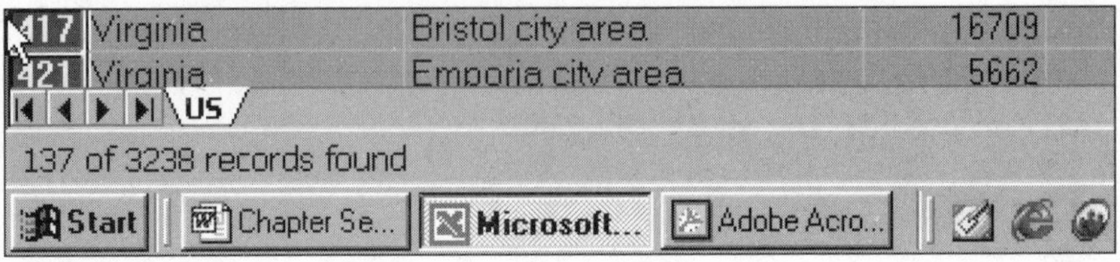

FIGURE 6.21

If we want to look at the average per-capita spending by county, there's a really quick way to do it. We define column D, then move down to the bottom of the page, and right-click, as shown in Fig. 6.22.

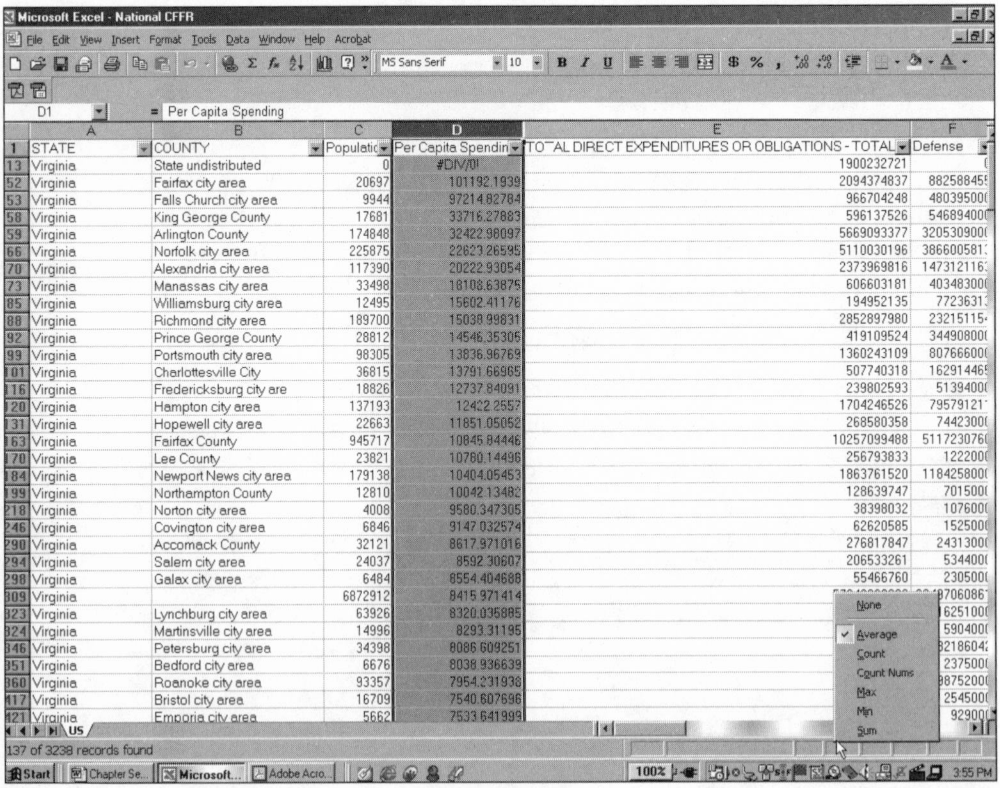

FIGURE 6.22

If we click on the "Average" button, Excel calculates the average for the defined area—assuming there aren't any nonnumeric characters. We'll have to delete the characters in cell D13 and take out the state totals to ensure accuracy. Once we do that, we see that the average per-capita amount in Virginia is $7,388.62.

You can also use custom filters. Within Virginia, let's say we just wanted to look at city areas. We'd click on the filter pull-down in the "County" column and select "Custom." We can use the pull-down menu on the upper left-hand side for a number of options (see Fig. 6.23).

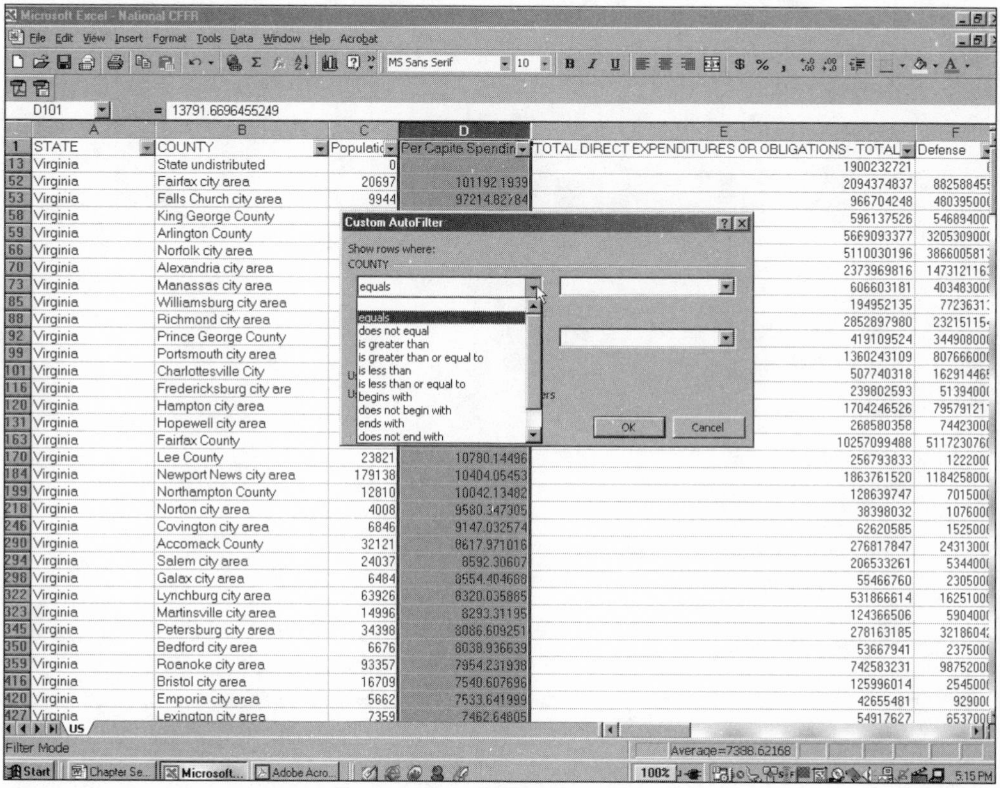

FIGURE 6.23

In this case, since we want "city area" only, we'll select "ends with" and enter "city area" (see Fig. 6.24).

When we click on "OK," we can see that the filter works because specific city areas appear in column B. We also see that the average per-capita

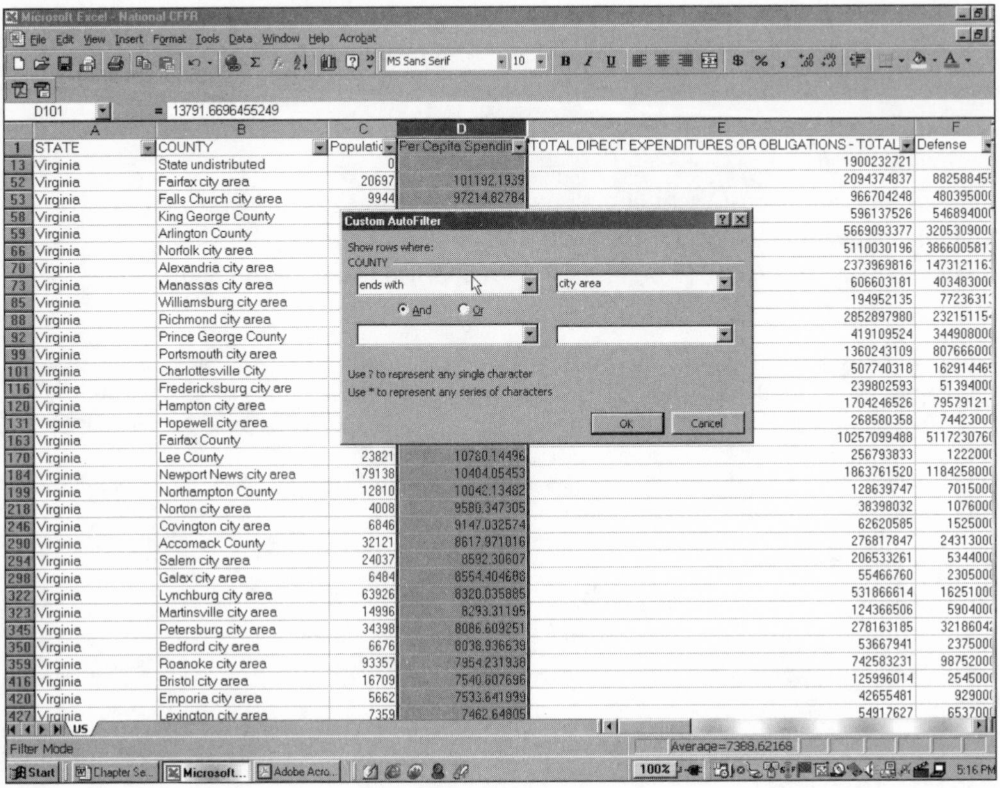

FIGURE 6.24

spending has changed at the bottom of the screen: It is now $13,880.15 (see Fig. 6.25).

There are other ways we can calculate formulas on spreadsheets besides using the approach illustrated in Figs. 6.13 and 6.14. The "Paste Function" button can be used for a wide array of formulas. If you go to a blank cell at the bottom of the spreadsheet and click on it, you get an idea of its scope (see Fig. 6.26).

Let's try using the "Sum" function to calculate the total federal spending in city areas. If we go to the bottom of the spreadsheet, at cell D3239, and click on the "Paste Function" button, we can select the "Sum" option from either the "All" or "Math & Trig" function categories. Excel will automatically ask us for a range, as shown in Fig. 6.27. The range is automatically calculated, and the formula result is given at the bottom of the box.

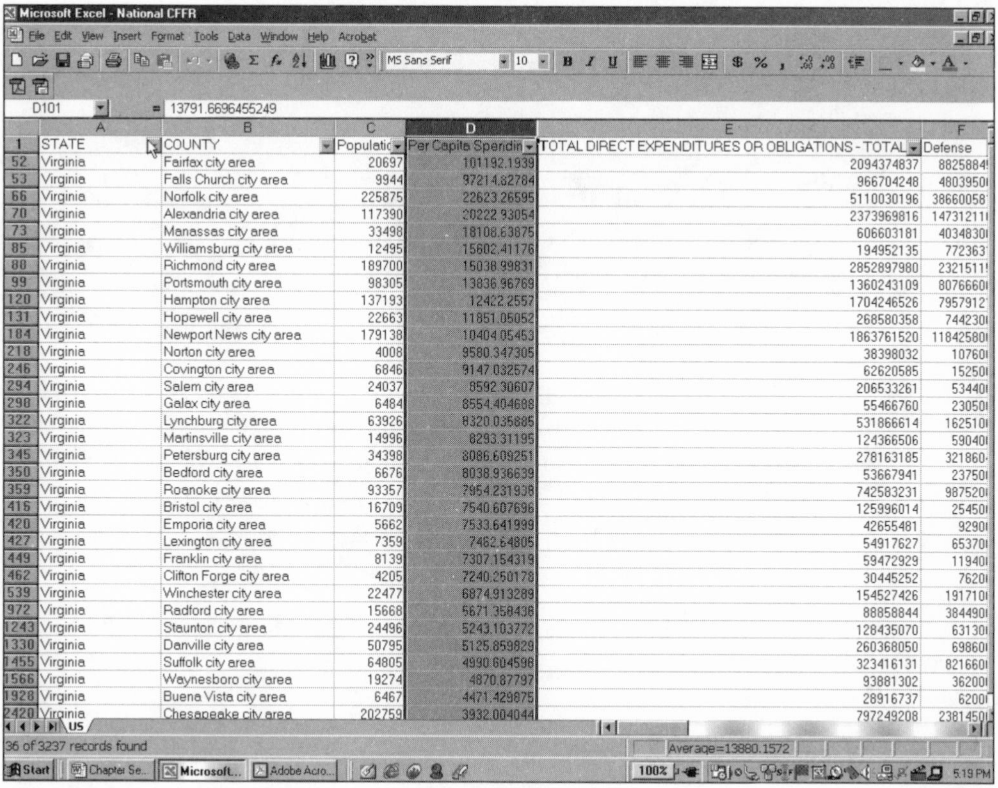

FIGURE 6.25

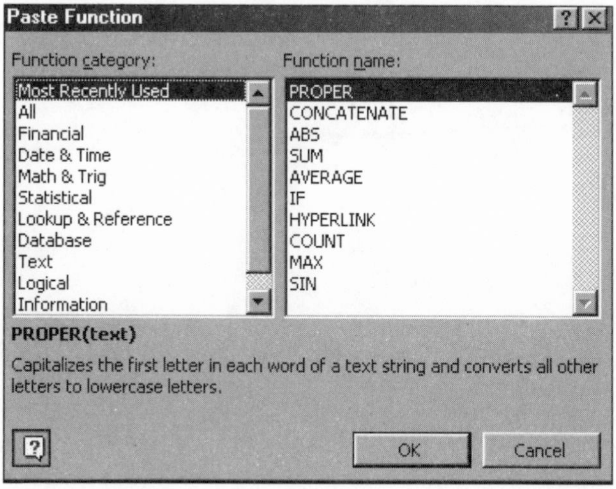

FIGURE 6.26

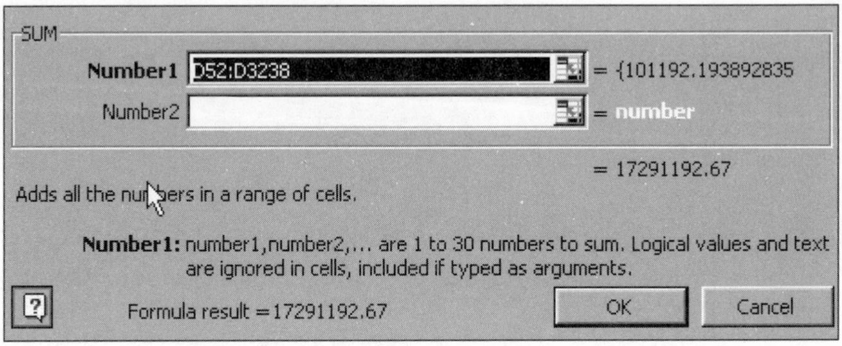

FIGURE 6.27

Of course, you can always use the raw formula to get the same result, but that's one of the beauties of a good spreadsheet program. A well-designed spreadsheet will have more than one way to get results, and in the end it doesn't matter how reporters calculate numbers—as long as they're correct.

CHAPTER SEVEN

Databases

So you've learned how to sort, rank, filter, and calculate with Excel. What more can a reporter need? Plenty, in today's world. Spreadsheets are great tools for reporters, but sometimes they're not enough. Let's look at a couple of scenarios where you might need something more.

A reporter has asked for prison records, or student loan data, or banking deposits from a federal agency. The files are in a *dbf (dBase) or *txt (text) format. No problem; those can be opened with a basic spreadsheet program, assuming that there aren't more than 69,000 records (which is roughly the most that any spreadsheet program will handle). But what if the data comes in separate files, and what if there aren't an equal number of records in each file?

To complicate things, what if the reporter wants to group the records? True, you can filter data in a spreadsheet all day long with today's software. But that's what you'd be doing if you have thousands of records that you wanted to group—you'd be filtering all day (if not all week), and most reporters just don't have that kind of time.

Database programs, such as Microsoft Access, FoxPro, or Paradox, are designed for those problems. First, they're relational database programs, which means they can relate one file to another—as long as there's a *unique* record number, such as a Social Security number or other identifier, in both tables. If, for example, you wanted to combine a database of school bus drivers with a database of convicted drunk drivers, you wouldn't want to do it using a "last name" field. What if you were looking at several hundred bus drivers named "Smith" in your state? How would you know you had the right one? You'd need something that's highly accurate, and matching the Social Security numbers (or drivers' license numbers) from a school bus drivers' database to a database of convicted drunk drivers is a lot safer than using last names. The idea is to get a *unique* identifier.

Let's look at a database of student loans. When we open the program in Microsoft Access, we see that there are four tables (see Fig. 7.1).

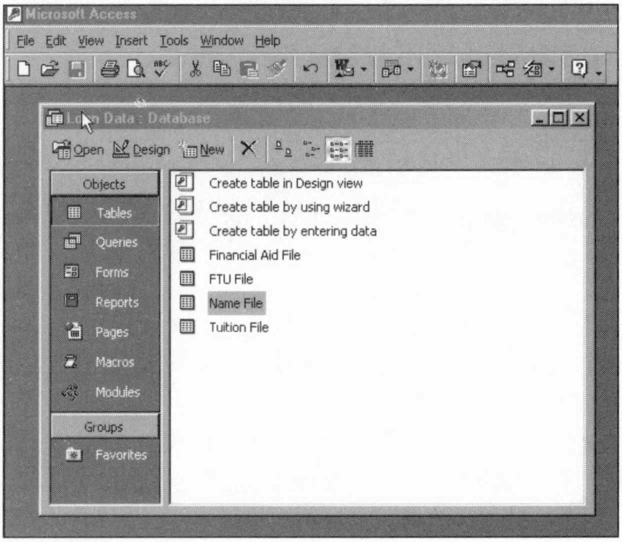

FIGURE 7.1

Next, open the "Name" table by double-clicking on it (or using the "Open" icon in the upper left-hand corner of the window) and see what's there. You may notice a strong resemblance to a spreadsheet (see Fig. 7.2).

At this point, it's always a good idea to look at the very bottom of the screen, where you'll see how many records are in the table. In this case, Access tells us there are 6,214 records in this particular table. What kind of records? You've been looking at the "Datasheet" view. Now, go to the upper left-hand corner of the window and click on the "Design" icon. When you do, you'll see that Access gives you not only the name of the columns, but also the type of character (see Fig. 7.3).

If you click on the "Data Type" column, you'll see that there are lots of options (see Fig. 7.4).

Now that you're somewhat familiar with the table, it's time to get to work. There's not a lot in this table, so working with it is a fairly straightforward exercise. The first thing we might want to do is to find out which

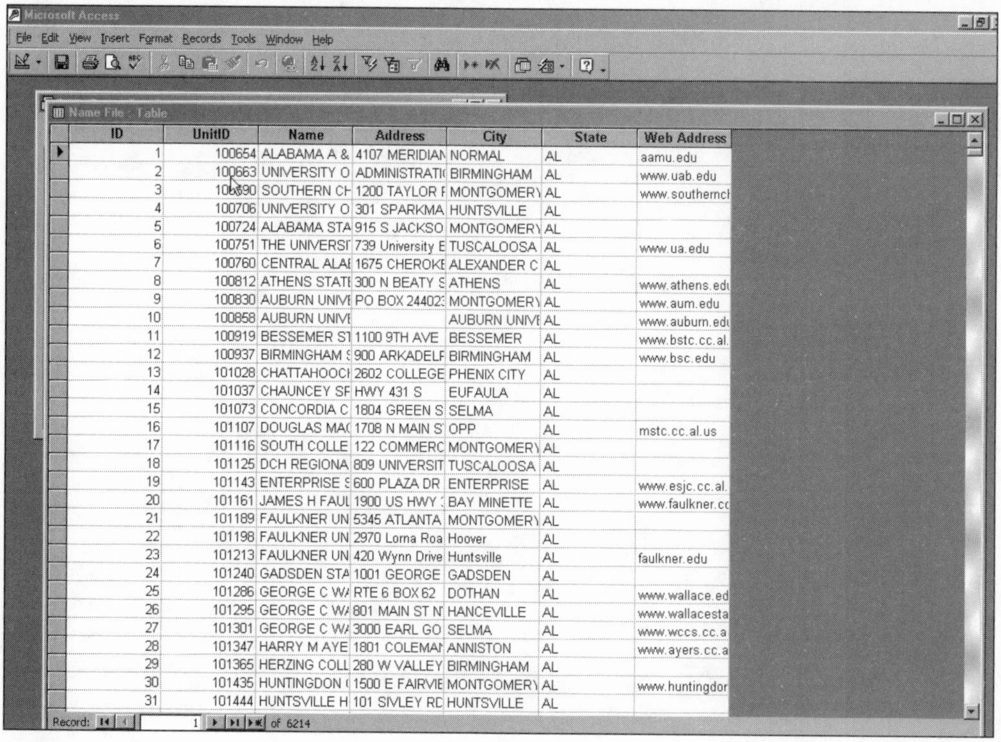

ID	UnitID	Name	Address	City	State	Web Address
1	100654	ALABAMA A &	4107 MERIDIAN	NORMAL	AL	aamu.edu
2	100663	UNIVERSITY O	ADMINISTRATI	BIRMINGHAM	AL	www.uab.edu
3	10[illegible]90	SOUTHERN CH	1200 TAYLOR F	MONTGOMERY	AL	www.southernch
4	100706	UNIVERSITY O	301 SPARKMA	HUNTSVILLE	AL	
5	100724	ALABAMA STA	915 S JACKSO	MONTGOMERY	AL	
6	100751	THE UNIVERSI	739 University E	TUSCALOOSA	AL	www.ua.edu
7	100760	CENTRAL ALAI	1675 CHEROKE	ALEXANDER C	AL	
8	100812	ATHENS STATI	300 N BEATY S	ATHENS	AL	www.athens.edu
9	100830	AUBURN UNIVE	PO BOX 24402	MONTGOMERY	AL	www.aum.edu
10	100858	AUBURN UNIVE		AUBURN UNIVE	AL	www.auburn.edu
11	100919	BESSEMER ST	1100 9TH AVE	BESSEMER	AL	www.bstc.cc.al.
12	100937	BIRMINGHAM S	900 ARKADELF	BIRMINGHAM	AL	www.bsc.edu
13	101028	CHATTAHOOCH	2602 COLLEGE	PHENIX CITY	AL	
14	101037	CHAUNCEY SF	HWY 431 S	EUFAULA	AL	
15	101073	CONCORDIA C	1804 GREEN S	SELMA	AL	
16	101107	DOUGLAS MAC	1708 N MAIN ST	OPP	AL	mstc.cc.al.us
17	101116	SOUTH COLLE	122 COMMERC	MONTGOMERY	AL	
18	101125	DCH REGIONA	809 UNIVERSIT	TUSCALOOSA	AL	
19	101143	ENTERPRISE S	600 PLAZA DR	ENTERPRISE	AL	www.esjc.cc.al.
20	101161	JAMES H FAUL	1900 US HWY	BAY MINETTE	AL	www.faulkner.cc
21	101189	FAULKNER UN	5345 ATLANTA	MONTGOMERY	AL	
22	101198	FAULKNER UN	2970 Lorna Roa	Hoover	AL	
23	101213	FAULKNER UN	420 Wynn Drive	Huntsville	AL	faulkner.edu
24	101240	GADSDEN STA	1001 GEORGE	GADSDEN	AL	
25	101286	GEORGE C WA	RTE 6 BOX 62	DOTHAN	AL	www.wallace.ed
26	101295	GEORGE C WA	801 MAIN ST N	HANCEVILLE	AL	www.wallacesta
27	101301	GEORGE C WA	3000 EARL GO	SELMA	AL	www.wccs.cc.a
28	101347	HARRY M AYE	1801 COLEMAN	ANNISTON	AL	www.ayers.cc.a
29	101365	HERZING COLL	280 W VALLEY	BIRMINGHAM	AL	
30	101435	HUNTINGDON	1500 E FAIRVIE	MONTGOMERY	AL	www.huntingdor
31	101444	HUNTSVILLE H	101 SIVLEY RD	HUNTSVILLE	AL	

FIGURE 7.2

state has the most schools. We could do that in Excel, but it would require doing 50 different filters and probably creating a new spreadsheet just to keep up with them all. So we'll try creating a basic "select" query in Access.

When you return to the main menu of the database by closing the design view, you'll see a "Query" tab when the "Objects" bar is selected. When you click on the "Query" tab, your table names will disappear. You should see a window that looks like the screen in Fig. 7.5.

Start by clicking on the "Create query in Design view" icon. We know the table we want is the Name File. So we'll highlight it, and click on "Add" and then "Close." You can make the boxes bigger for easier reading by clicking on the square in the upper right-hand corner of the Query1: Select Query box.

Next, we need to insert the fields that we want. In this case, we know we'll want the school and the state. So we'll click on "Name" and then "State." Our table should look like Fig. 7.6.

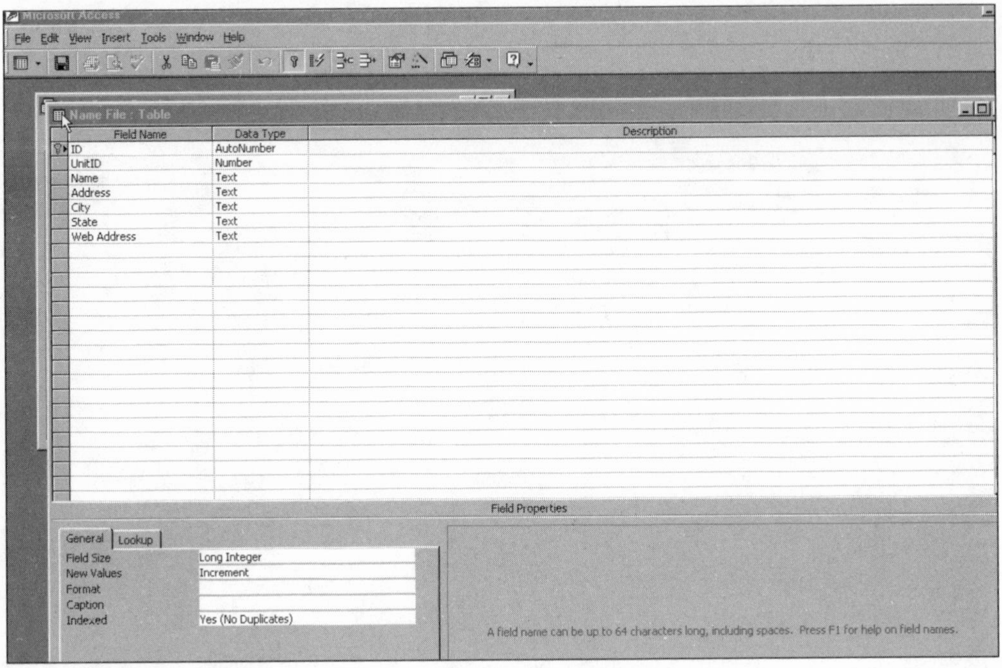

FIGURE 7.3

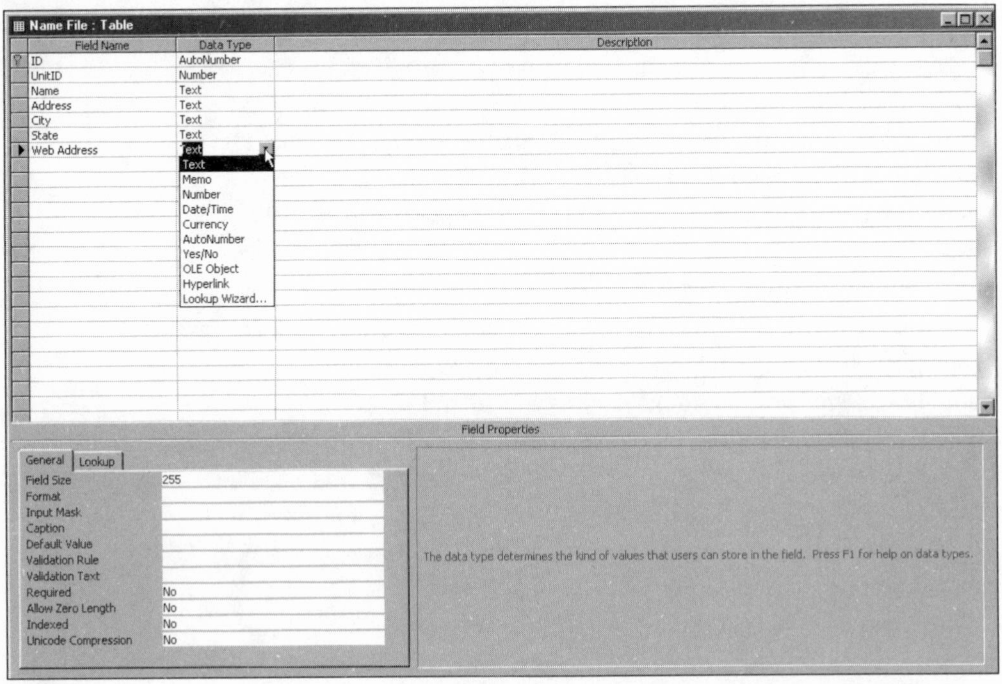

FIGURE 7.4

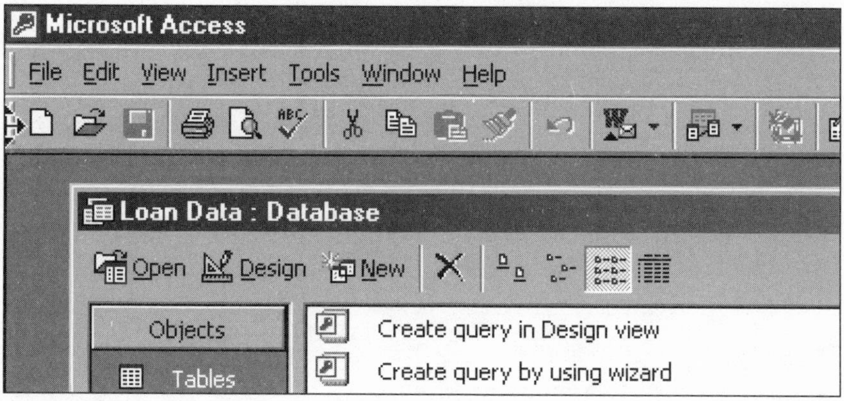

FIGURE 7.5

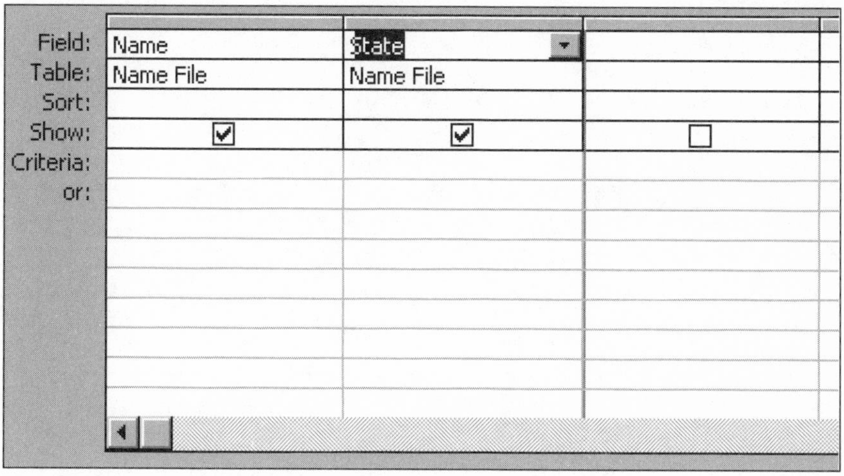

FIGURE 7.6

At this point, if we ran the query by clicking on the red exclamation mark, as seen in Fig. 7.7, we'd just get a list of all schools and states, which is not what we want.

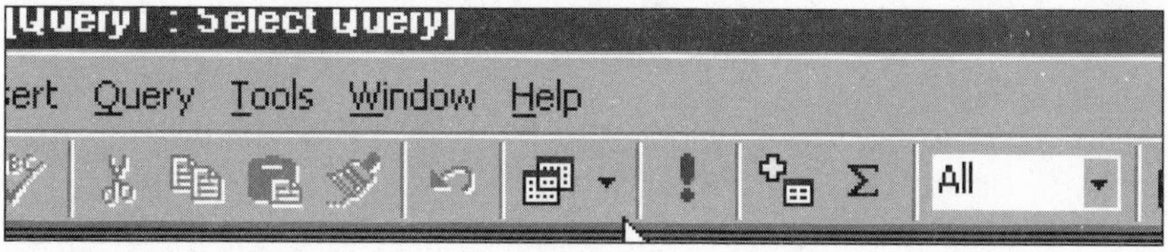

FIGURE 7.7

Instead, we want to "Group By state" and "Count" the number of schools in each state. Both "Group By" and "Count" have very specific meanings in Access. The way we group is to click on the Σ button to add a new row to our query. When we click on the button, we get this additional Total row (see Fig. 7.8).

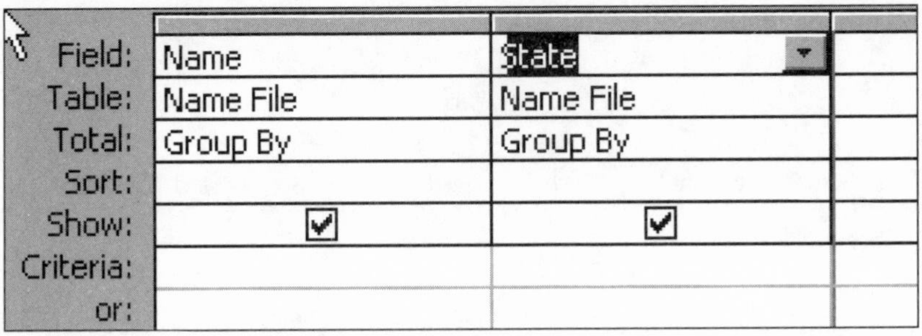

FIGURE 7.8

You can see that the default for the Total row is "Group By." If you click on the "Group By" cell, you'll see there are other options (see Fig. 7.9).

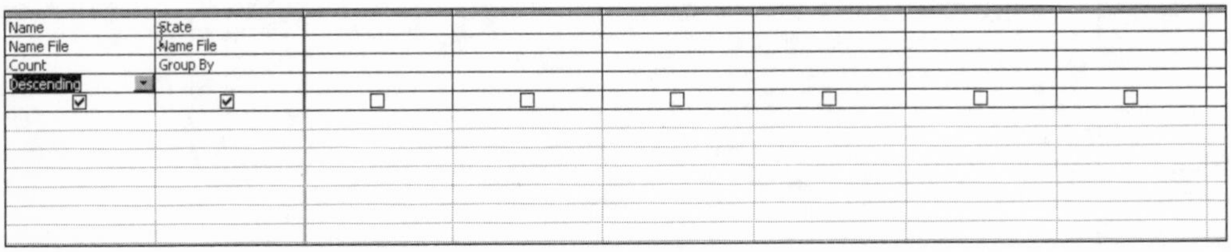

FIGURE 7.9

In this case, we want to "Count" the number of schools and "Group By" the number in each state. So our query table needs to look like Fig. 7.10.

When we run it by clicking on the red exclamation point, we get the result shown in Fig. 7.11.

This is nice enough, but we'd like it sorted. We can go back to the "Query Design" menu by clicking on the "Design View" icon (the blue triangle at the upper right-hand corner) and then click on the "Sort" cell. We want to go from greatest to least, so we'll highlight "Descending" and rerun the query (see Fig. 7.12).

When we do, our results look a little better (see Fig. 7.13).

To save your query, click on the diskette icon, just to the right of the "Design View" icon. It will prompt you for a name. As a general rule, it's a

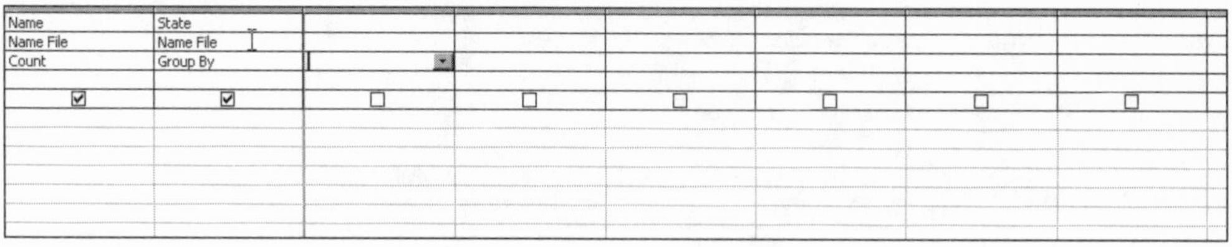

FIGURE 7.10

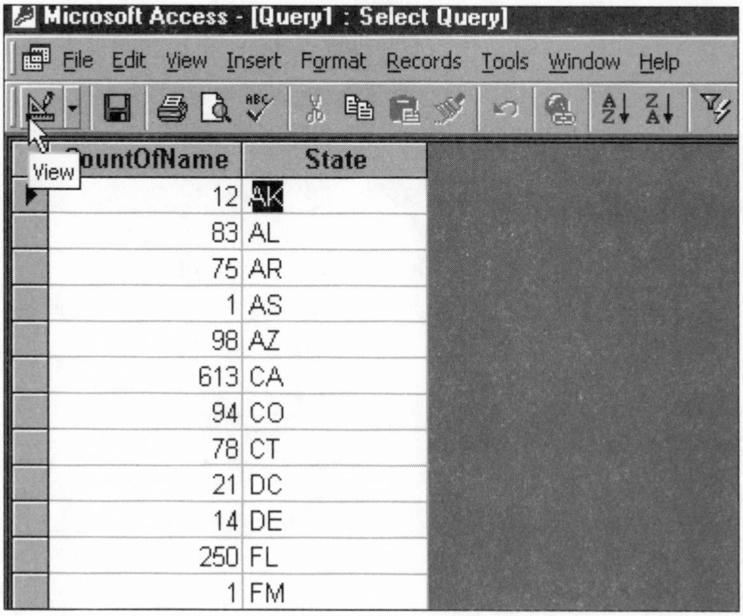

Microsoft Access - [Query1 : Select Query]
File Edit View Insert Format Records Tools Window Help
View
CountOfName
State
12 AK
83 AL
75 AR
1 AS
98 AZ
613 CA
94 CO
78 CT
21 DC
14 DE
250 FL
1 FM

FIGURE 7.11

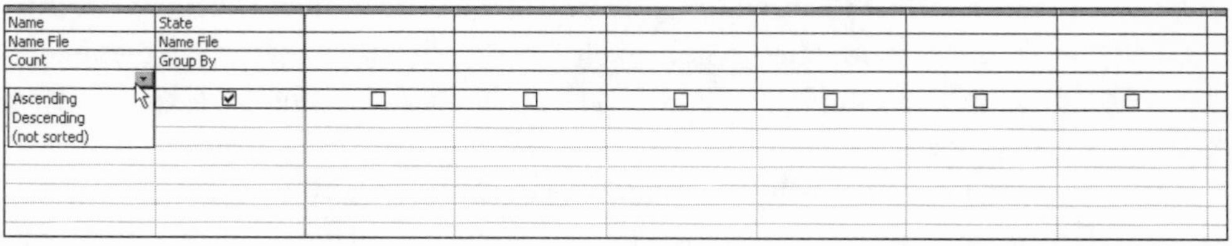

FIGURE 7.12

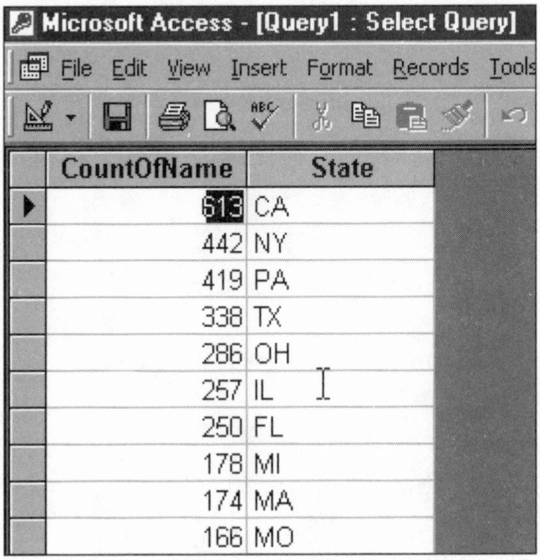

FIGURE 7.13

good idea to preface your query name with the type of specific query you've just done. For general queries, something like "qry" might be appropriate (see Fig. 7.14).

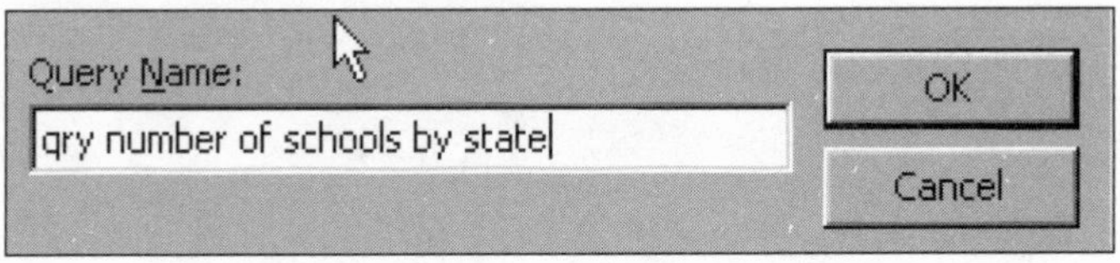

FIGURE 7.14

So we've got some useful information, but not enough. What if we wanted to find out which school had the highest tuition for out-of-state residents? We'd need two files—the Name file and the Tuition file. But we have to join them—and to join them, we need a unique identifier. In this case, after looking at both tables, it's fairly easy to see that the unique identifier will be the UnitID field. We'll start by going back to the query window.

This time, we'll add both the Name file and the Tuition file. By default, Access might try to join the two ID fields; you'll need to delete the default join. To delete the join, just right-click on the line connecting the two ID files, then select "Delete."

After you've deleted the join, create a new join. Click on the "UnitID" field in one file and while holding the left mouse key down, drag it over the "UnitID" field in the other file. The new join should look like Fig. 7.15.

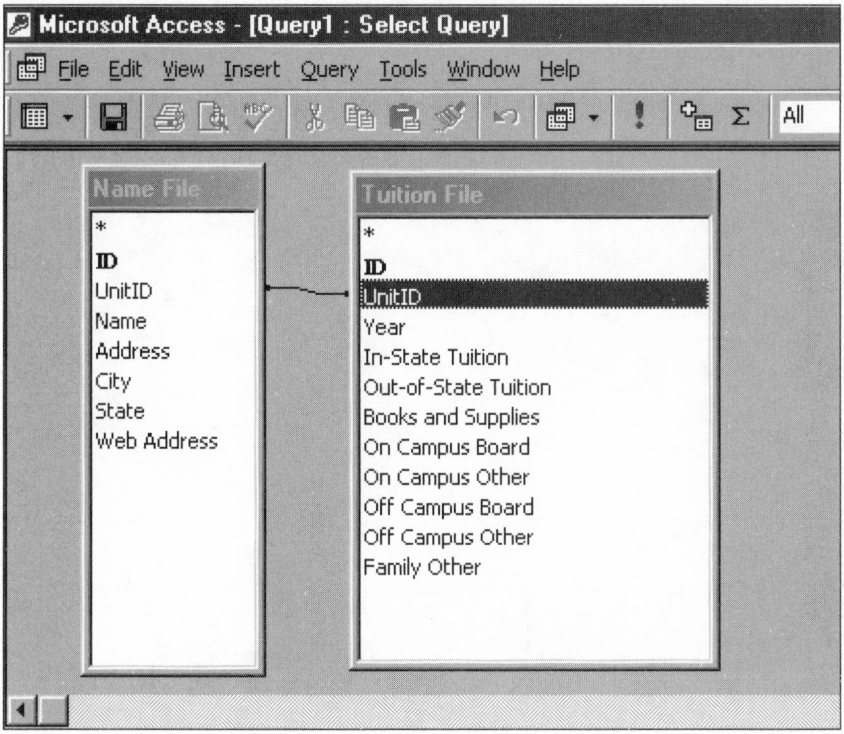

FIGURE 7.15

Now, you're ready to join. Select the fields you want from each table. For the first one, we'll select the "Name" field. From the second, we'll select "Out-of-State Tuition." When we run the query—being sure to sort in descending order—we find that Cornell University has the highest out-of-state tuition rates of any school in the database (see Fig. 7.16).

As usual, we'll save our query.

For a variation on this theme, we could find out which state has the highest average out-of-state tuition rates. To do that, we'd need to "group" the states by the "average" out-of-state tuitions. So select the "State" field from the Name file and the "Out-of-State Tuition" field from the Tuition file. Finally, we make sure that the "Out-of-State Tuition" field is sorted in

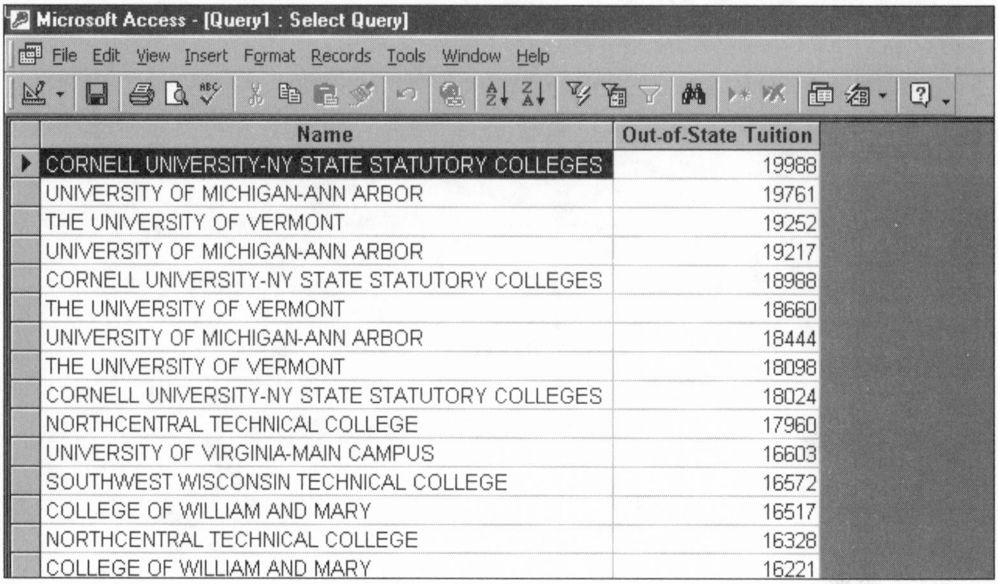

Microsoft Access - [Query1 : Select Query]

Name	Out-of-State Tuition
CORNELL UNIVERSITY-NY STATE STATUTORY COLLEGES	19988
UNIVERSITY OF MICHIGAN-ANN ARBOR	19761
THE UNIVERSITY OF VERMONT	19252
UNIVERSITY OF MICHIGAN-ANN ARBOR	19217
CORNELL UNIVERSITY-NY STATE STATUTORY COLLEGES	18988
THE UNIVERSITY OF VERMONT	18660
UNIVERSITY OF MICHIGAN-ANN ARBOR	18444
THE UNIVERSITY OF VERMONT	18098
CORNELL UNIVERSITY-NY STATE STATUTORY COLLEGES	18024
NORTHCENTRAL TECHNICAL COLLEGE	17960
UNIVERSITY OF VIRGINIA-MAIN CAMPUS	16603
SOUTHWEST WISCONSIN TECHNICAL COLLEGE	16572
COLLEGE OF WILLIAM AND MARY	16517
NORTHCENTRAL TECHNICAL COLLEGE	16328
COLLEGE OF WILLIAM AND MARY	16221

FIGURE 7.16

descending order. We run our query by clicking on the exclamation point, and get the result shown in Fig. 7.17.

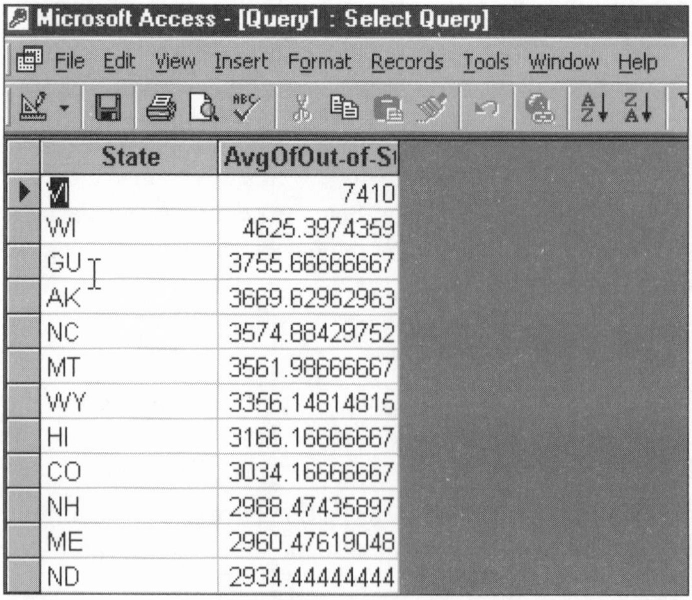

Microsoft Access - [Query1 : Select Query]

State	AvgOfOut-of-St
VI	7410
WI	4625.3974359
GU	3755.66666667
AK	3669.62962963
NC	3574.88429752
MT	3561.98666667
WY	3356.14814815
HI	3166.16666667
CO	3034.16666667
NH	2988.47435897
ME	2960.47619048
ND	2934.44444444

FIGURE 7.17

What if we wanted to see how many schools were included in the average out-of-state tuition figures? Easy. We'd just add another field to our query—this time, one to "count" the number of schools in each state.

When we run the query, we can see one reason why the Virgin Islands' average out-of-state tuition is so high, namely, only three schools are contributing to the average (see Fig. 7.18).

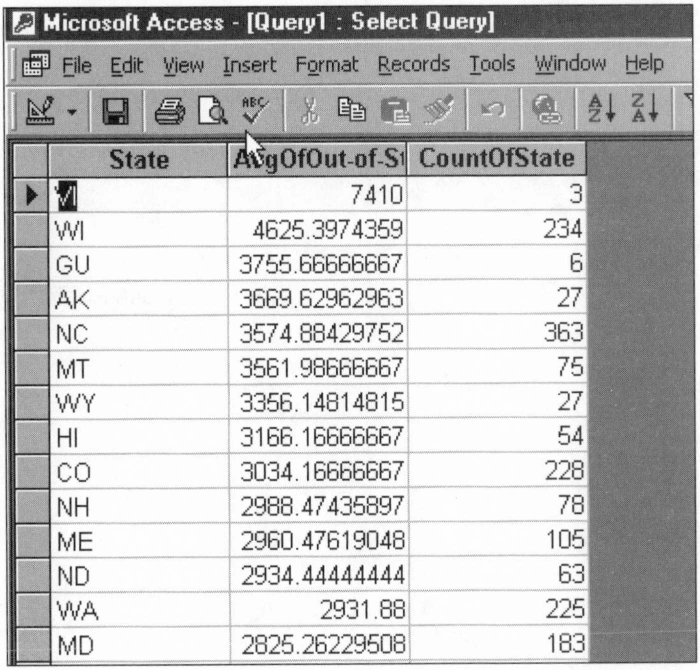
Microsoft Access - [Query1 : Select Query]

State	AvgOfOut-of-S	CountOfState
VI	7410	3
WI	4625.3974359	234
GU	3755.66666667	6
AK	3669.62962963	27
NC	3574.88429752	363
MT	3561.98666667	75
WY	3356.14814815	27
HI	3166.16666667	54
CO	3034.16666667	228
NH	2988.47435897	78
ME	2960.47619048	105
ND	2934.44444444	63
WA	2931.88	225
MD	2825.26229508	183

FIGURE 7.18

Of course, it's possible to join more than two tables. If you wanted to add the total number of full-time undergraduates (or "sum" them), you could join all three tables as in Fig. 7.19.

The result of this query is given in Fig. 7.20.

Here's a problem, though: These numbers aren't right. If we go back into the "Out-of-State Tuition" field in the Tuition table, we see some negative numbers (see Fig. 7.21).

Since no students (or at least, very few) are paid \$1 or \$2 or \$3 to go to school, we can safely assume that these are some type of codes. Sometimes, the people who use government databases will use negative numbers for codes in a numeric field; sometimes, they'll use something like

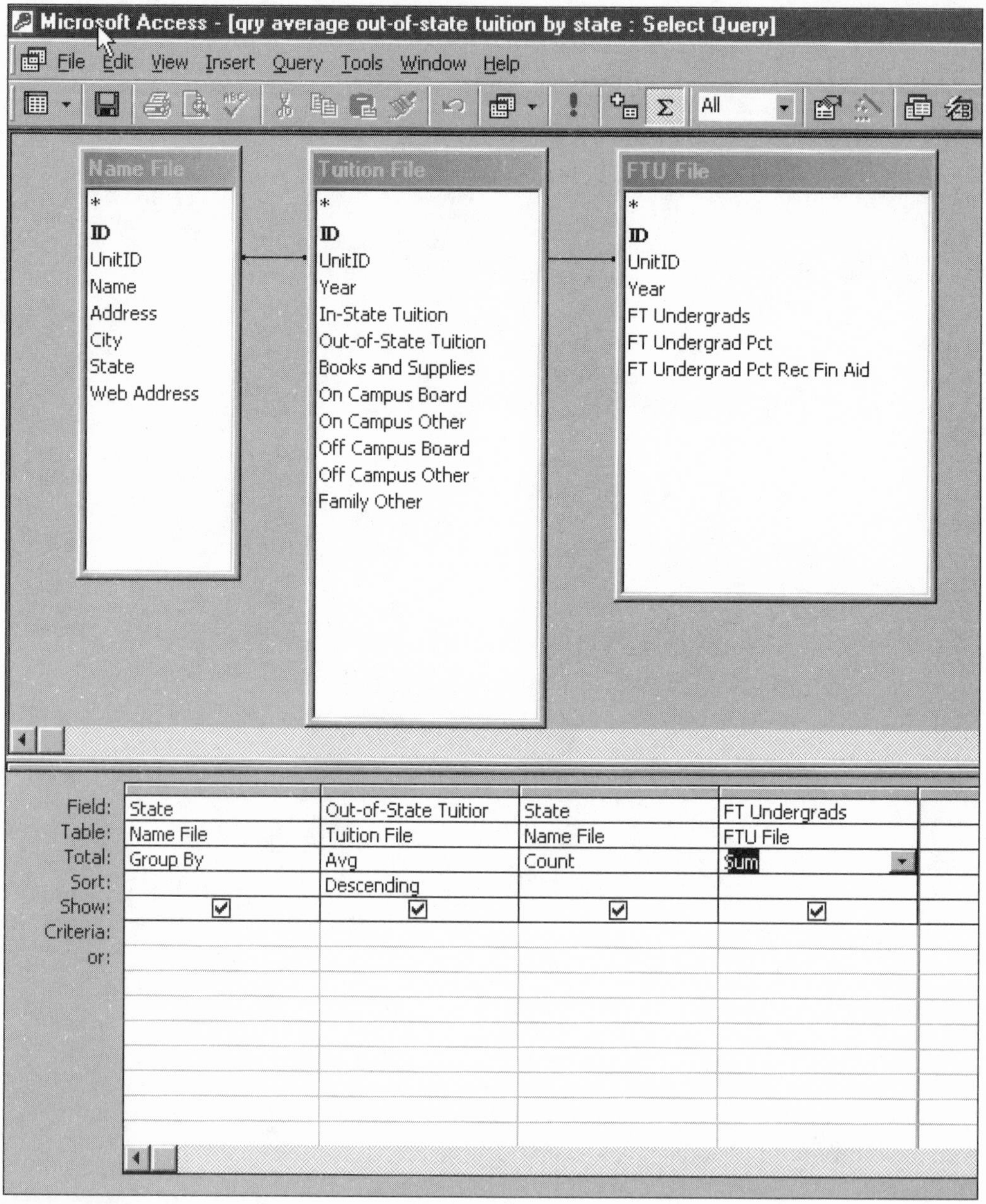
Microsoft Access - [qry average out-of-state tuition by state : Select Query]
File Edit View Insert Query Tools Window Help
All
Name File
*
ID
UnitID
Name
Address
City
State
Web Address
Tuition File
*
ID
UnitID
Year
In-State Tuition
Out-of-State Tuition
Books and Supplies
On Campus Board
On Campus Other
Off Campus Board
Off Campus Other
Family Other
FTU File
*
ID
UnitID
Year
FT Undergrads
FT Undergrad Pct
FT Undergrad Pct Rec Fin Aid
Field:
Table:
Total:
Sort:
Show:
Criteria:
or:
State
Name File
Group By
Out-of-State Tuitior
Tuition File
Avg
Descending
State
Name File
Count
FT Undergrads
FTU File
Sum

FIGURE 7.19

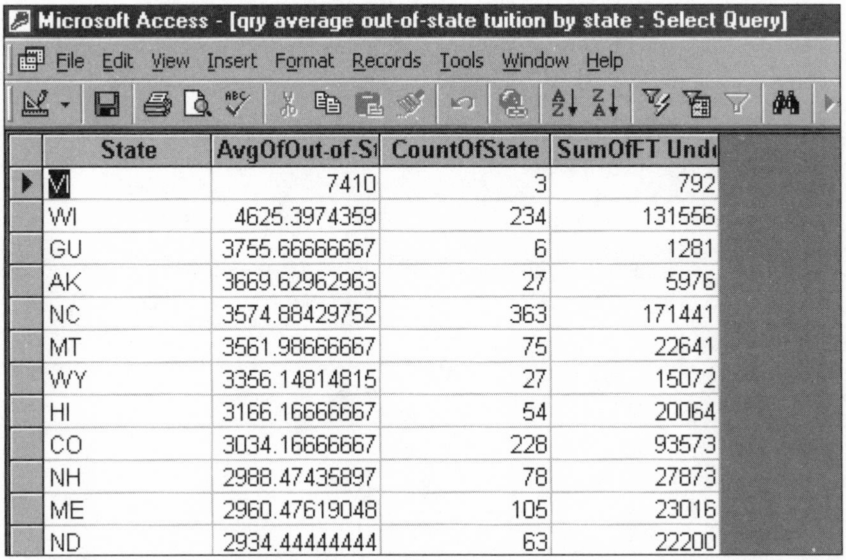

Microsoft Access - [qry average out-of-state tuition by state : Select Query]

State	AvgOfOut-of-St	CountOfState	SumOfFT Und
VI	7410	3	792
WI	4625.3974359	234	131556
GU	3755.66666667	6	1281
AK	3669.62962963	27	5976
NC	3574.88429752	363	171441
MT	3561.98666667	75	22641
WY	3356.14814815	27	15072
HI	3166.16666667	54	20064
CO	3034.16666667	228	93573
NH	2988.47435897	78	27873
ME	2960.47619048	105	23016
ND	2934.44444444	63	22200

FIGURE 7.20

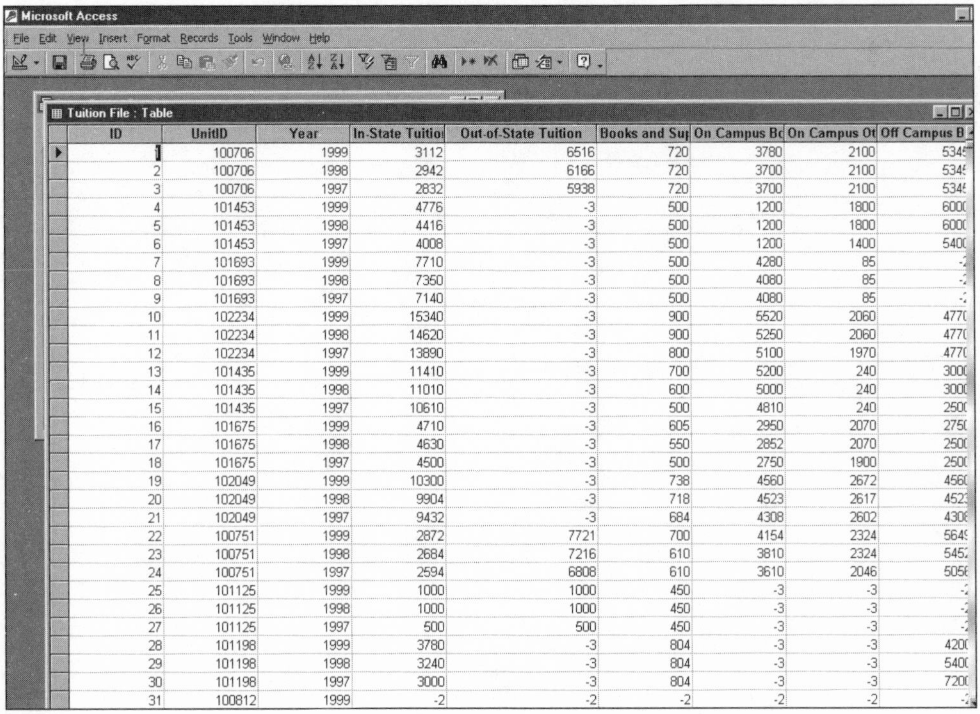

Microsoft Access — Tuition File : Table

ID	UnitID	Year	In-State Tuitio	Out-of-State Tuition	Books and Su	On Campus Bo	On Campus Ot	Off Campus B
1	100706	1999	3112	6516	720	3780	2100	534
2	100706	1998	2942	6166	720	3700	2100	534
3	100706	1997	2832	5938	720	3700	2100	534
4	101453	1999	4776	-3	500	1200	1800	600
5	101453	1998	4416	-3	500	1200	1800	600
6	101453	1997	4008	-3	500	1200	1400	540
7	101693	1999	7710	-3	500	4280	85	-
8	101693	1998	7350	-3	500	4080	85	-
9	101693	1997	7140	-3	500	4080	85	-
10	102234	1999	15340	-3	900	5520	2060	477
11	102234	1998	14620	-3	900	5250	2060	477
12	102234	1997	13890	-3	800	5100	1970	477
13	101435	1999	11410	-3	700	5200	240	300
14	101435	1998	11010	-3	600	5000	240	300
15	101435	1997	10610	-3	500	4810	240	250
16	101675	1999	4710	-3	605	2950	2070	275
17	101675	1998	4630	-3	550	2852	2070	250
18	101675	1997	4500	-3	500	2750	1900	250
19	102049	1999	10300	-3	738	4560	2672	456
20	102049	1998	9904	-3	718	4523	2617	452
21	102049	1997	9432	-3	684	4308	2602	430
22	100751	1999	2872	7721	700	4154	2324	564
23	100751	1998	2684	7216	610	3810	2324	545
24	100751	1997	2594	6808	610	3610	2046	505
25	101125	1999	1000	1000	450	-3	-3	-
26	101125	1998	1000	1000	450	-3	-3	-
27	101125	1997	500	500	450	-3	-3	-
28	101198	1999	3780	-3	804	-3	-3	420
29	101198	1998	3240	-3	804	-3	-3	540
30	101198	1997	3000	-3	804	-3	-3	720
31	100812	1999	-2	-2	-2	-2	-2	-

FIGURE 7.21

"9999". Either way, it's always a good idea to check to see if codes exist. You can do this with a simple query if it's a really big database; just run a query to "group" the amounts, and see if anything looks suspicious. In this case, it does, so we're going to re-run the query, except with criteria to throw out any number less than 0. The revised query looks like Fig. 7.22 (note the >0 condition at the bottom).

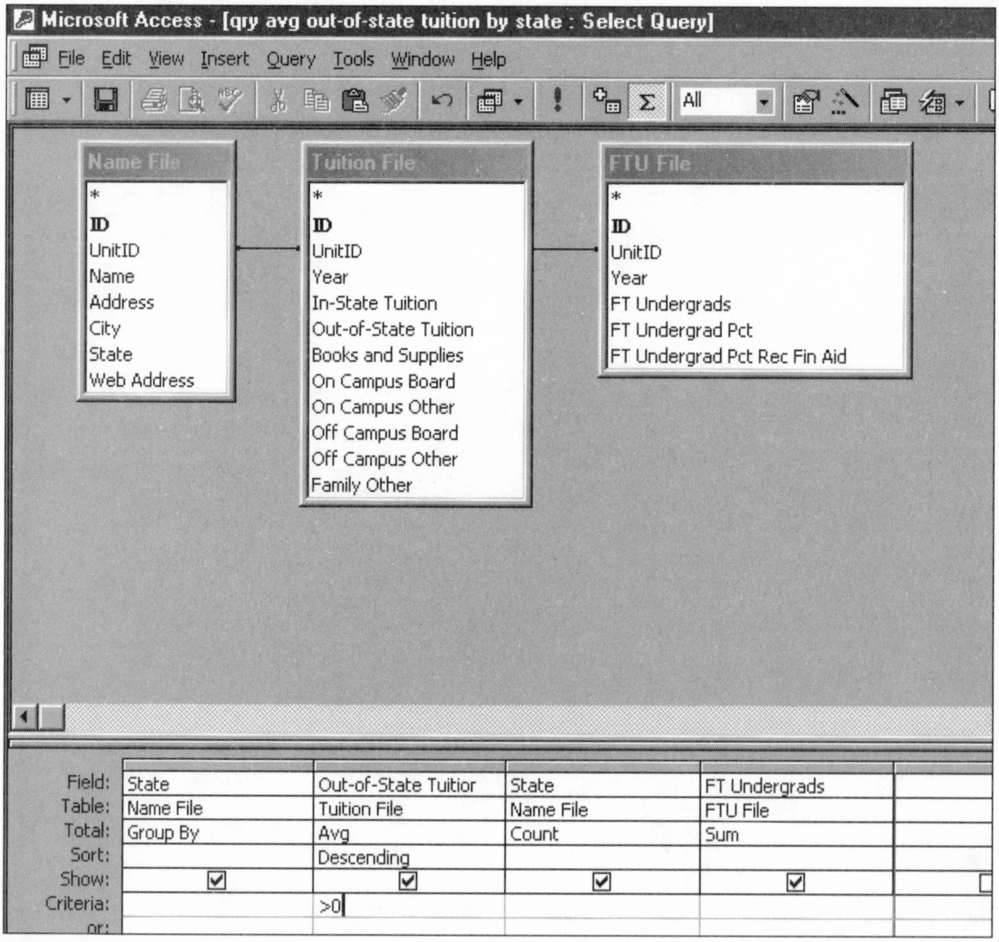

FIGURE 7.22

When we run the query, we've gotten rid of the negative numbers. Although the results from the top states may be the same, some numbers may have changed.

You also don't have to restrict criteria to numbers. Let's say we wanted to look at the average out-of-state tuition in the New England states. We'd define them by their postal codes (from the "State" field) and create a query that looks like Fig. 7.23.

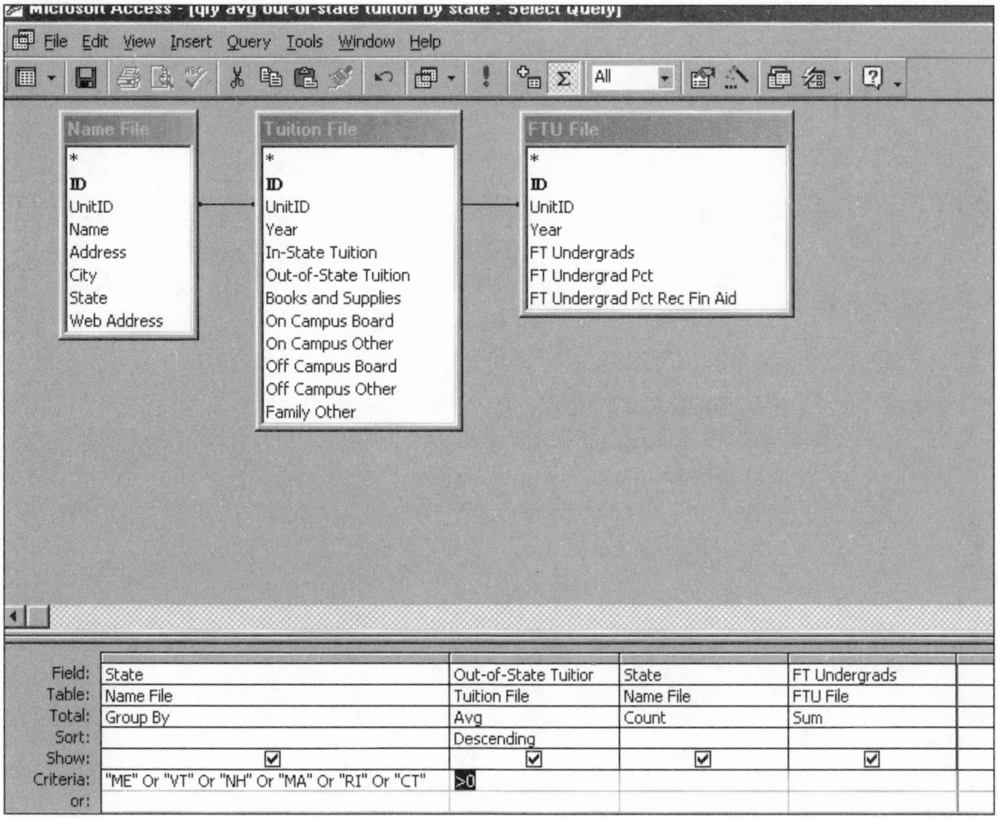

FIGURE 7.23

When inserting criteria, you don't have to type the quotation marks. Access recognizes that you're entering text and will adjust the criteria field appropriately. When we run the query, we get the result shown in Fig. 7.24.

Theoretically, you can join as many tables as you have unique identifiers for. One major barrier, though, is that most database programs tend to slow down with a greater number of joins. Size is also a factor. Access, for example, begins to slow down at roughly 1GB of data. One way of getting around that is to use a "Make Table" query. Make-table queries come

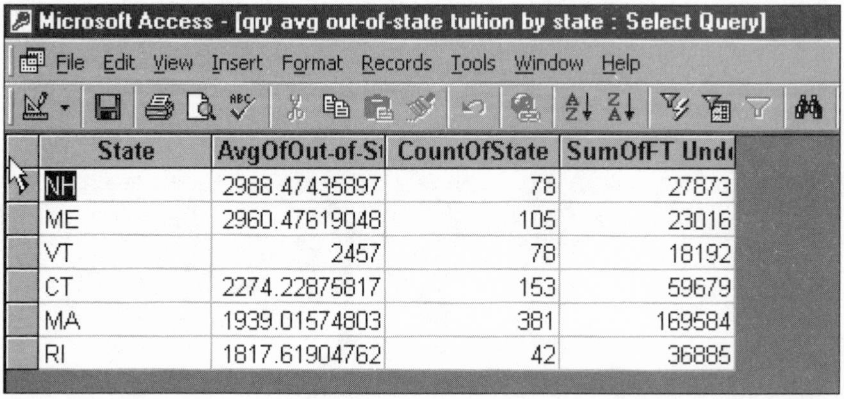

FIGURE 7.24

in handy for generating tables that will be queried later. To make a table out of the above query, for example, you'd open it in "Design View" and use the pull-down "Query" menu to select the "Make Table" query option.

Next, you give the new table a name (as with queries, it's usually a good idea to give it a recognizable prefix that will identify it for future use). When you run the query, nothing much will happen at first. You'll get a brief warning like that in Fig. 7.25.

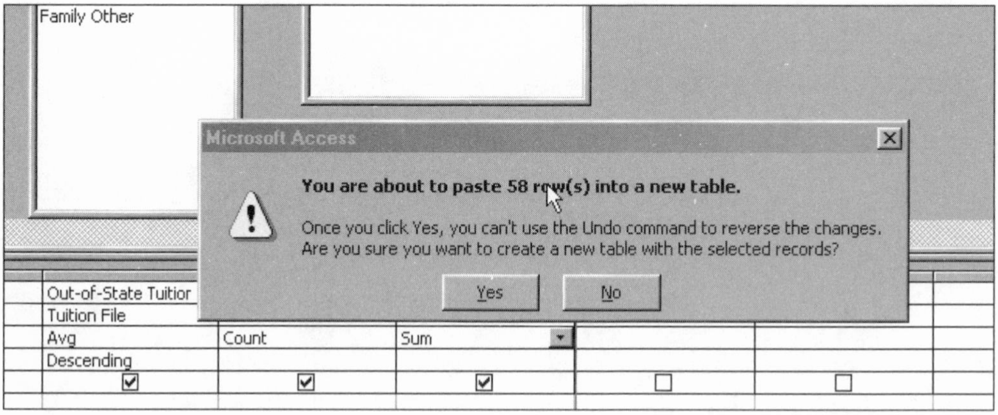

FIGURE 7.25

After clicking on "Yes," you'll want to save your table, close it, and double-check the "Tables" tab to make sure that there weren't any problems with the table.

Sometimes, it's useful to be able to run an update query on a table. Generally, people use update queries to change code names; for example, if 1 is "male" and 2 is "female," you might run an update query so you don't have to remember which is which. For example, let's say that you wanted to change the postal codes for New England states in the Name file to a generic New England description. You'd start a new query from the Name file, using only the "State" field and select "Update Query" from the "Query" menu.

When you select the update query option, you'll see that the query grid changes slightly (see Fig. 7.26).

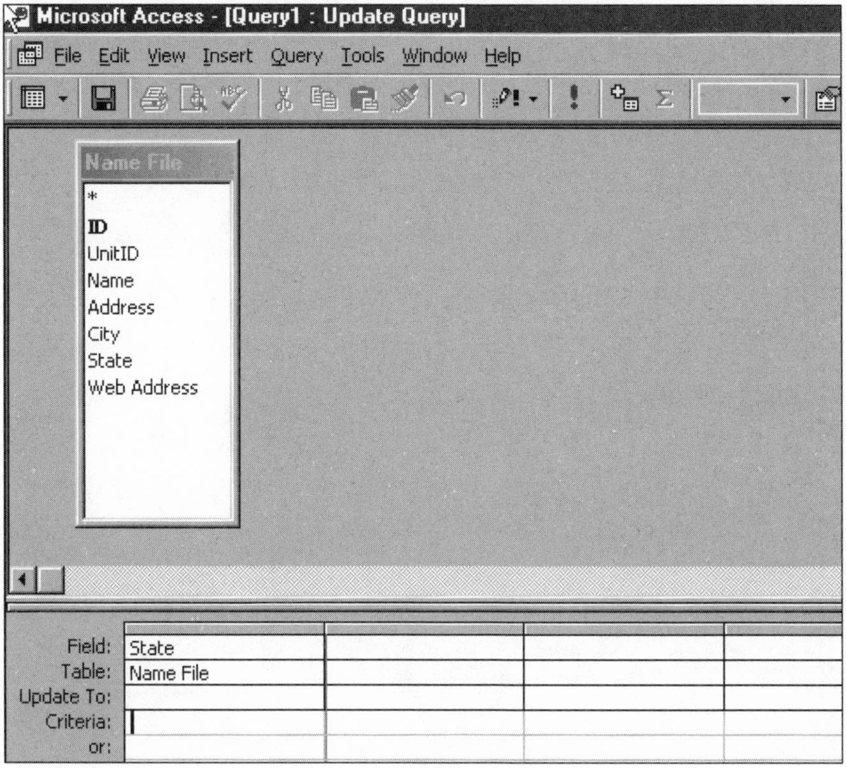

FIGURE 7.26

We'll fill in the "Update To" box with "New England." Next, we'll add criteria (see Fig. 7.27).

Again, you'll get a standard warning like that in Fig. 7.28.

And when you run the query, nothing much will happen. But if you go back to the Name file, you can see that the state postal codes for the New England states have been replaced (see Fig. 7.29).

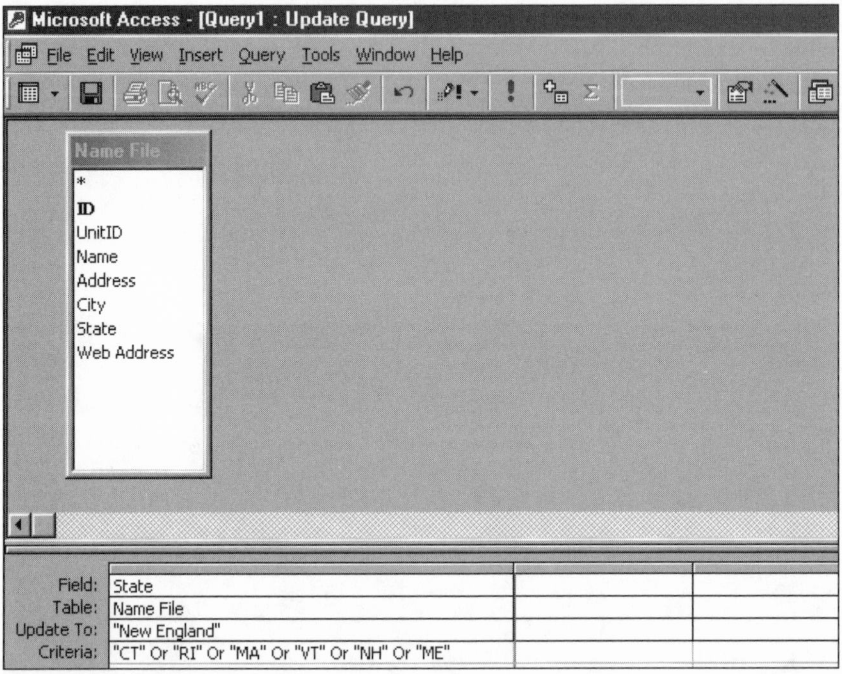

FIGURE 7.27

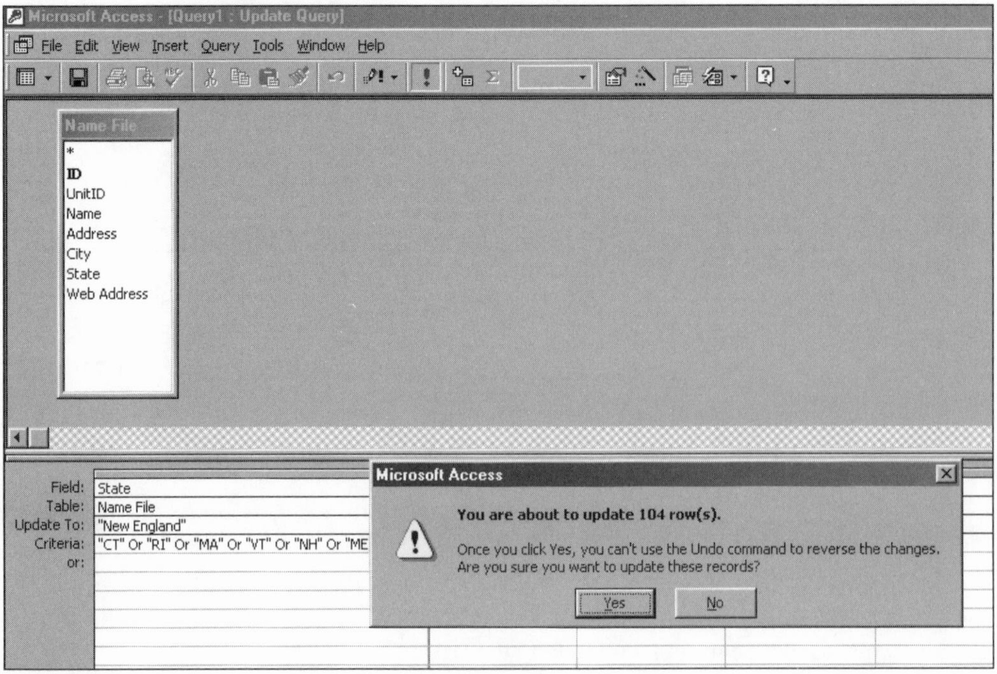

FIGURE 7.28

719	128151	T H PICKENS T	500 AIRPORT E	AURORA	CO	
720	128179	TECHNICAL TR	2315 E PIKES I	COLORADO SF	CO	
721	128188	TECHNICAL TR	772 HORIZON D	GRAND JUNCT	CO	(970) 245-8101
722	128203	ULTIMA COLLE	3049 W 74 AVE	WESTMINSTEF	CO	
723	128258	TRINIDAD STAT	600 PROSPEC	TRINIDAD	CO	www.tsjc.cccoe
724	128328	UNITED STATE	HQ USAFA/XPF	COLORADO SF	CO	
725	128391	WESTERN STA		GUNNISON	CO	
726	128425	YESHIVA TORA	1555 STUART S	DENVER	CO	
727	128498	ALBERTUS MA	700 PROSPEC	NEW HAVEN	New England	
728	128540	AMERICAN AC.	28 KEELER ST	DANBURY	New England	
729	128577	ASNUNTUCK C	170 ELM ST	ENFIELD	New England	www.asctc.com
730	128586	BAIS BINYOMII	132 PROSPEC	STAMFORD	New England	
731	128674	BRANFORD HA	1 SUMMIT PL	BRANFORD	New England	
732	128683	BRIARWOOD C	2279 MT VERN	SOUTHINGTON	New England	WWW.BRIARW
733	128744	UNIVERSITY O	380 UNIVERSIT	BRIDGEPORT	New England	
734	128762	BUTLER BUSIN	2710 NORTH A'	BRIDGEPORT	New England	
735	128771	CENTRAL CON	1615 STANLEY	NEW BRITAIN	New England	www.ccsu.edu
736	128780	CHARTER OAK	55 Paul J. Mana	New Britain	New England	www.cosc.edu
737	128896	CONNECTICUT	75 KITTS LN	NEWINGTON	New England	www.ccmt.com
738	128902	CONNECTICUT	270 MOHEGAN	NEW LONDON	New England	www.conncoll.e
739	128957	CONNECTICUT	1000 MAIN ST	EAST HARTFO	New England	www.naccas.org

FIGURE 7.29

There are also a few other types of queries. Occasionally, you'll want to delete a field from a table (use the "Delete" query) or add a field to a table (use the "Append" query). But nine times out of ten, a simple "Select" query will work wonders for a reporter's story—and for the time they'll spend researching it.

CHAPTER EIGHT

Mapping

It's one thing to analyze numbers; it's another thing to see them, visually. Even the best reporters who know their areas well can miss trends if they're buried in a stack of numbers. This is where knowing how to map the numbers can help. Mapping also helps clarify stories that otherwise would be overloaded with numbers. In a business where a picture is worth 1,000 words and 1,000 words is a lot for an editor (and a reader) to wade through, a good map can be worth its weight in gold. So while mapping software can be expensive, for those reasons alone, it's a good thing for reporters to have a working knowledge of mapping software.

Two things are worth knowing immediately about mapping software. First, it takes up a lot of hard drive space and a lot of random access memory (RAM). A good mapping program won't work well on a machine with less than 128MB of RAM. The second thing to know is that a basic understanding of relational database theory is essential for anyone who wants to properly use mapping software.

A knowledge of relational database theory is important because mapping essentially involves joining two databases—the one with your data and the one with the mapping attributes. And when you join two databases, you need a common field. The trick to joining your database with the mapping attribute database is to find—or create—that common field.

Although there are many different kinds of mapping software, the program used most frequently by reporters and government agencies is ESRI's ArcView. It's a large program and rather expensive—a single copy costs around $1,000 for a newsroom—but it is the most flexible and it easily handles other data and mapping file formats.

Start by creating a new "project" in ArcView (see Fig. 8.1).

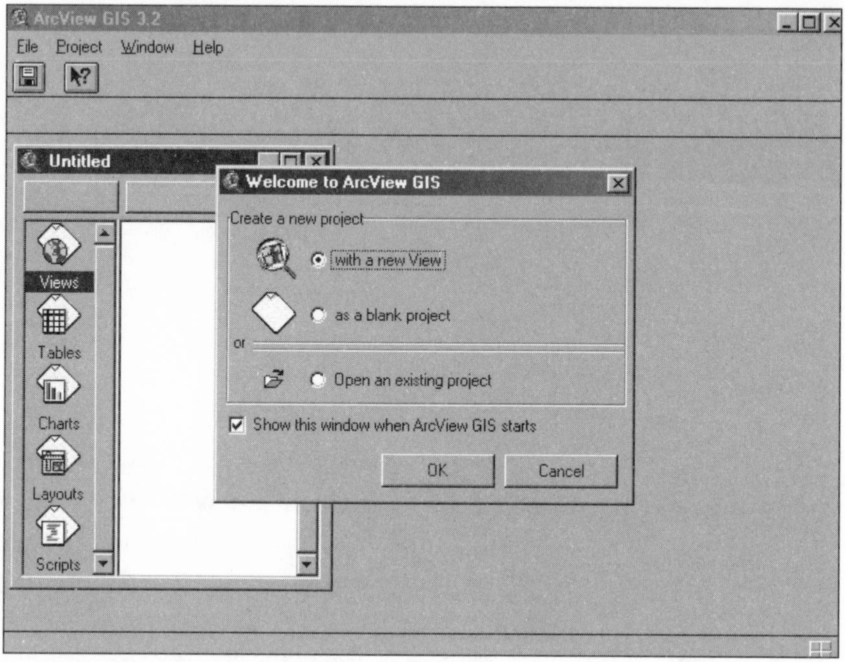

FIGURE 8.1

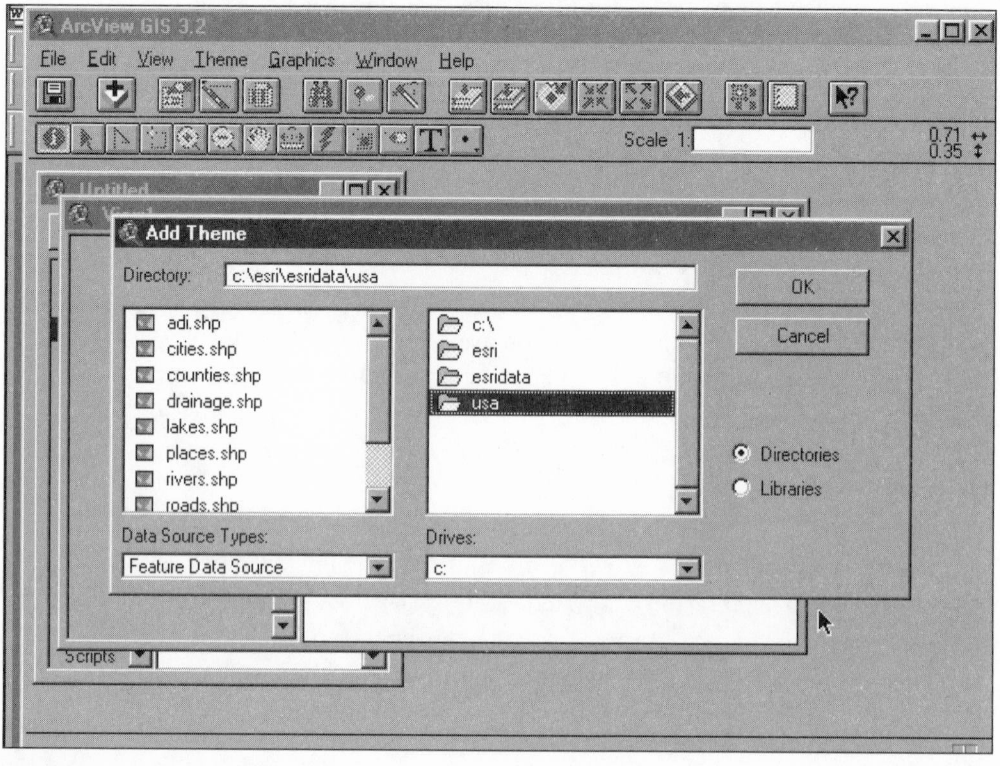

FIGURE 8.2

When we create the new view, ArcView will ask for data. We'll browse to it and add data, called a "theme" in ArcView. Since we're looking at federal spending by county, we'll add a national map of counties that's available in ArcView (see Fig. 8.2).

When we add the Counties theme—which is a file called a "shapefile" and has a *shp extension—we get a window that has all states listed. We can move the box to a more convenient location by clicking on the "View1" box and dragging it to the side (see Fig. 8.3). We can also resize the box by using the cursor to drag the lower right-hand corner to expand it.

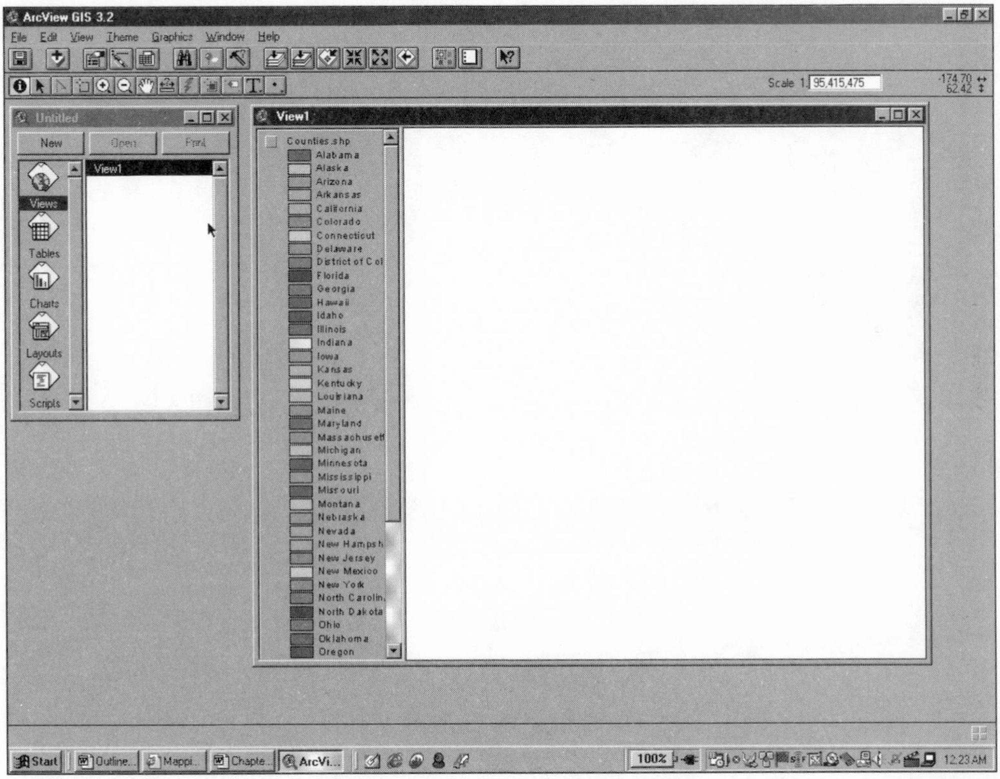

FIGURE 8.3

Finally, we need to see the actual map itself. To do that, we need to check the box next to "Counties.shp." When we do, we see a national map of counties, as shown in Fig. 8.4. (We can make the map a little larger by clicking on the "zoom" button at the top of the menu.)

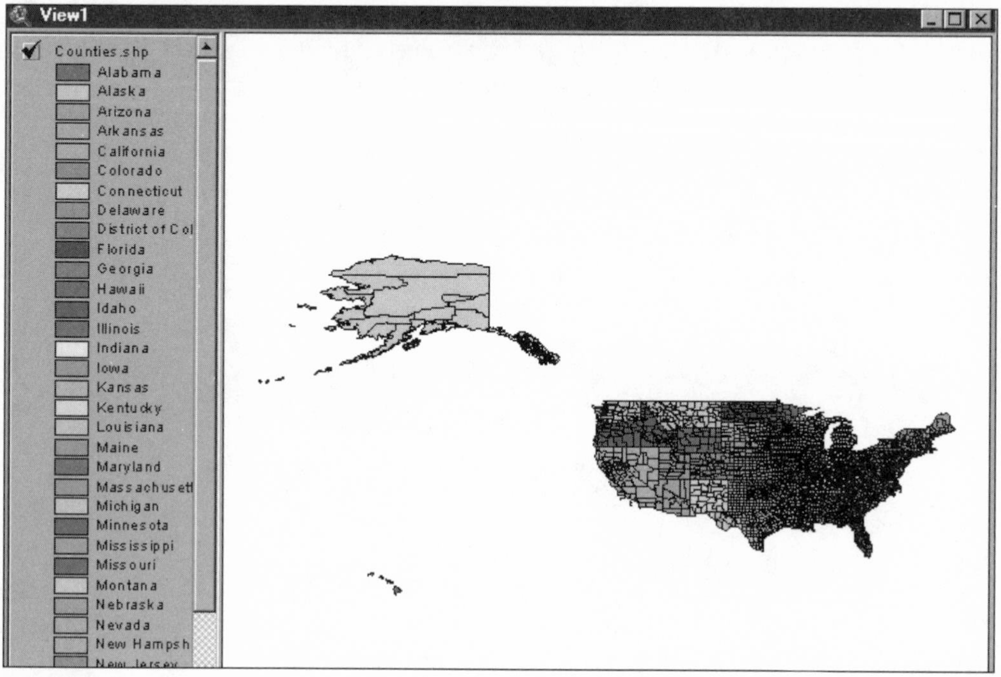

FIGURE 8.4

Finally, we want to look at the attributes of the shapefile. To do that, we go to the menu and click on the "Open Theme Table" button (see Fig. 8.5).

Attributes of Counties.shp

Shape	Name	State_name	State_fips	Cnty_fips	Fips	Area	Pop1990	Pop1999	Pop90_sqm
Polygon	Lake of the Woods	Minnesota	27	077	27077	1784.0634	4076	4597	
Polygon	Ferry	Washington	53	019	53019	2280.2319	6295	7150	
Polygon	Stevens	Washington	53	065	53065	2529.9794	30948	39965	1
Polygon	Okanogan	Washington	53	047	53047	5306.1800	33350	38596	
Polygon	Pend Oreille	Washington	53	051	53051	1445.0286	8915	11788	
Polygon	Boundary	Idaho	16	021	16021	1279.2987	8332	9840	
Polygon	Lincoln	Montana	30	053	30053	3746.0908	17481	18691	
Polygon	Flathead	Montana	30	029	30029	5232.0306	59218	72458	1

FIGURE 8.5

Looking back at the Excel table we used in the previous chapter, we can see there's a problem here. The only field that we can possibly use to join to the attribute table is the "Name" field. But that won't join, because the names aren't exactly the same (see Fig. 8.6).

To make the fields join, we need to do a search-and-replace in Excel to eliminate the "County," "City Area," "Borough," "Parish," and everything

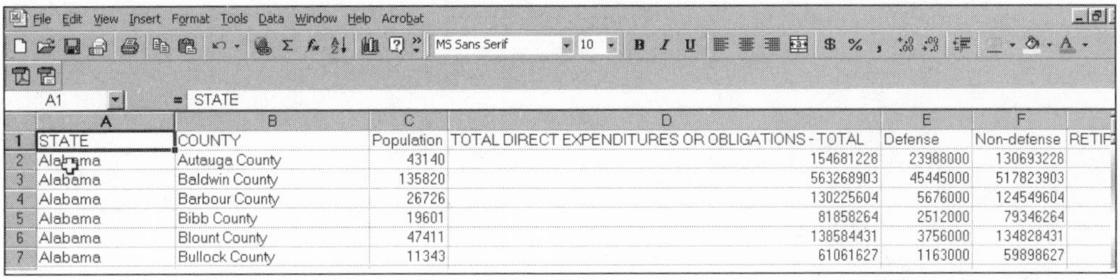

FIGURE 8.6

that's not a name. Tedious work, but it has to be done. To do a search-and-replace, we start by defining the entire spreadsheet (click on the gray box to the left of column A and just above row 1). Then go to the "Edit" menu and click on "Replace." We'll start with "County," and replace it with a blank (see Fig. 8.7).

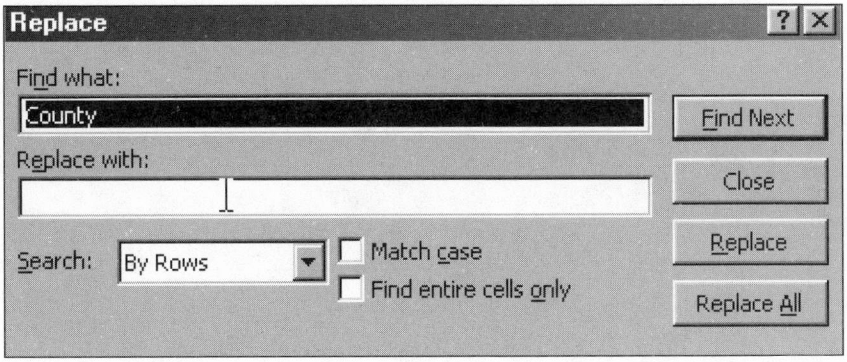

FIGURE 8.7

Once you've replaced all the extraneous wording, it's time to join it to the attribute table. Because ArcView will only join its attribute table with text or *dbf files, you need to save the Excel table as one of those. To save the Excel file as a *dbf file, simply click on "File," then "Save As," and then define the file type as a dBASE III file.

Once you've saved your Excel file as a dBASE file, you'll want to add it to the project. To add a table, go to the window shown in Fig. 8.8.

Click on "Add," browse to your file's location, and make sure the proper file type has been selected, as in Fig. 8.9.

When you find your file, click on "OK."

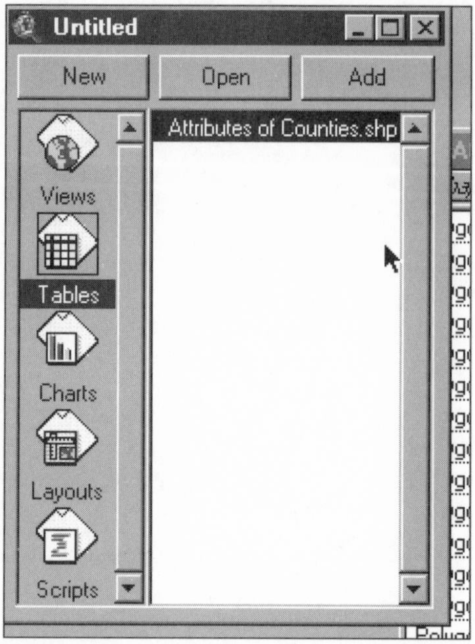

FIGURE 8.8

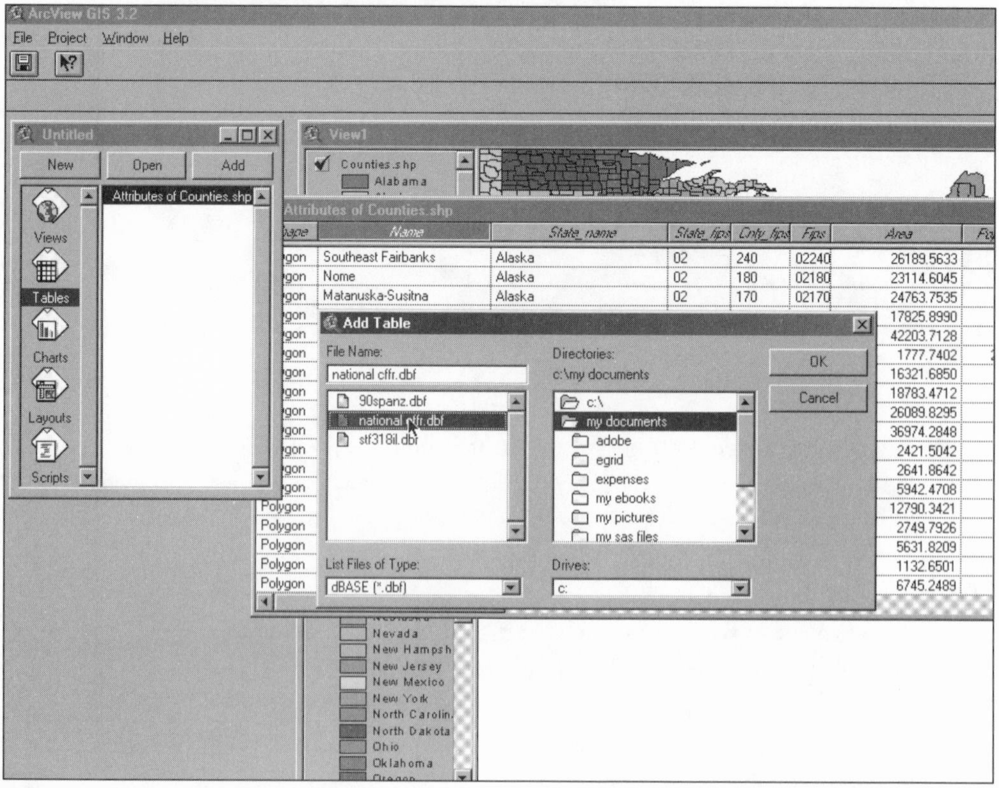

FIGURE 8.9

Your newly created *dbf file should pop up quickly. You'll note that some of your columns have been truncated; that's a common limitation in *dbf files. If you have a table with very long names, sometimes it's best to use a tab-delimited table (see Fig. 8.10).

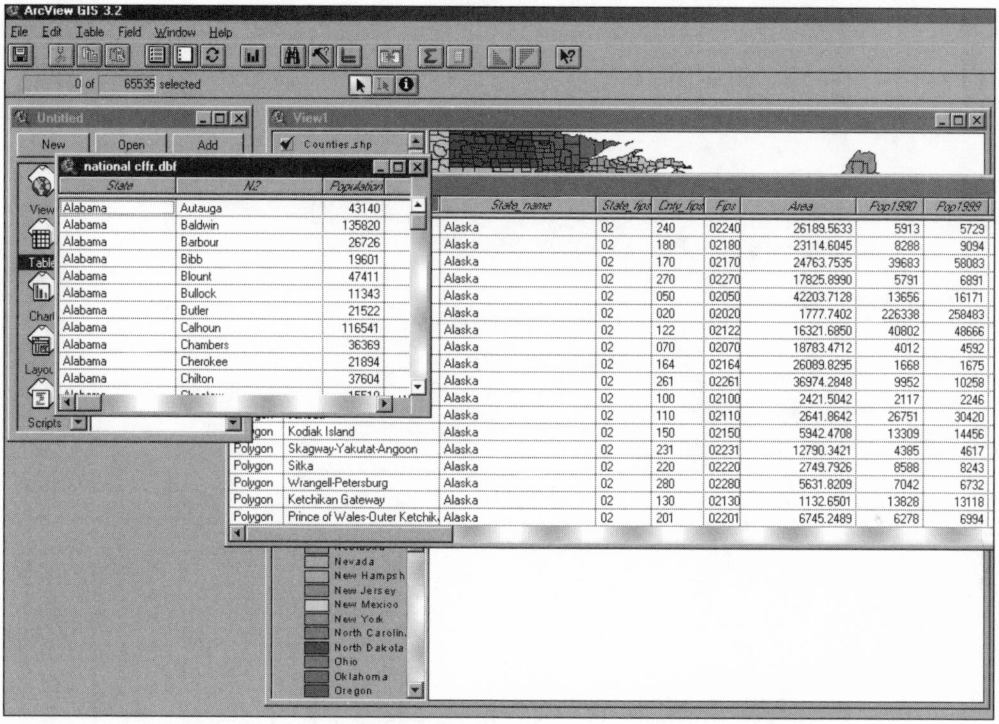

FIGURE 8.10

Finally, we need to join the tables. The way to join tables is to click on the field that you'll use to join from your table; the box should turn gray. Next, click on the field that you're joining (the attribute table). That box should turn gray, too.

Then click on the "Join" icon. The two tables should merge into one. If you scroll all the way over to the right, you can see that the spending data have been merged with the attribute table (see Fig. 8.11).

For purposes of this exercise, we'll look at defense spending by county. We'll start by clicking on the "Legend Editor," as shown in Fig. 8.12.

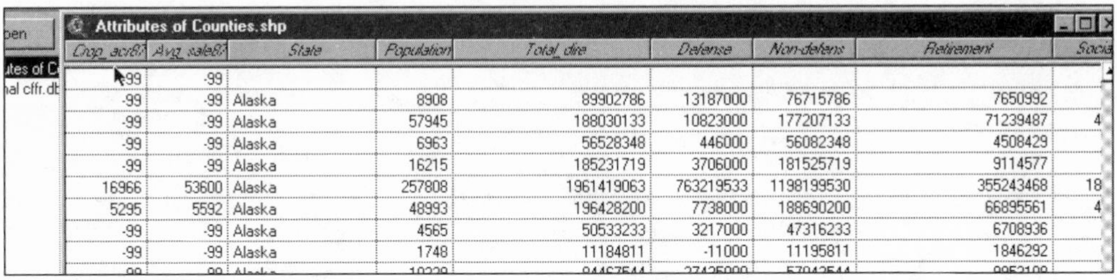
Attributes of Counties.shp
Crop_acr87
Avg_sale87
State
Population
Total_dire
Defense
Non-defens
Retirement
-99 -99
-99 -99 Alaska 8908 89902786 13187000 76715786 7650992
-99 -99 Alaska 57945 188030133 10823000 177207133 71239487
-99 -99 Alaska 6963 56528348 446000 56082348 4508429
-99 -99 Alaska 16215 185231719 3706000 181525719 9114577
16966 53600 Alaska 257808 1961419063 763219533 1198199530 355243468
5295 5592 Alaska 48993 196428200 7738000 188690200 66895561
-99 -99 Alaska 4565 50533233 3217000 47316233 6708936
-99 -99 Alaska 1748 11184811 -11000 11195811 1846292

FIGURE 8.11

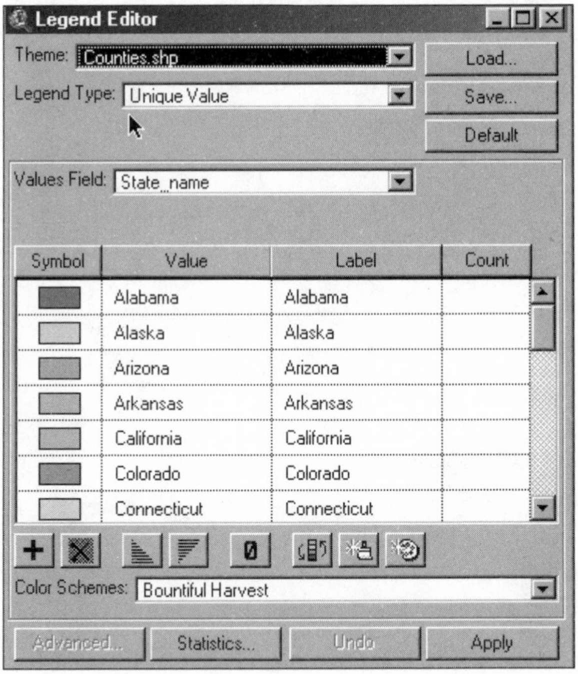

FIGURE 8.12

Since we don't want to map every unique value, we need to change the "Legend Type." The "Graduated Color" option probably works best (see Fig. 8.13).

We also need to change the "Classification Field" to "Defense Spending" (see Fig. 8.14).

ArcView will automatically calculate the quintiles when you select graduated color (although you can change that).

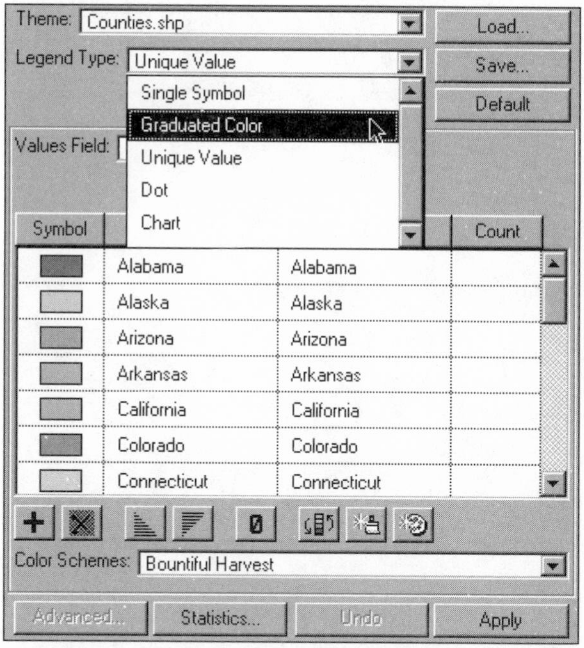

FIGURE 8.13

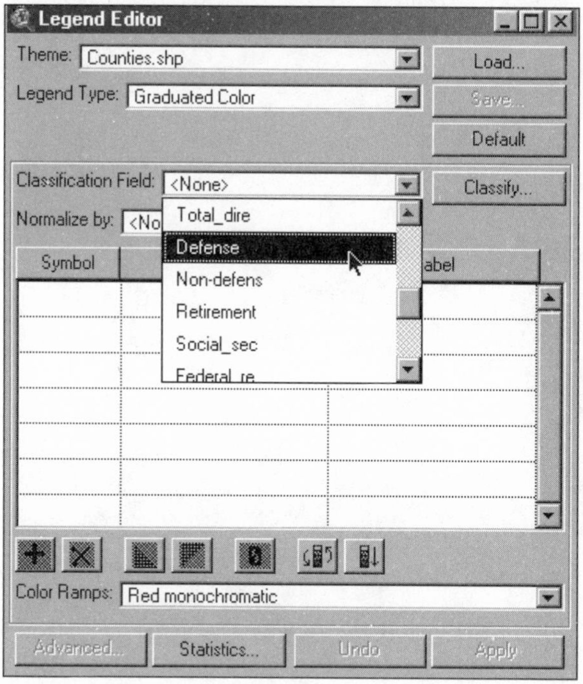

FIGURE 8.14

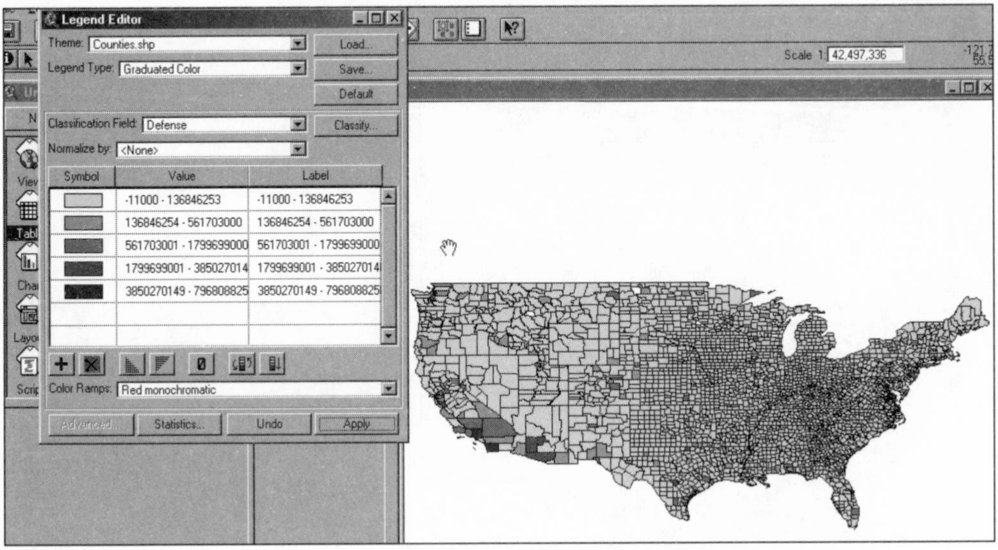

FIGURE 8.15

When we click on "Apply," we can see where defense spending is concentrated across the nation's more than 3,000 counties (see Fig. 8.15).

This is a useful map. But what if we were only interested in seeing how California fared in defense spending? We can select an individual state using ArcView's query tool, from the top of the menu. When we click on it, we get a dialog box. If we highlight the "State_name" field on the left, we get a list of all states (see Fig. 8.16).

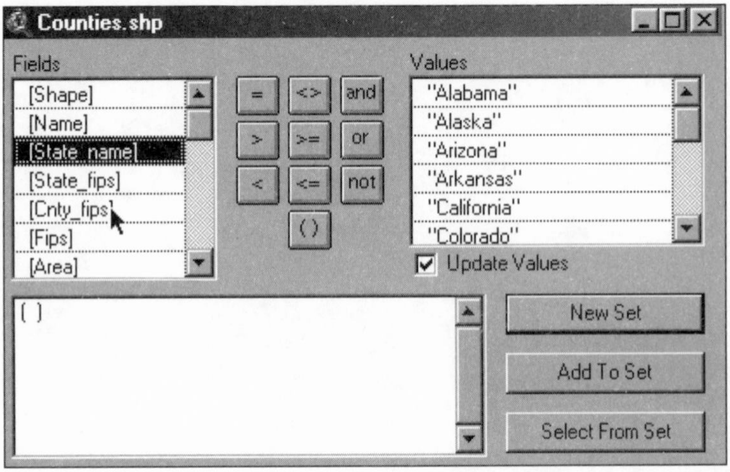

FIGURE 8.16

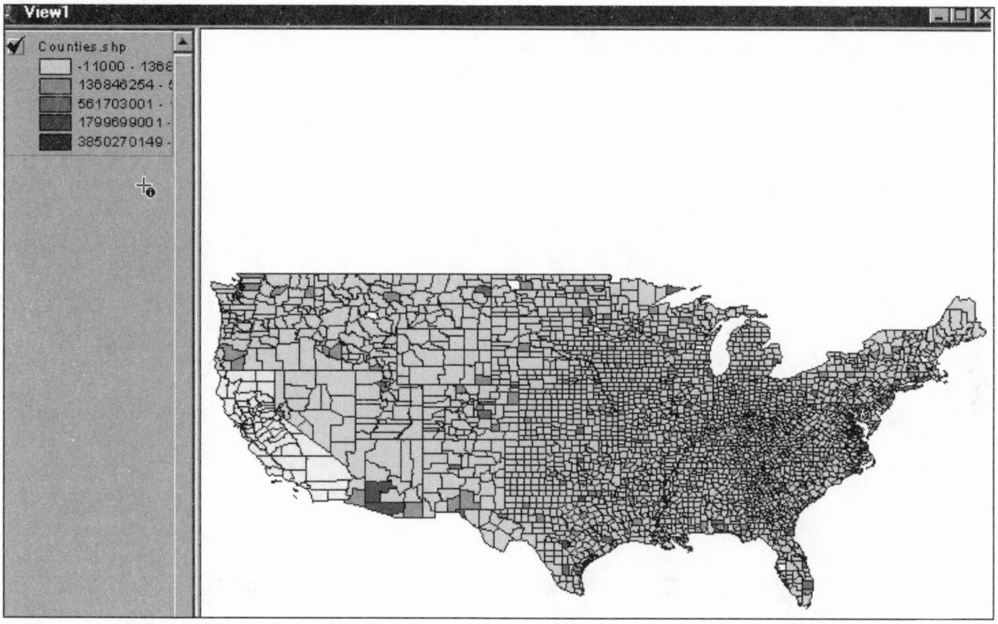

FIGURE 8.17

We'll select "California" from the right and click on the "New Set" button before closing the "Query Builder" dialog box.

If we look at our map, we can see that California is now shaded in Fig. 8.17.

To be sure that you've selected properly, open the theme table and click on the "Promote" button. California counties should be at the top (see Fig. 8.18).

Next, we'll convert these California data into a separate shapefile. Make the "View1" window active by clicking on it and select "Convert to Shapefile," as shown in Fig. 8.19.

ArcView will ask where you'd like to save the file. Give it a name and save it in a folder where it will be easily found (see Fig. 8.20).

Next, you'll be asked if you want to add the new shapefile to your current project. You do. When you add it, you'll see that there's now a "California" option in your "View" window (see Fig. 8.21).

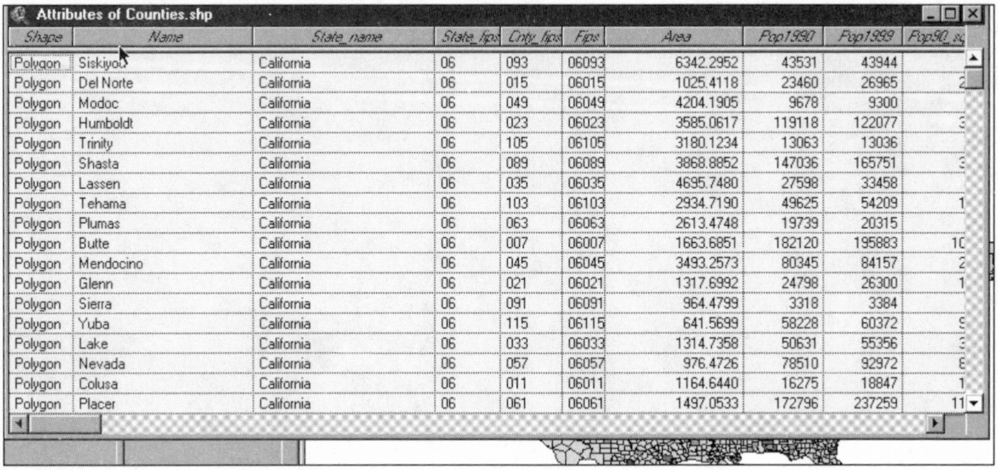

Attributes of Counties.shp

Shape	Name	State_name	State_fips	Cnty_fips	Fips	Area	Pop1990	Pop1999	Pop90_sq
Polygon	Siskiyou	California	06	093	06093	6342.2952	43531	43944	
Polygon	Del Norte	California	06	015	06015	1025.4118	23460	26965	2
Polygon	Modoc	California	06	049	06049	4204.1905	9678	9300	
Polygon	Humboldt	California	06	023	06023	3585.0617	119118	122077	3
Polygon	Trinity	California	06	105	06105	3180.1234	13063	13036	
Polygon	Shasta	California	06	089	06089	3868.8852	147036	165751	3
Polygon	Lassen	California	06	035	06035	4695.7480	27598	33458	
Polygon	Tehama	California	06	103	06103	2934.7190	49625	54209	1
Polygon	Plumas	California	06	063	06063	2613.4748	19739	20315	
Polygon	Butte	California	06	007	06007	1663.6851	182120	195883	1C
Polygon	Mendocino	California	06	045	06045	3493.2573	80345	84157	2
Polygon	Glenn	California	06	021	06021	1317.6992	24798	26300	1
Polygon	Sierra	California	06	091	06091	964.4799	3318	3384	
Polygon	Yuba	California	06	115	06115	641.5699	58228	60372	9
Polygon	Lake	California	06	033	06033	1314.7358	50631	55356	3
Polygon	Nevada	California	06	057	06057	976.4726	78510	92972	8
Polygon	Colusa	California	06	011	06011	1164.6440	16275	18847	1
Polygon	Placer	California	06	061	06061	1497.0533	172796	237259	11

FIGURE 8.18

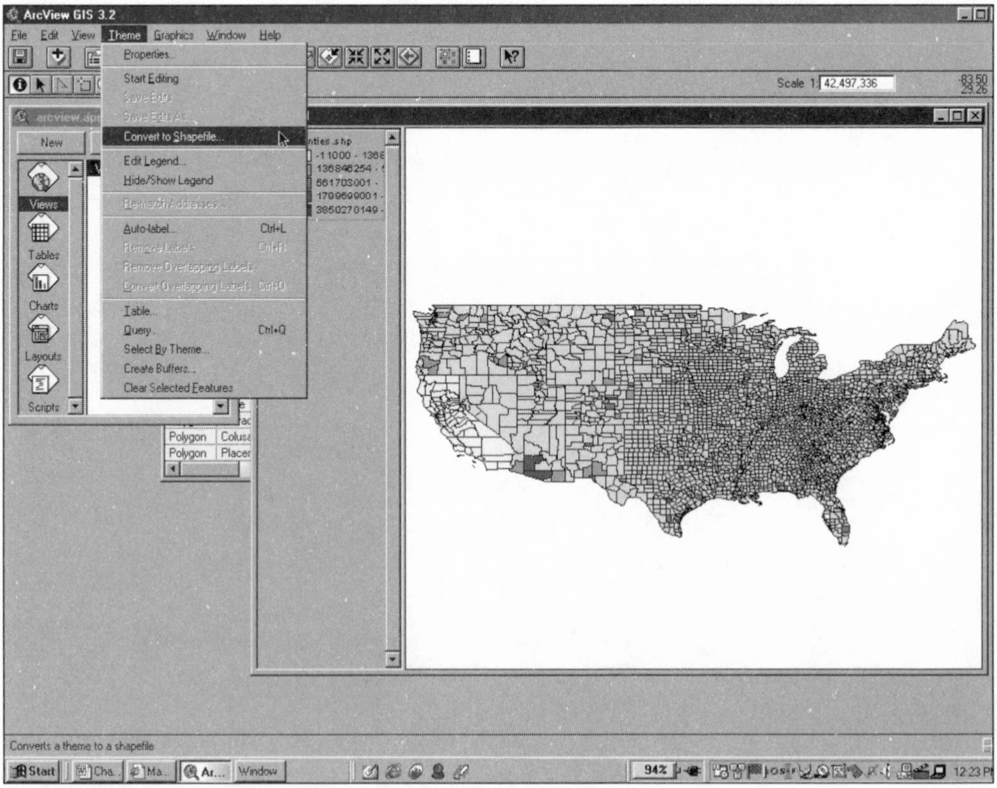

FIGURE 8.19

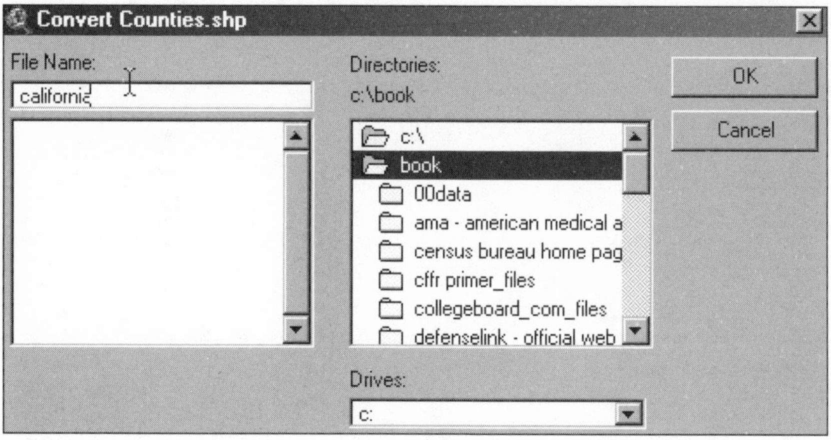

FIGURE 8.20

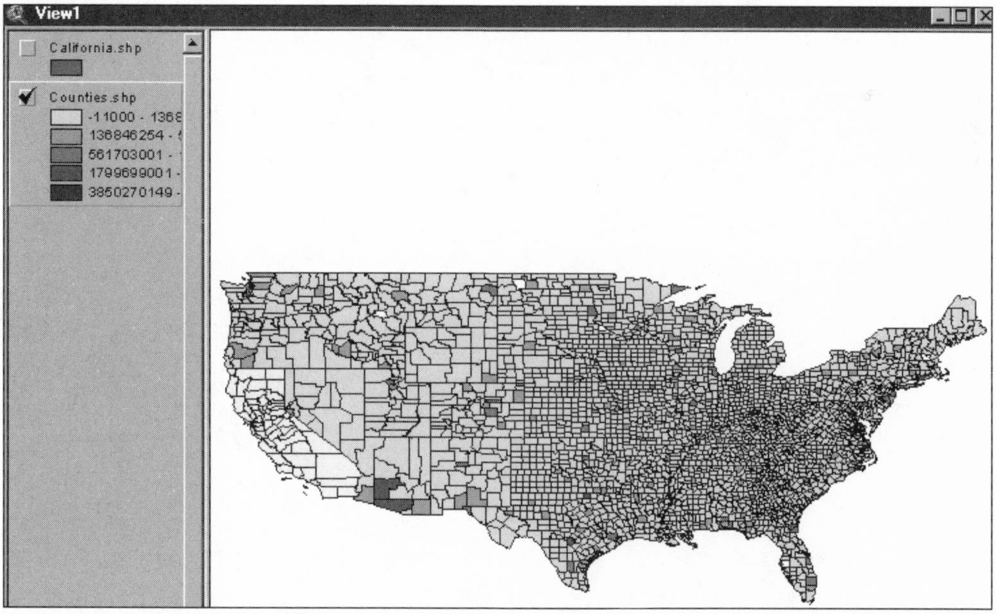

FIGURE 8.21

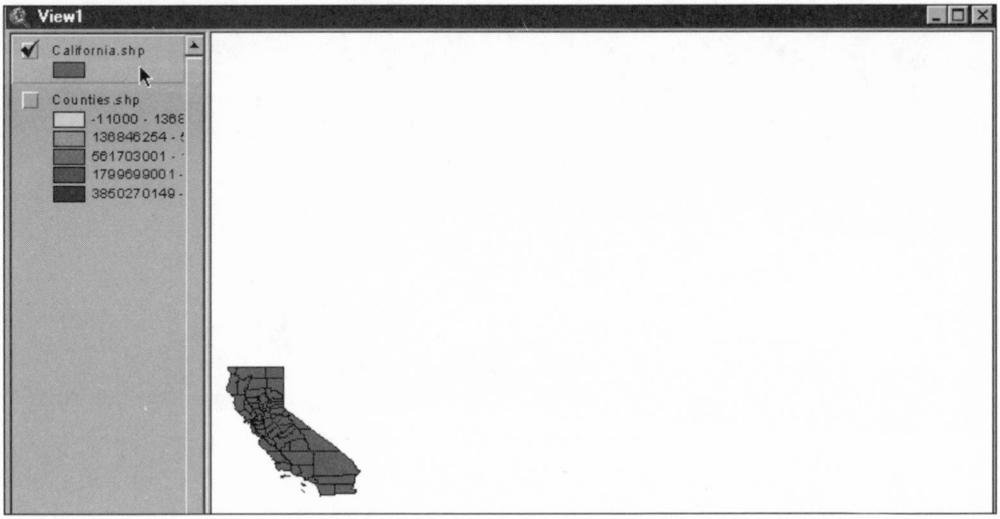

FIGURE 8.22

If you want to get rid of everything but "California," check the "California" box and uncheck the "Counties.shp" box. You should also click on the invisible rectangle that surrounds the "California" box to make it the active theme (see Fig. 8.22).

After expanding and centering the California image, it's time to use the "Legend Editor" again. Figure 8.23 gives us a much better idea of where defense spending is going in the state.

Next, you'll want to save your project by clicking on "File," then "Save." Finally, you can export the graphic by clicking on "File," then "Export" (see Fig. 8.24).

When you click on "Export," you'll get a dialog box with several options, as in Fig. 8.25. Select the one that makes the most sense for your newsroom.

You have now navigated your way through ArcView, joined two databases, and saved them for future reference. This relatively straightforward manipulation of data has yielded useful analysis that you can now use in your reporting.

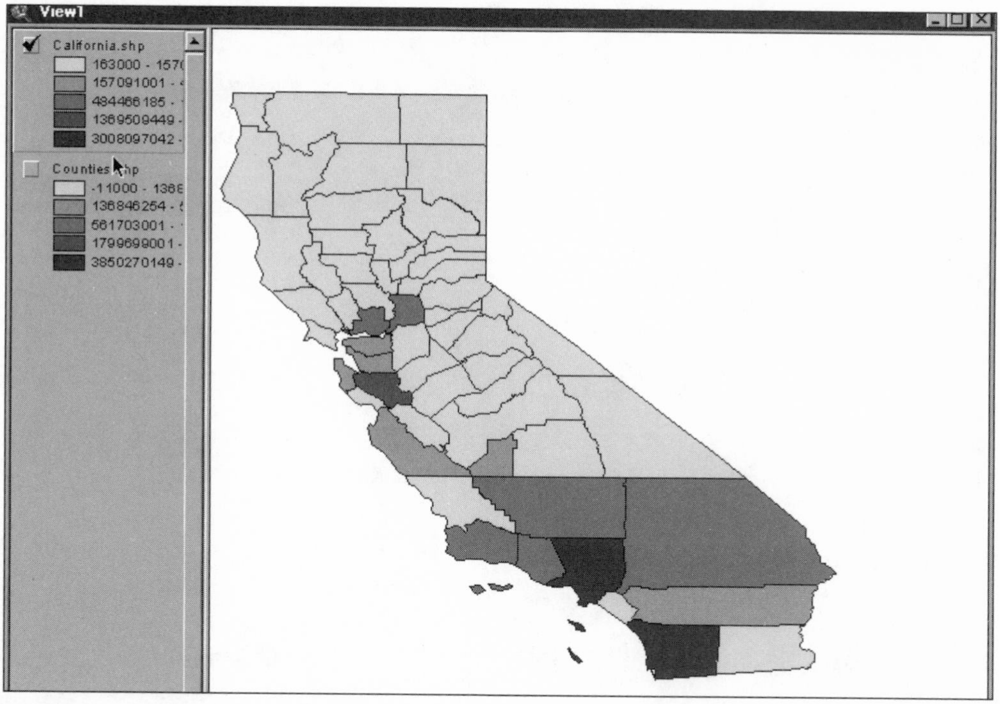

FIGURE 8.23

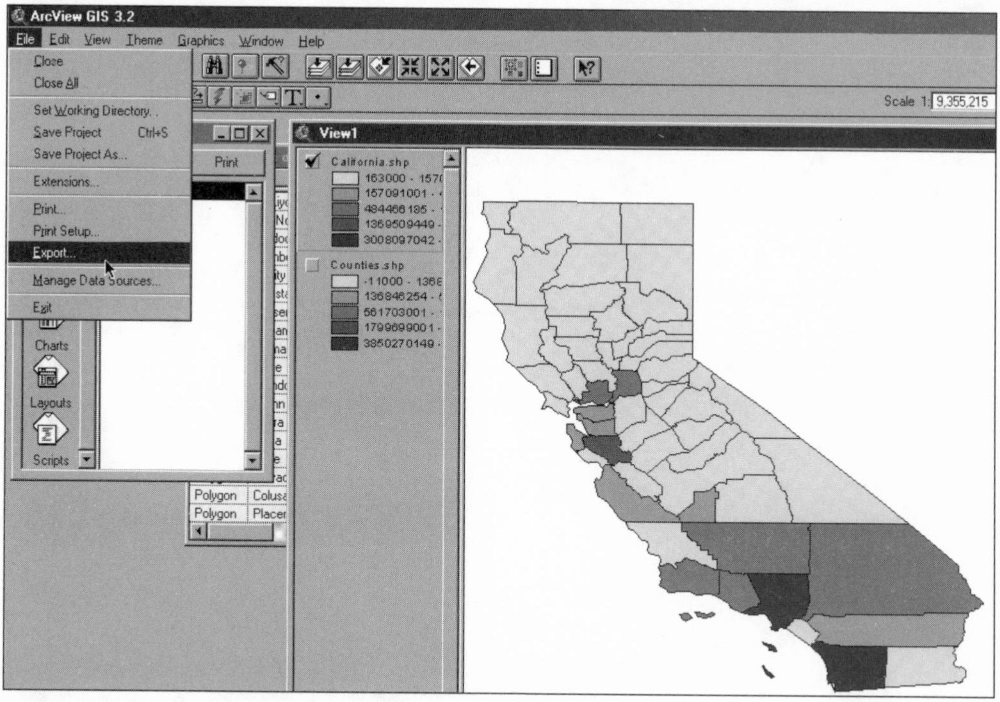

FIGURE 8.24

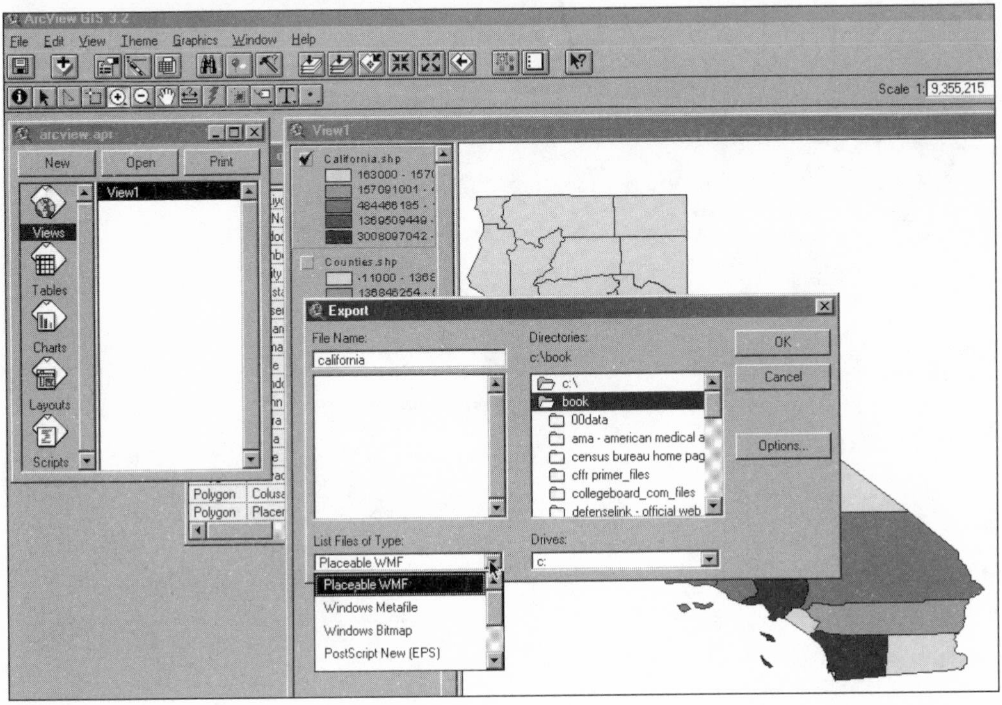
ArcView GIS 3.2
File Edit View Theme Graphics Window Help
Scale 1: 9,355,215
arcview.apr
New Open Print
Views
Tables
Charts
Layouts
Scripts
View1
California.shp
Counties.shp
Polygon
Export
File Name:
california
Directories:
c:\book
c:\
book
00data
ama - american medical a
census bureau home pag
cffr primer_files
collegeboard_com_files
defenselink - official web
OK
Cancel
Options...
List Files of Type:
Placeable WMF
Windows Metafile
Windows Bitmap
PostScript New (EPS)
Drives:
c:

FIGURE 8.25

CHAPTER NINE

Statistics

Statistics often get a bad rap in newsrooms. But statistics don't kill stories—editors (and careless reporters) kill stories.

Certainly, one can argue that statistics are inherently risky animals and should perhaps be regulated, and possibly even phased out of existence among the civilian population. But advocates of greater precision in journalism argue that statistics, when properly used, can act as a deterrent against criticism of controversial stories.

Perhaps the best argument for becoming more conversant with statistics, however, has come from Phil Meyer, the former reporter and now University of North Carolina professor who wrote *Precision Journalism.* Journalists who rely solely on sources to obtain, interpret, and provide statistics, he wrote, are simply not being good journalists. In his 1990 update of the book, Meyer wrote: "The trouble with being a passive and innocent journalist is that, like any passive and innocent person, one can be too easily taken advantage of."

Few academics (and even fewer editors) will argue that their staffs should become completely fluent in statistical techniques. It might be great fun to calculate the negative binomial distribution—the probability that there will be x number of failures before a certain success—of the Boston Red Sox baseball team, but it's most likely not something that the average newspaper reader, broadcast viewer, or listener will want to know about. Still, every reporter and editor should have a basic understanding of a number of statistical concepts.

Percentages

The first statistical concept that every reporter should learn is percentage calculations. It should be an easy concept—percent simply means "per 100"—but figuring percentages has been the bane of many journalists.

It's easy enough: If I have written three of five stories on the front page, I've got 60 percent (3 divided by 5 = 0.6). And to our credit, most reporters get the most basic percentage calculations right.

But when it comes to calculating percentage changes, many reporters struggle. Let's say the population of a city has grown from 200,000 to 250,000 over a 10-year period. What's the percentage change? Here's the formula:

Percentage change = (New number – old number)/old number, or
Percentage change = (250,000 – 200,000)/200,000, or
Percentage change = 0.25, or 25 percent.

Here's a simple mnemonic to help out. Remember the "Just Say No" antidrug campaign of the early 1980s? Just say (N-O)/O, for

(New – old)/old.

One issue often comes up in journalism statistics classes. Why the parentheses? If you didn't have them, you're simply subtracting 1 from your new number, because you're dividing the old number by the old number. If you didn't have the parentheses in the above example, your percentage change would equal 249,000 percent.

Another potential pitfall bears mentioning. Let's say the population of Town A has increased by 25 percent over the last 10 years, from 10,000 to 12,500 people. During the same time, the population of Town B has increased 50 percent, from 10,000 to 15,000 people. Does that mean that the population of the two towns has increased 75 percent? Of course not. We can use our formula to calculate percentage change:

Percentage change =
[(12,500 + 15,000) – (10,000 + 10,000)]/(10,000 + 10,000)

We find that the percentage change of the two cities actually is 37.5 percent—a far cry from the 75 percent that we might have guessed if we'd just added the two percentages together.

Finally, don't confuse percentage change with percentage difference. If the rate of inflation was 10 percent in 1999 and 20 percent in 2000, the percentage change over the two years would be 100 percent. The percentage difference would be 10 percent. Small change in wording, big change in meaning.

Means, Medians, and Modes

Next to percentage change calculations, means, medians, and modes are almost certainly the most commonly misused statistics by reporters. The average, or mean, is probably the most frequently used but the least understood of the three. It's likely that means are misused because they're so easy to calculate; you just add up all the numbers, and divide by the total count of numbers. For example, if we have three houses valued at $100,000, $200,000, and $300,000, then our formula looks like this:

$$\begin{aligned} \text{Average} &= (\$100{,}000 + \$200{,}000 + \$300{,}000)/3 \\ &= (\$600{,}000)/3 \\ &= \$200{,}000. \end{aligned}$$

This is an honest enough use of statistics. But what if you have three houses in a neighborhood, with one worth $100,000, one worth $200,000, and one worth $1,200,000? Is it fair to say that the average homeowner has a house that's worth $500,000? This conundrum can also be encountered when analyzing job salaries if a handful of top executives are paid millions of dollars—but the average worker takes home $45,000. So what to do? This is generally where a median is handy. Simply put, a median is the middle number. In the preceding housing example, the median would be $200,000, which is probably more representative of the values of the homes than the mean.

Finally, we read a lot about modes, although they're seldom mentioned. Put simply, the mode is just the most frequent number in a list.

Per Capita

Per-capita rates may be one of the most easily understood but little-used statistics in journalism. It's a shame, because it's one measurement that can be used to clear up misperceptions rather quickly.

Let's consider federal spending in California. The federal government spends roughly $43 billion in Los Angeles County, which has about 9 million people. Does that mean that the average Angeleno is faring better than other Californians when it comes to getting state funds? Not necessarily; the per-capita amount spent, or the amount per person, is about $4,600. By contrast, the average resident of Inyo County, in northern California, which has about 18,000 people, gets nearly $14,500 from the federal government.

As always, there are caveats when dealing with such numbers. Because of its sparse population, Alaska will almost always wind up at the top (or bottom) of statewide per-capita rankings. Where necessary, smart reporters will often compare nearby states or states with similar demographics to avoid "outliers," or figures that fall either very far under or very far over the mean.

Weighting

Reporters spend more time writing about the results of surveys than they do actually conducting their own surveys. And being reporters, almost everyone who looks at a survey cares about one thing: Where do we rank?

"Rankings," writes Sarah Cohen, a database editor at the *Washington Post* and author of a book on newsroom statistics, "cause no end of trouble in a newsroom. . . . They're land mines in the news."

Cohen and other statisticians warn that the key element of rankings is "weighting," or how much importance is assigned to each component of a ranking. For example, a survey about the best newspapers in a state might be based on several components: circulation, editorial quality, number of advertisements, and so on. But they might not all be equally considered in ranking newspapers. Circulation might be responsible for 25 percent of the newspaper's total score, editorial quality for 50 percent, and advertisements for 10 percent. So it's always a good idea to ask how each component is weighted, and like Sherlock Holmes in "The Adventure of Silver Blaze," always look for the dog that didn't bark—or in this case, the component in the ranking that wasn't listed.

Probability

Probably the most frequent probability problem for reporters involves state lotteries (also known as the state tax on poor math students). At its most basic level, a probability is simply a ratio. If a reporter buys one of 500,000 tickets sold for a $68 million lottery, that reporter has a 1-in-500,000 chance of winning the lottery. If the same reporter buys two tickets, there's a 1-in-250,000 chance of winning the prize. Four tickets narrows the chances down to 1-in-125,000.

A word about lottery combinations: They generally involve something called factorials, which are, appropriately enough, represented by an exclamation mark. To determine the possible number of combinations in a nine-digit lottery game—one that would allow you to select any combination of nine numbers—you would calculate 9!, which is equivalent to

$$9 \ 8 \ 7 \ 6 \ 5 \ 4 \ 3 \ 2 \ 1,$$

or 362,880 possible combinations.

Polling

Most reporters don't do their own polling. But that doesn't mean that they should ignore the statistics behind the polls. One of the most important statistics is the "margin of error," or the percentage that the findings might be off. A poll with a 95 percent margin of error, for example, means that 5 percent of the answers may be incorrect or incomplete. Margins of error become particularly important during political campaigns, when races can be very close. If one candidate has 43 percent of the vote in a poll, for example, and another has 45 percent, and the poll has a margin of error of 5 percent, then it's safe to write that the race is too close to call, according to the poll.

One other thing to keep in mind when writing about polls: Consider the source. In general, a poll about firearms from the National Rifle Association is going to have very different results than a poll from the National Handgun Control Association. In most cases, poll results are directly determined by the questions that are asked, and how they're asked—or not asked. Election tracking polls used by politicians in the heat of a campaign are particularly egregious examples of how polls can be misused.

CHAPTER TEN

Importing Data

One of the trickiest problems for reporters trying to analyze data is bringing it into an understandable and compatible format with their existing software. Although reporters can get spreadsheet- and database-ready data more often now, a lot of government data still are available only in text or other formats. At times, it can seem as though it would be quicker just to make a printout and enter everything by hand. For some data, that's possible. But for most, it's a waste of time.

In this chapter, we're going to look at five kinds of importing:

1. Fixed-width text files into spreadsheets
2. Delimited text files into spreadsheets
3. Web pages into spreadsheets
4. PDF files into spreadsheets
5. Text and other files into databases

For purposes of consistency, we'll work with Microsoft Excel and Access.

Fixed-Width Text Files

In many ways, fixed-width files are the easiest files to import, and a type that many beginners first encounter. A fixed-width file has the same number of characters in each column, so if you've got a record layout—a must-have for anyone working with data—you always know where the column breaks go. Fixed-width files, however, do carry some perils. It's very easy to misplace a column break and wind up with a wrong result, or a number that doesn't make sense, or a column that mixes characters and numbers.

Of the major spreadsheet programs, Excel probably does the best job of alerting reporters to potential pitfalls with fixed-width data. To open a fixed-width file, you first open Excel. Next, you need to either click on the "Open File" icon (the folder) or go to "File," then "Open," and find the fixed-width file (see Fig. 10.1).

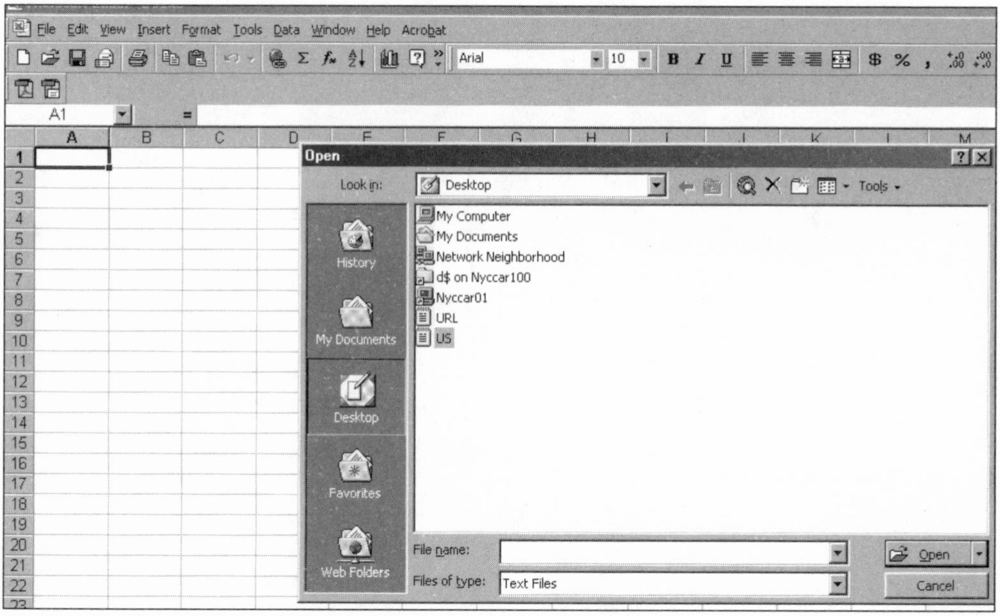

FIGURE 10.1

When we click on the correct file, we'll get the dialog box shown in Fig. 10.2.

We can choose either delimited or fixed width; we'll choose fixed width here. Usually, Excel will guess properly about whether you're dealing with a fixed-width or delimited file. It will also try to guess where the column breaks should go (not always with a great deal of success). In some cases, Excel will leave it up to you to put the breaks in their proper places. To create a column break, simply click on "Next" to go to Step 2 of the Import Wizard. You can see in Fig. 10.3 that Excel has had mixed success in assigning column breaks, doing well with the numbers.

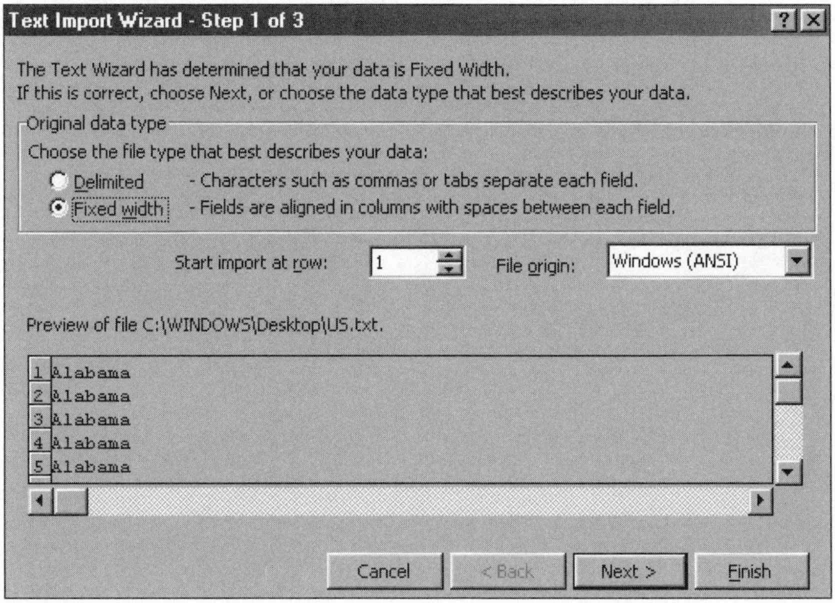

FIGURE 10.2

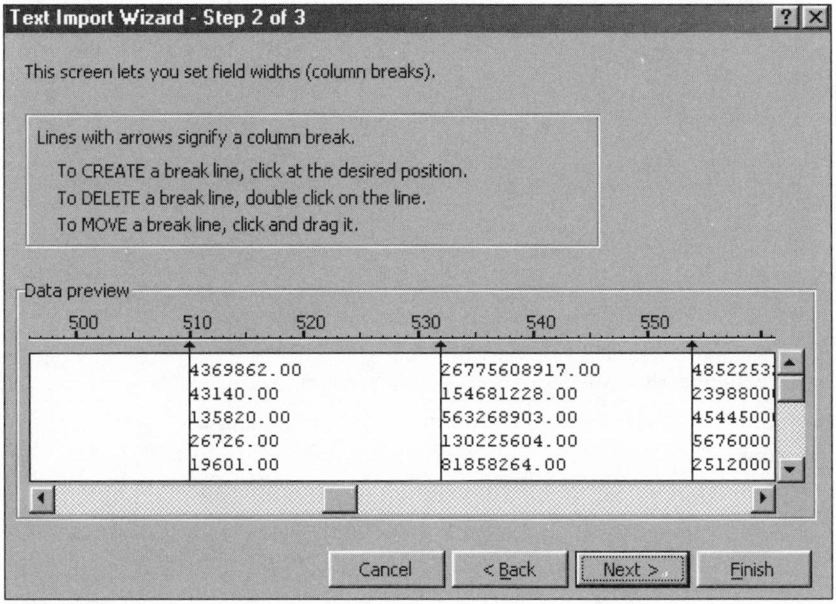

FIGURE 10.3

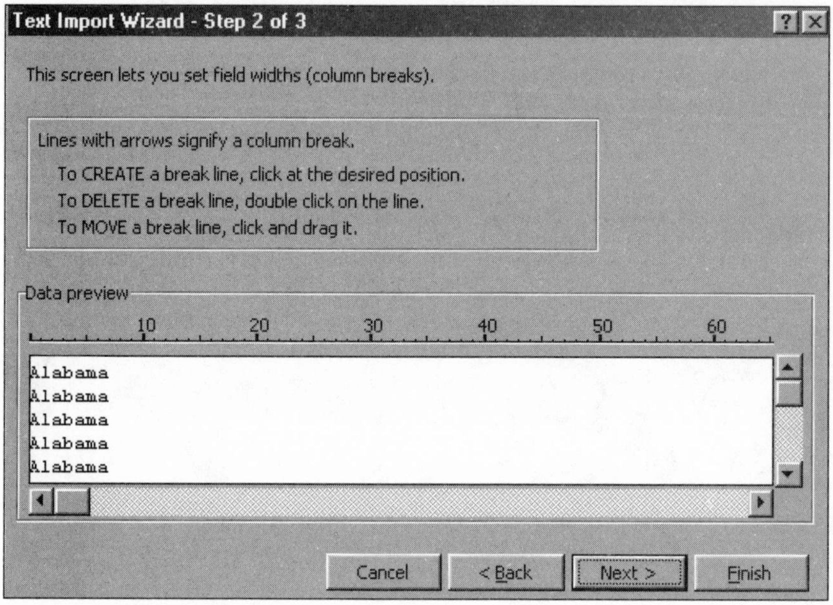

FIGURE 10.4

But it doesn't always do that well. Let's look at the first column (see Fig. 10.4).

It starts out well, but goes on and on . . . all the way out to column 130. That's a bit more than we need, so let's move the cursor back to column 25. To do that, we move the cursor until it's just on top of the line, as in Fig. 10.5.

Then drag it back to column 25, as in Fig. 10.6.

To get rid of all the extra space, we're going to go to the "Counties" column, and place a line right before it. To do that, go where you want to put the line (see Fig. 10.7).

Next, click on the column where you want the line—in this case, column 255—and the line will appear. Don't worry if you put the line in the wrong place. You can double-click on a column break line to make it go away (see Fig. 10.8).

Now, we'll click on "Next" to go to the final step (see Fig. 10.9).

This part lets us specify what kinds of values we want in a column—or whether we want the column at all. For example, we don't want the sec-

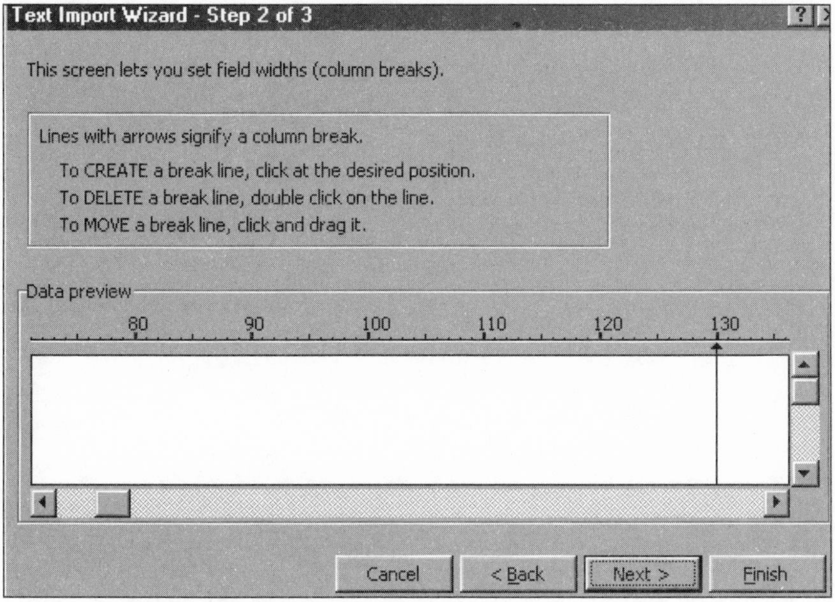

FIGURE 10.5

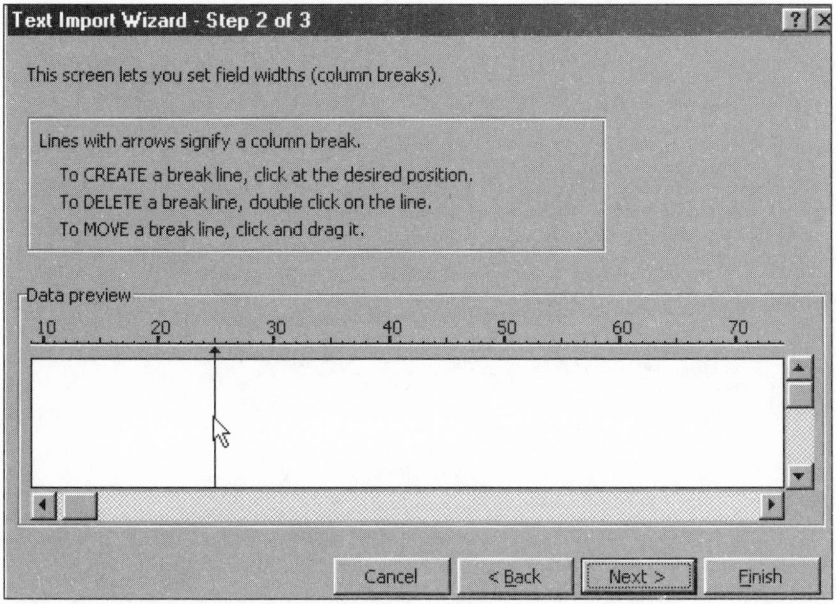

FIGURE 10.6

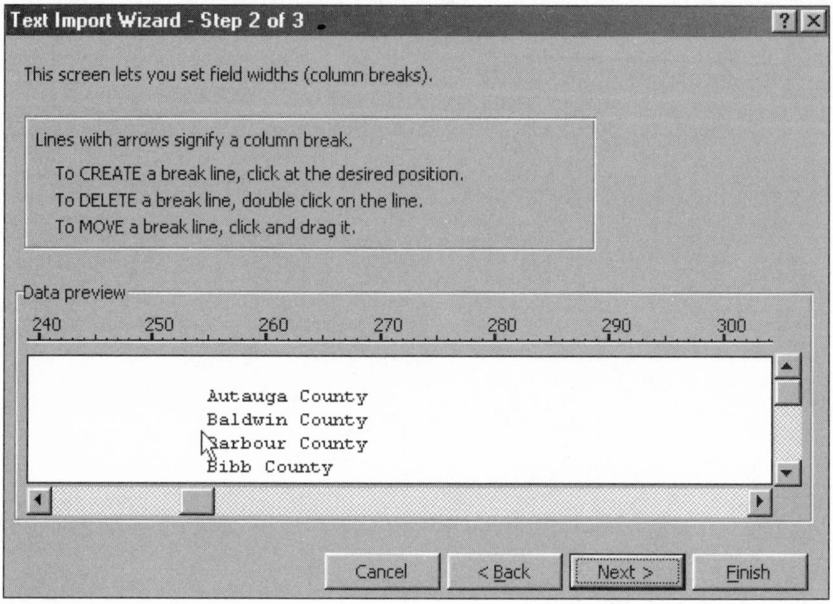

FIGURE 10.7

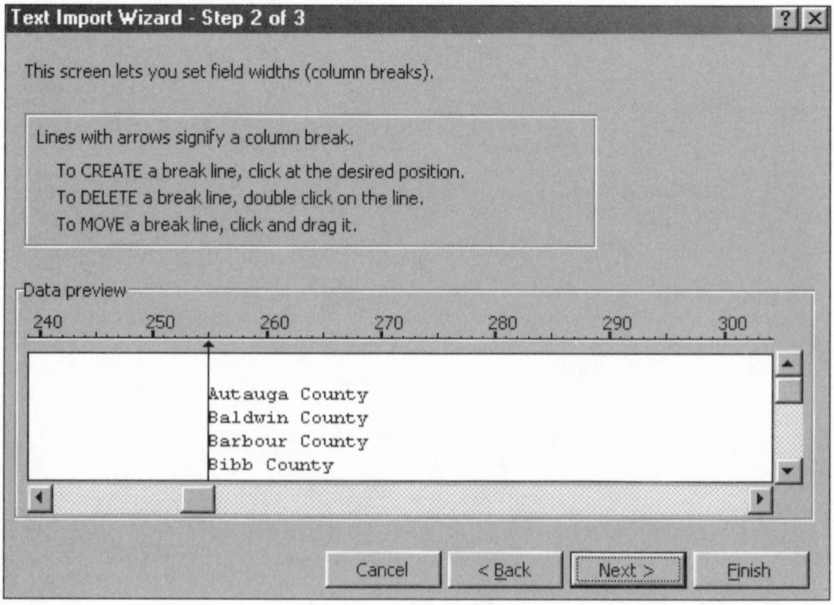

FIGURE 10.8

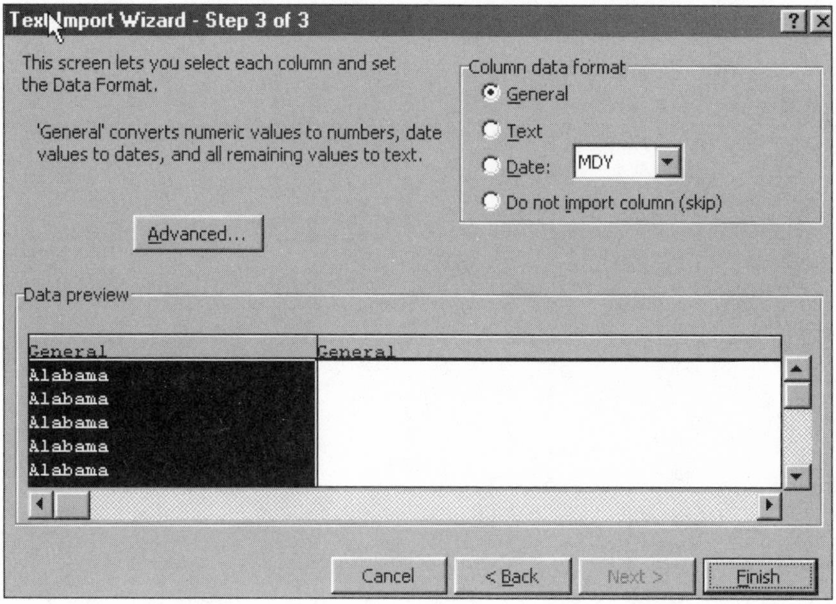

FIGURE 10.9

ond column, so we'd highlight it by clicking on "General" above it and select the "Do not import column (skip)" button.

Sometimes, it's necessary to change a column from a general format to a text format, especially in databases that have leading zeros, such as zip codes, Social Security numbers, and government FIPS (federal information processing standards) codes. It's not necessary here, so we'll click on "Finish." Our spreadsheet now appears in Fig. 10.10.

To put the column headers in, you can click on row 1, right-click, and "Insert" a row. You'll then type in column headers. To make the spreadsheet wider, you can just define it all by clicking in the gray box above row 1 and to the left of column A, go to "Format," "Column," and "AutoFit Selection" (see Fig. 10.11). If importing fixed-width files seems a little arcane at first, don't worry. Like everything else with computer-assisted reporting, it takes a few times to master.

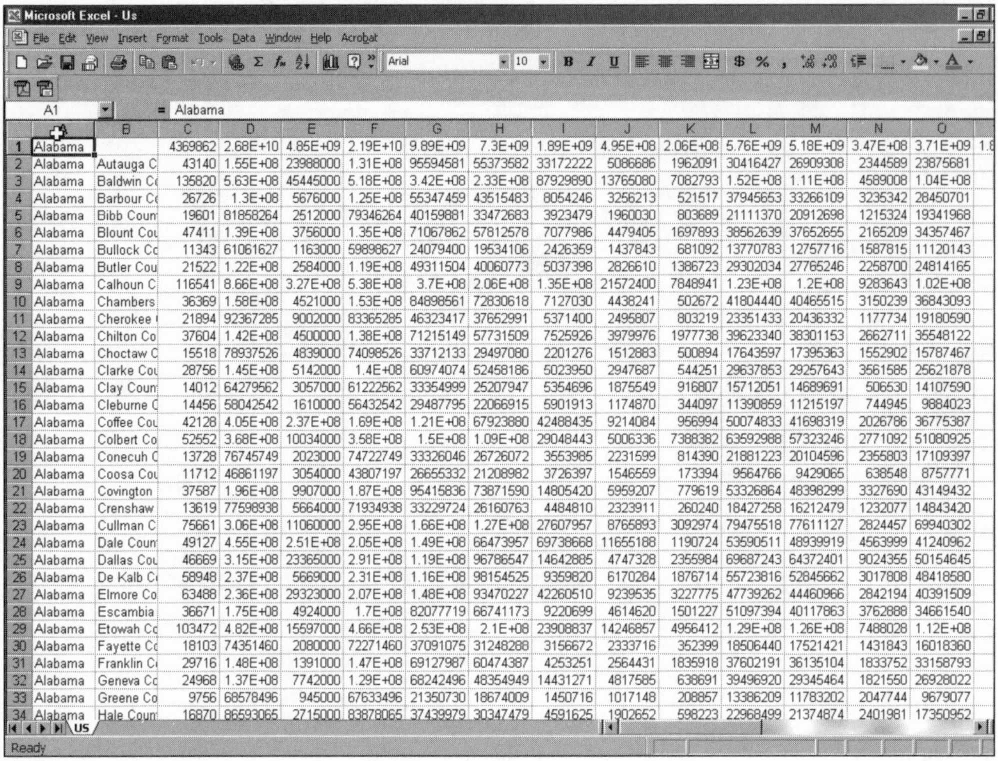

	A	B	C	D	E	F	G	H	I	J	K	L	M	N	O	
1	Alabama		4369862	2.68E+10	4.85E+09	2.19E+10	9.89E+09	7.3E+09	1.89E+09	4.95E+08	2.06E+08	5.76E+09	5.18E+09	3.47E+08	3.71E+09	1.8
2	Alabama	Autauga C	43140	1.55E+08	23988000	1.31E+08	95594581	55373582	33172222	5086686	1962091	30416427	26909308	2344589	23875681	
3	Alabama	Baldwin Co	135820	5.63E+08	45445000	5.18E+08	3.42E+08	2.33E+08	87929890	13765080	7082793	1.52E+08	1.11E+08	4589008	1.04E+08	
4	Alabama	Barbour Co	26726	1.3E+08	5676000	1.25E+08	55347459	43515483	8054246	3256213	521517	37945653	33266109	3235342	28450701	
5	Alabama	Bibb Coun	19601	81858264	2512000	79346264	40159881	33472683	3923479	1960030	803689	21111370	20912698	1215324	19341968	
6	Alabama	Blount Cou	47411	1.39E+08	3756000	1.35E+08	71067862	57812578	7077986	4479405	1697893	38562639	37652655	2165209	34357467	
7	Alabama	Bullock Co	11343	61061627	1163000	59898627	24079400	19534106	2426359	1437843	681092	13770783	12757716	1587815	11120143	
8	Alabama	Butler Cou	21522	1.22E+08	2584000	1.19E+08	49311504	40060773	5037398	2826610	1386723	29302034	27765246	2258700	24814165	
9	Alabama	Calhoun C	116541	8.66E+08	3.27E+08	5.38E+08	3.7E+08	2.06E+08	1.35E+08	21572400	7848941	1.23E+08	1.2E+08	9283643	1.02E+08	
10	Alabama	Chambers	36369	1.58E+08	4521000	1.53E+08	84898561	72830618	7127030	4438241	502672	41804440	40465515	3150239	36843093	
11	Alabama	Cherokee	21894	92367285	9002000	83365285	46323417	37652991	5371400	2495807	803219	23351433	20436332	1177734	19180590	
12	Alabama	Chilton Co	37604	1.42E+08	4500000	1.38E+08	71215149	57731509	7525926	3979976	1977738	39623340	38301153	2662711	35548122	
13	Alabama	Choctaw C	15518	78937526	4839000	74098526	33712133	29497080	2201276	1512883	500894	17643597	17395363	1552902	15787467	
14	Alabama	Clarke Cou	28756	1.45E+08	5142000	1.4E+08	60974074	52458186	5023950	2947687	544251	29637853	29257643	3561585	25621878	
15	Alabama	Clay Coun	14012	64279562	3057000	61222562	33354999	25207947	5354696	1875549	916807	15712051	14689691	506530	14107590	
16	Alabama	Cleburne C	14456	58042542	1610000	56432542	29487795	22066915	5901913	1174870	344097	11390859	11215197	744945	9884023	
17	Alabama	Coffee Cou	42128	4.05E+08	2.37E+08	1.69E+08	1.21E+08	67923880	42488435	9214084	956994	50074833	41698319	2026786	36775387	
18	Alabama	Colbert Co	52552	3.68E+08	10034000	3.58E+08	1.5E+08	1.09E+08	29048443	5006336	7388382	63592988	57323246	2771092	51080925	
19	Alabama	Conecuh C	13728	76745749	2023000	74722749	33326046	26726072	3553985	2231599	814390	21881223	20104596	2355803	17109397	
20	Alabama	Coosa Cou	11712	46861197	3054000	43807197	26655332	21208982	3726397	1546559	173394	9564766	9429065	638548	8757771	
21	Alabama	Covington	37587	1.96E+08	9907000	1.87E+08	95415836	73871590	14805420	5959207	779619	53326864	48398299	3327690	43149432	
22	Alabama	Crenshaw	13619	77598938	5664000	71934938	33229724	26160763	4484810	2323911	260240	18427258	16212479	1232077	14843420	
23	Alabama	Cullman C	75661	3.06E+08	11060000	2.95E+08	1.66E+08	1.27E+08	27607957	8765893	3092974	79475518	77611127	2824457	69940302	
24	Alabama	Dale Coun	49127	4.55E+08	2.51E+08	2.05E+08	1.49E+08	66473957	69738668	11655188	1190724	53590511	48939919	4563999	41240962	
25	Alabama	Dallas Cou	46669	3.15E+08	23365000	2.91E+08	1.19E+08	96786547	14642885	4747328	2355984	69687243	64372401	9024355	50154645	
26	Alabama	De Kalb Co	58948	2.37E+08	5669000	2.31E+08	1.16E+08	98154525	9359820	6170284	1876714	55723816	52845662	3017808	48418580	
27	Alabama	Elmore Co	63488	2.36E+08	29323000	2.07E+08	1.48E+08	93470227	42260510	9239535	3227775	47739262	44460966	2842194	40391509	
28	Alabama	Escambia	36671	1.75E+08	4924000	1.7E+08	82077719	66741173	9220699	4614620	1501227	51097394	40117863	3762888	34661540	
29	Alabama	Etowah Co	103472	4.82E+08	15597000	4.66E+08	2.53E+08	2.1E+08	23908837	14246857	4956412	1.29E+08	1.26E+08	7488028	1.12E+08	
30	Alabama	Fayette Co	18103	74351460	2080000	72271460	37091075	31248288	3156672	2333716	352399	18506440	17521421	1431843	16018360	
31	Alabama	Franklin C	29716	1.48E+08	1391000	1.47E+08	69127987	60474387	4253251	2564431	1835918	37602191	36135104	1833752	33158793	
32	Alabama	Geneva Co	24968	1.37E+08	7742000	1.29E+08	68242496	48354949	14431271	4817585	638691	39496920	29345464	1821550	26928022	
33	Alabama	Greene Co	9756	68578496	945000	67633496	21350730	18674009	1450716	1017148	208857	13386209	11783202	2047744	9679077	
34	Alabama	Hale Coun	16870	86593065	2715000	83878065	37439979	30347479	4591625	1902652	598223	22968499	21374874	2401981	17350952	

FIGURE 10.10

Delimited Text Files

If fixed-width files are easy to import into Excel, delimited text files are even easier. The primary thing that you need to know is the delimiter. Is it a comma? A space? A tab? Some other character? A delimiter can be almost anything, although it helps if the people who create the delimited file understand the database. For example, if the database has numbers that contain commas, a comma-delimited data file isn't the best option. Likewise, a database that has spaces between names probably isn't the best candidate for a space-delimited file.

Let's look at a delimited-text version of the Consolidated Federal Funds Report. When we open it up in Excel, we see the usual Text Import Wizard (see Fig. 10.12).

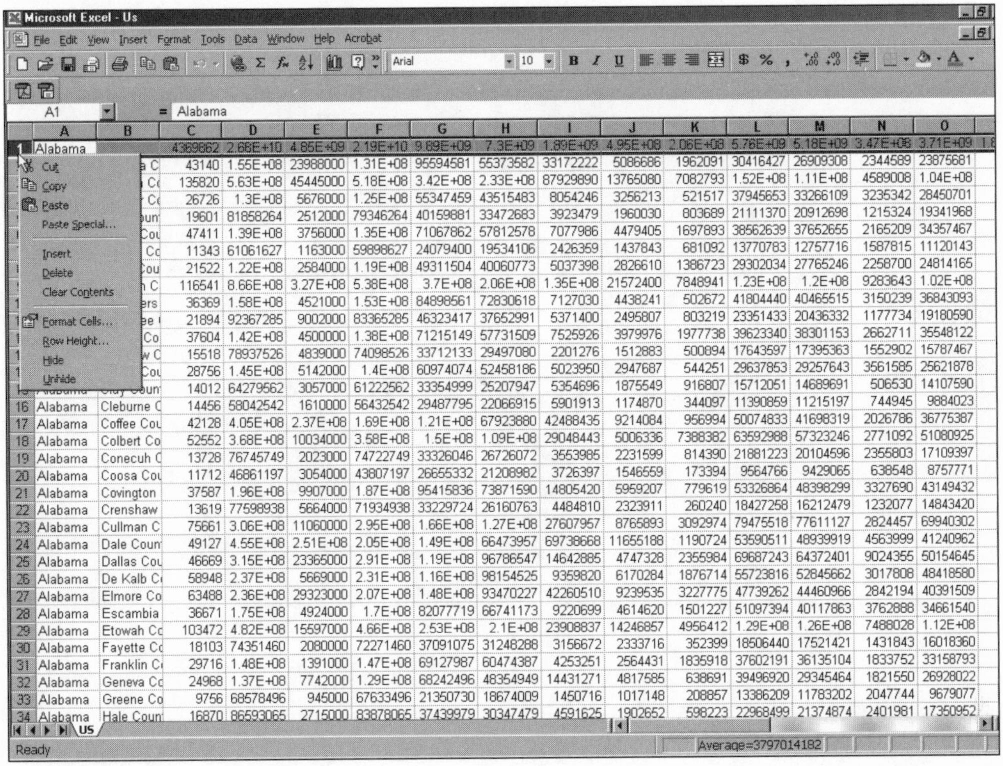

FIGURE 10.11

Again, Excel has guessed. This time, it's guessed correctly—this is a delimited file. Of course, you could have guessed that by the commas between the field. We'll click on "Next" and see a different step in the Import Wizard (see Fig. 10.13).

Next, we need to check the "Comma" box and make sure that the text qualifier is properly defined (see Fig. 10.14). The text qualifier tells Excel that a certain column is a text column. Obviously, the "State" column should be text, but it was apparently defined as a general format column. No harm done.

When we click on "Next," we get a final preview of the spreadsheet. And when we click on "Finish," the spreadsheet opens as shown in Fig. 10.15.

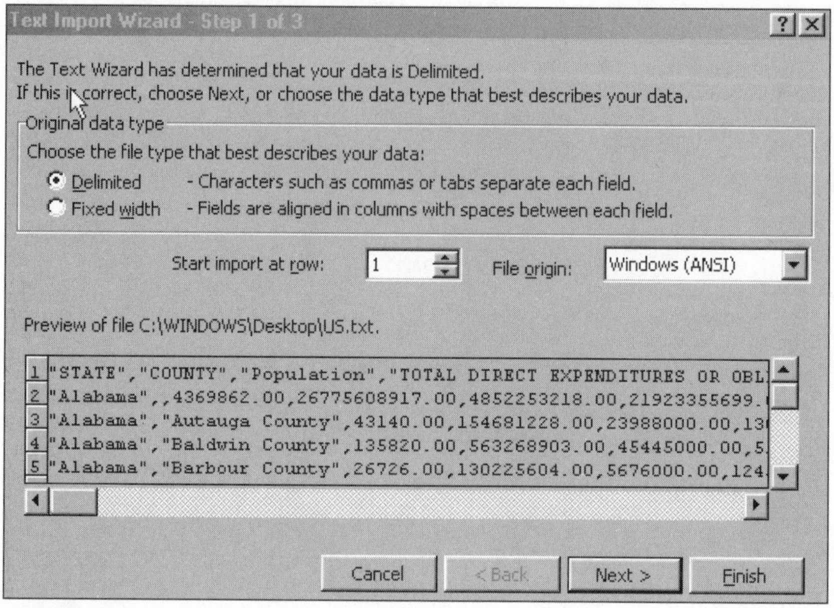

FIGURE 10.12

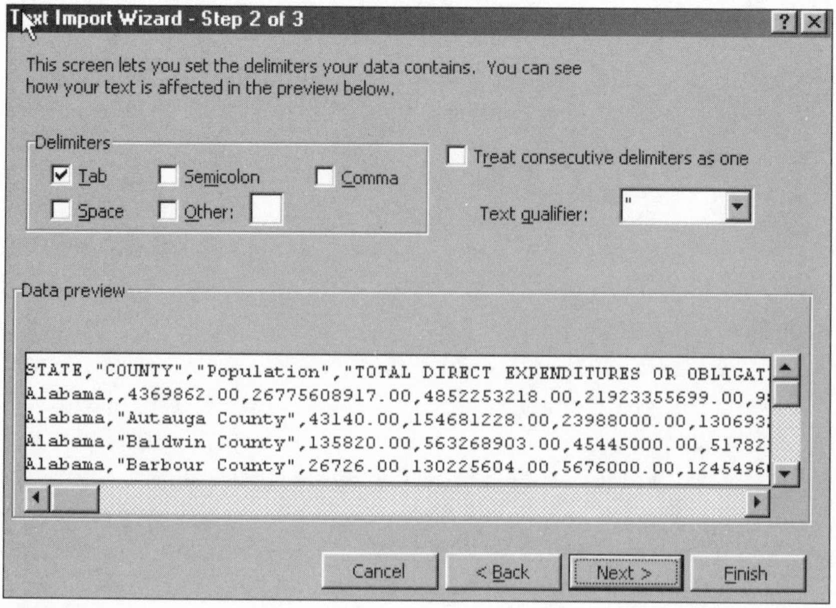

FIGURE 10.13

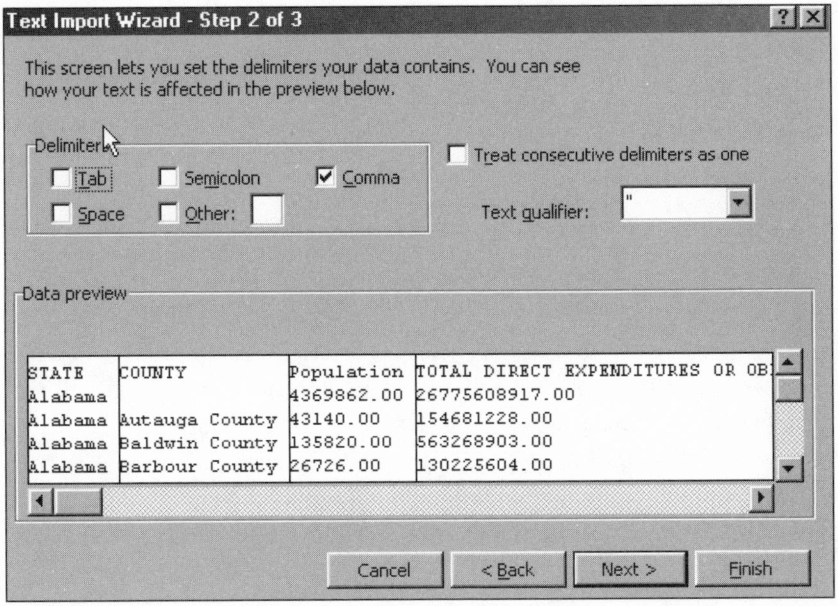

FIGURE 10.14

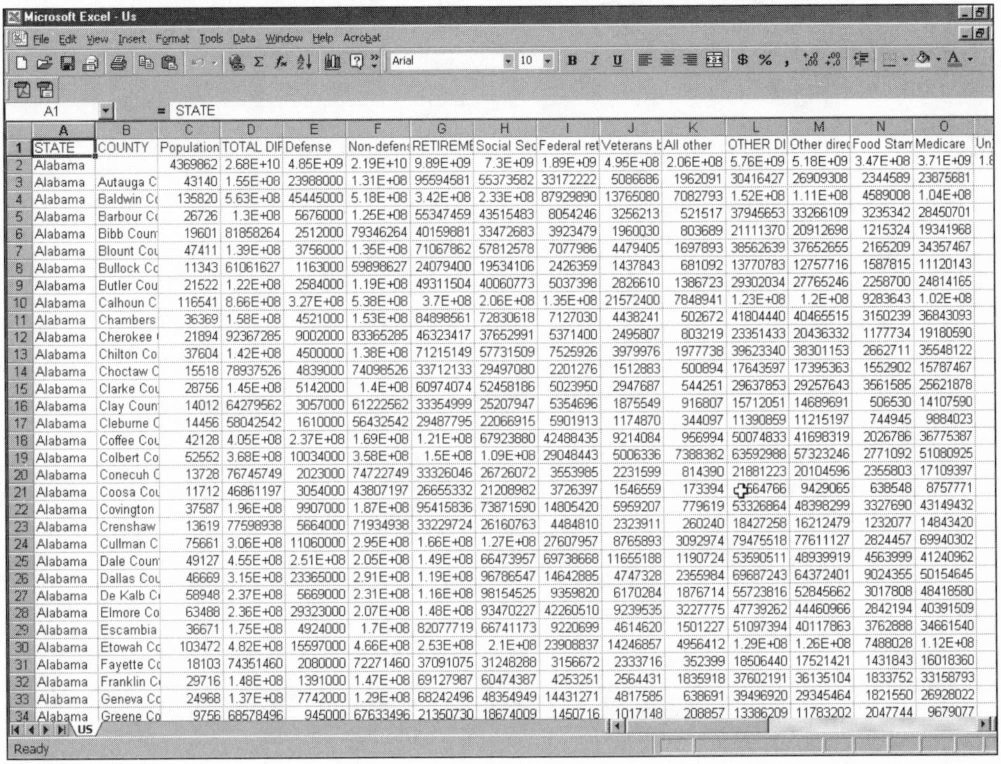

FIGURE 10.15

Again, you can get a better look at the spreadsheet by defining everything, and then going to "Format," "Columns," and "AutoFit Selection."

Web Pages

Importing Web pages can be difficult or easy, depending on the program used to create them and the format they're in. Tables created in HTML usually aren't that difficult to open; some will open directly into Excel without any manipulation. Others, however, can be more difficult. Let's look at 1999 population estimates for Alabama, which are available at www.census.gov/population/estimates/county/co–99–1/99C1_01.txt. Technically, this isn't a Web page at all; it's a text page that's been loaded onto the Internet (see Fig. 10.16).

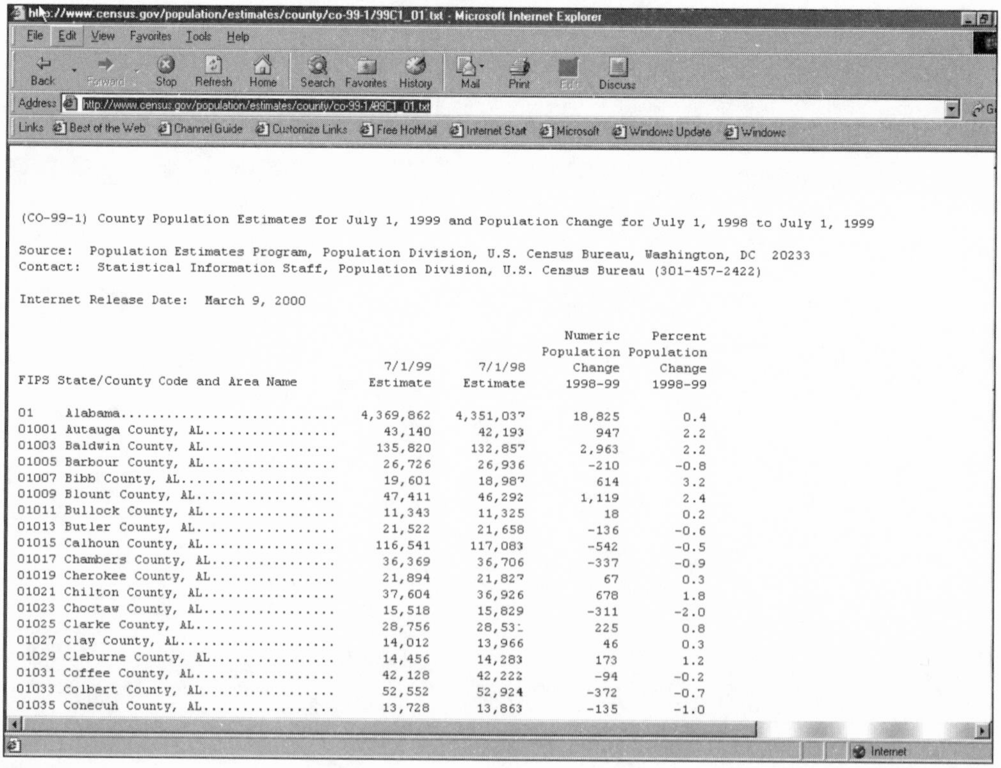

(CO-99-1) County Population Estimates for July 1, 1999 and Population Change for July 1, 1998 to July 1, 1999

Source: Population Estimates Program, Population Division, U.S. Census Bureau, Washington, DC 20233
Contact: Statistical Information Staff, Population Division, U.S. Census Bureau (301-457-2422)

Internet Release Date: March 9, 2000

FIPS State/County Code and Area Name	7/1/99 Estimate	7/1/98 Estimate	Numeric Population Change 1998-99	Percent Population Change 1998-99
01 Alabama............................	4,369,862	4,351,037	18,825	0.4
01001 Autauga County, AL................	43,140	42,193	947	2.2
01003 Baldwin County, AL................	135,820	132,857	2,963	2.2
01005 Barbour County, AL................	26,726	26,936	-210	-0.8
01007 Bibb County, AL...................	19,601	18,987	614	3.2
01009 Blount County, AL.................	47,411	46,292	1,119	2.4
01011 Bullock County, AL................	11,343	11,325	18	0.2
01013 Butler County, AL.................	21,522	21,658	-136	-0.6
01015 Calhoun County, AL................	116,541	117,083	-542	-0.5
01017 Chambers County, AL...............	36,369	36,706	-337	-0.9
01019 Cherokee County, AL...............	21,894	21,827	67	0.3
01021 Chilton County, AL................	37,604	36,926	678	1.8
01023 Choctaw County, AL................	15,518	15,829	-311	-2.0
01025 Clarke County, AL.................	28,756	28,531	225	0.8
01027 Clay County, AL...................	14,012	13,966	46	0.3
01029 Cleburne County, AL...............	14,456	14,283	173	1.2
01031 Coffee County, AL.................	42,128	42,222	-94	-0.2
01033 Colbert County, AL................	52,552	52,924	-372	-0.7
01035 Conecuh County, AL................	13,728	13,863	-135	-1.0

FIGURE 10.16

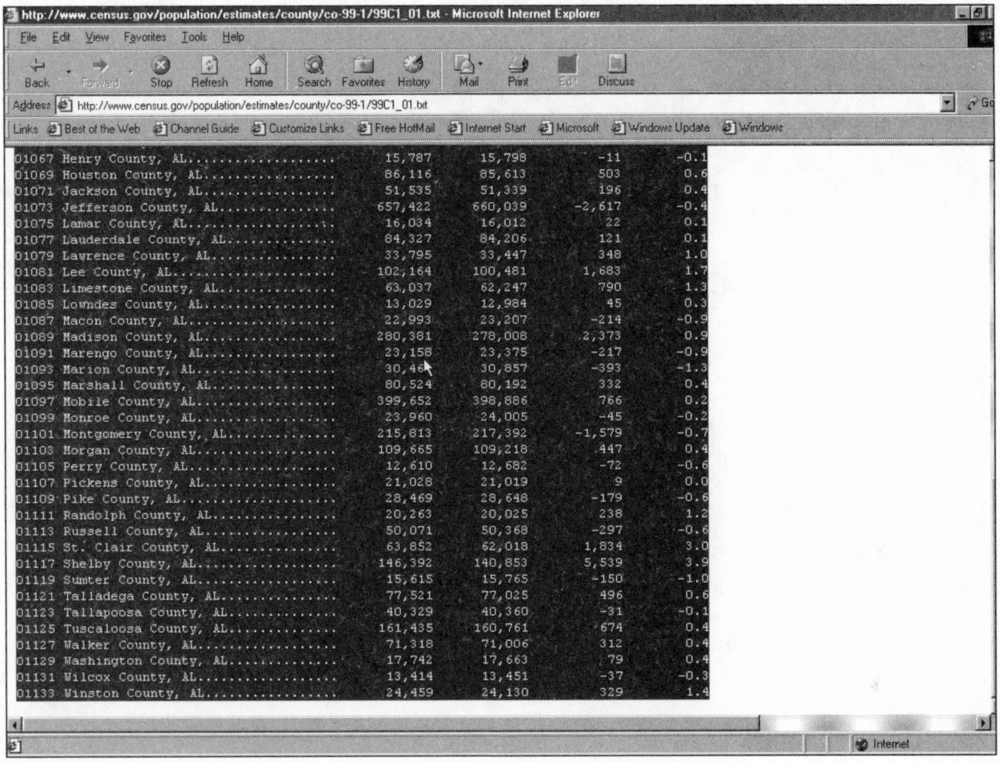

01067 Henry County, AL..................	15,787	15,798	-11	-0.1
01069 Houston County, AL................	86,116	85,613	503	0.6
01071 Jackson County, AL................	51,535	51,339	196	0.4
01073 Jefferson County, AL..............	657,422	660,039	-2,617	-0.4
01075 Lamar County, AL..................	16,034	16,012	22	0.1
01077 Lauderdale County, AL.............	84,327	84,206	121	0.1
01079 Lawrence County, AL...............	33,795	33,447	348	1.0
01081 Lee County, AL....................	102,164	100,481	1,683	1.7
01083 Limestone County, AL..............	63,037	62,247	790	1.3
01085 Lowndes County, AL................	13,029	12,984	45	0.3
01087 Macon County, AL..................	22,993	23,207	-214	-0.9
01089 Madison County, AL................	280,381	278,008	2,373	0.9
01091 Marengo County, AL................	23,158	23,375	-217	-0.9
01093 Marion County, AL.................	30,46	30,857	-393	-1.3
01095 Marshall County, AL...............	80,524	80,192	332	0.4
01097 Mobile County, AL.................	399,652	398,886	766	0.2
01099 Monroe County, AL.................	23,960	24,005	-45	-0.2
01101 Montgomery County, AL.............	215,813	217,392	-1,579	-0.7
01103 Morgan County, AL.................	109,665	109,218	447	0.4
01105 Perry County, AL..................	12,610	12,682	-72	-0.6
01107 Pickens County, AL................	21,028	21,019	9	0.0
01109 Pike County, AL...................	28,469	28,648	-179	-0.6
01111 Randolph County, AL...............	20,263	20,025	238	1.2
01113 Russell County, AL................	50,071	50,368	-297	-0.6
01115 St. Clair County, AL..............	63,852	62,018	1,834	3.0
01117 Shelby County, AL.................	146,392	140,853	5,539	3.9
01119 Sumter County, AL.................	15,615	15,765	-150	-1.0
01121 Talladega County, AL..............	77,521	77,025	496	0.6
01123 Tallapoosa County, AL.............	40,329	40,360	-31	-0.1
01125 Tuscaloosa County, AL.............	161,435	160,761	674	0.4
01127 Walker County, AL.................	71,318	71,006	312	0.4
01129 Washington County, AL.............	17,742	17,663	79	0.4
01131 Wilcox County, AL.................	13,414	13,451	-37	-0.3
01133 Winston County, AL................	24,459	24,130	329	1.4

FIGURE 10.17

We start by defining the relevant parts. Just hold down on your left mouse key and drag it down and over until the area you want to import has been defined. The next step is to copy the data; you can do that by right-clicking and selecting "Copy" (see Fig. 10.17).

Once that's been done, switch to a blank Excel worksheet. Place the cursor in cell A1 and right-click on "Paste." The data should appear on the worksheet as illustrated in Fig. 10.18.

We can see a bit of a problem, though. If we look in the formula bar, we can see that cell A1 now consists of the words "Numeric" and "Percent." We'll have to do a little better job of separating the columns. Fortunately, there's a good Excel tool for doing that. Go to "Data," and select "Text to Columns." When you do, the dialog box in Fig. 10.19 will appear.

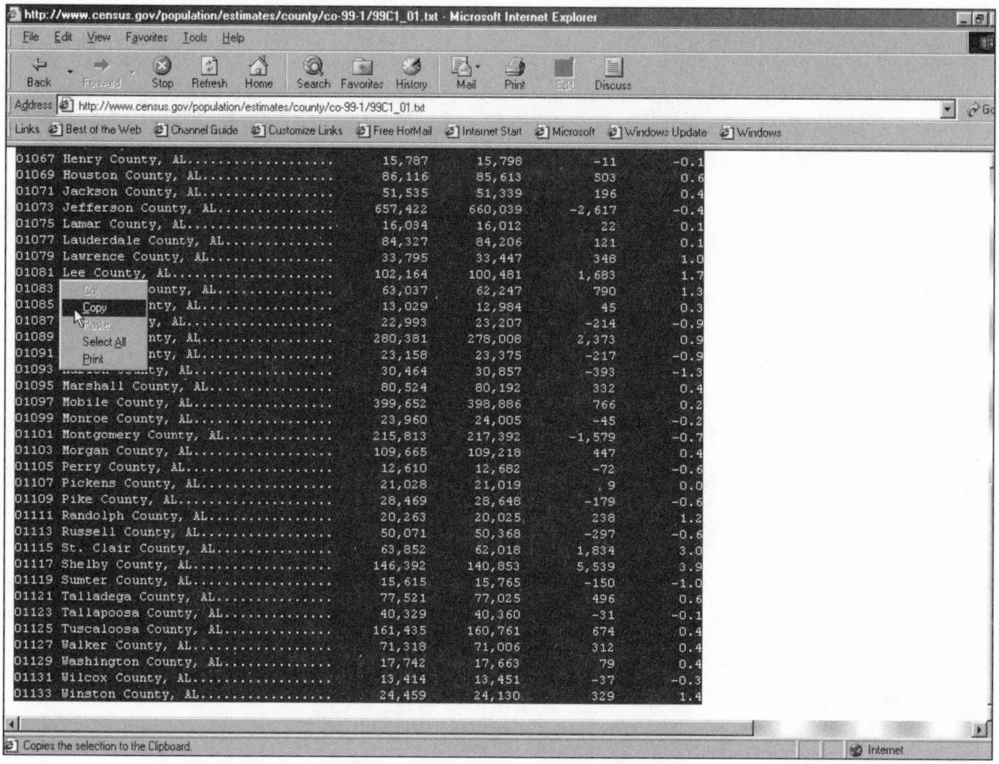

FIGURE 10.18

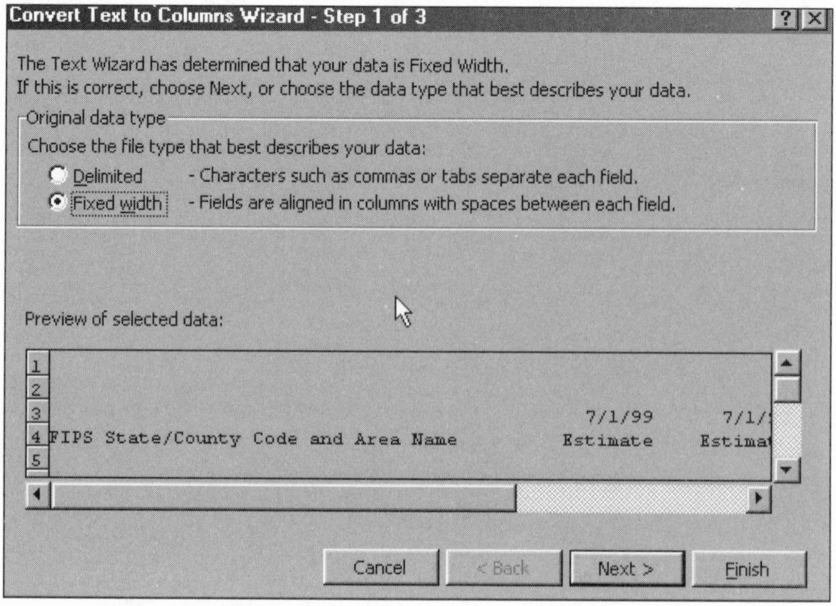

FIGURE 10.19

From looking at the Web page, we can tell this is a fixed-width database. So we'll stick with the "Fixed width" option and click on "Next" (see Fig. 10.20).

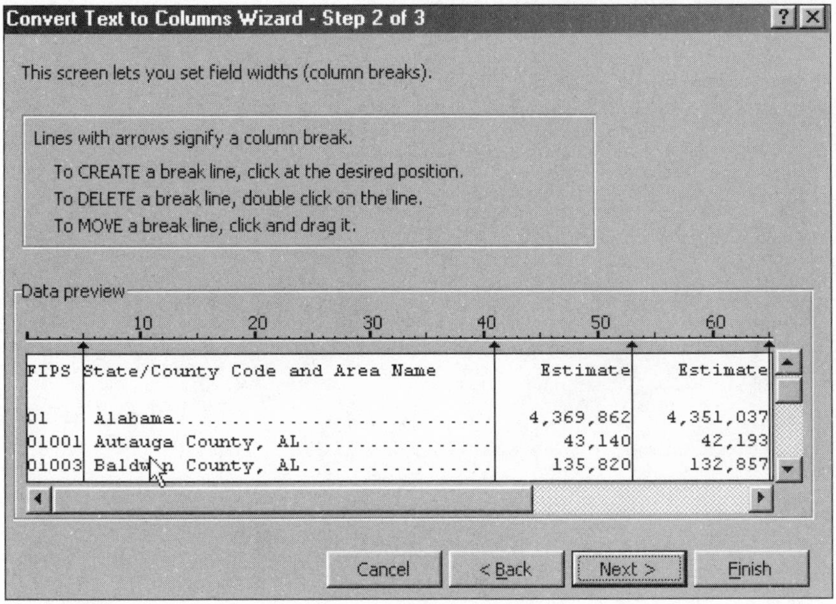

FIGURE 10.20

When we do, we can tell that Excel has guessed correctly on all the columns (it isn't always this easy). Now let's click on "Next" (see Fig. 10.21).

Here's a formatting problem. If we let the first column remain a "general" format, we'll lose all our leading zeroes. We don't want to do that, so we'll change the data type for the first (FIPS) column to a text format. Then, we'll click on "Finish" (see Fig. 10.22).

Now, all we need to do is clean up our column headers and eliminate the blank spaces and we'll get the spreadsheet shown in Fig. 10.23.

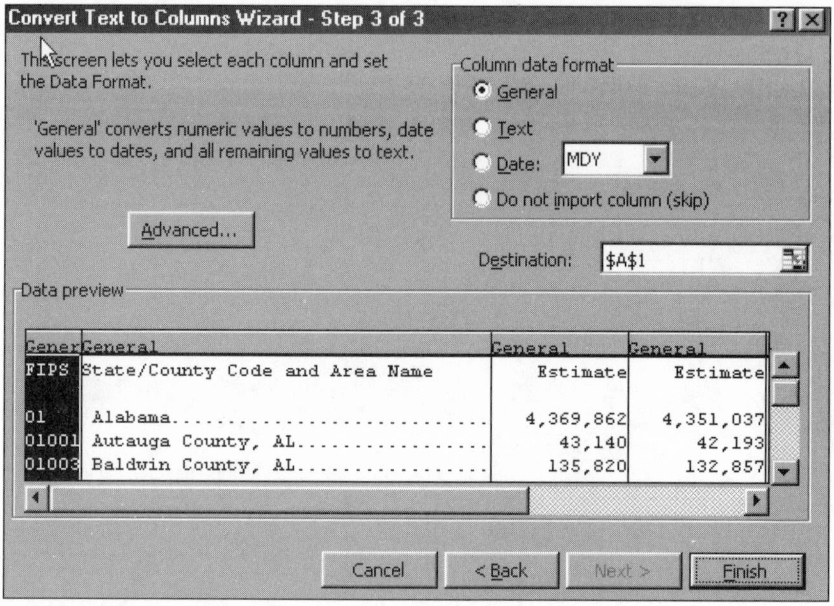

FIGURE 10.21

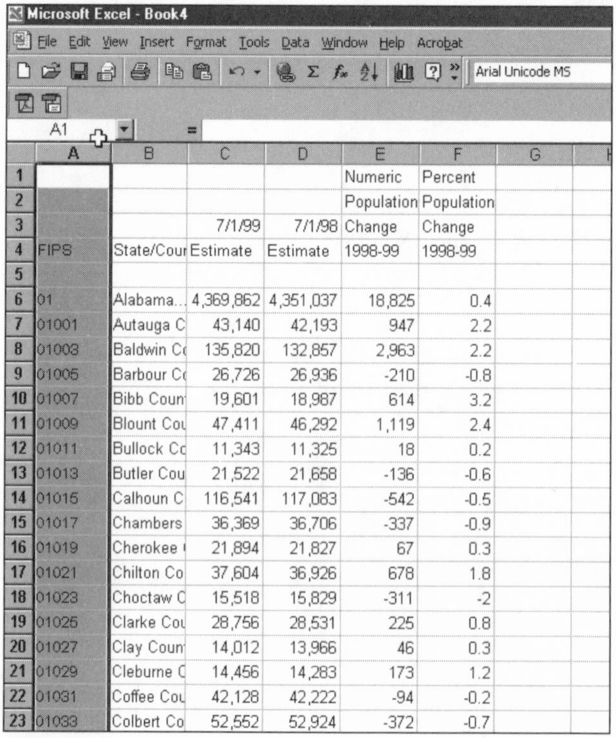

FIGURE 10.22

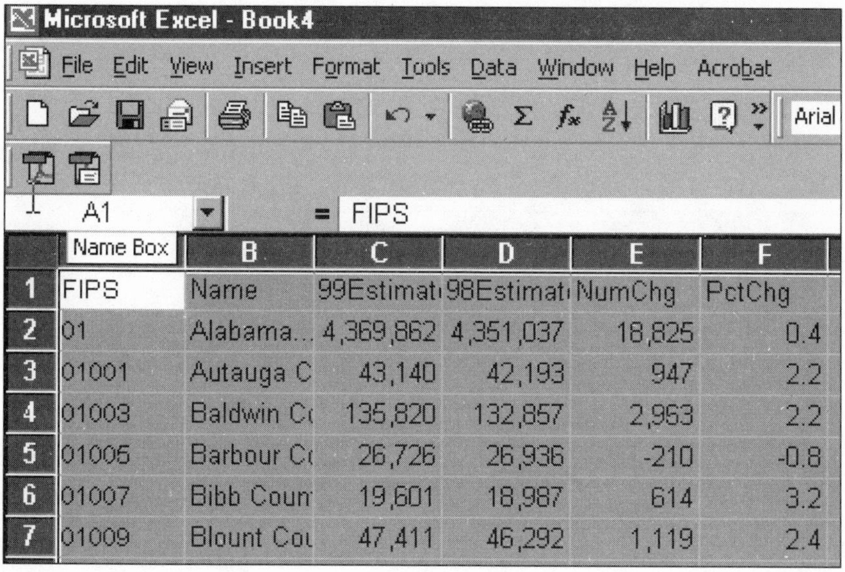

FIGURE 10.23

PDF Files

Of all the file formats, PDF (or portable document format) files can be the most maddening. Unfortunately, they're also becoming the most prevalent. Although Adobe makes available a free PDF reader at its Web site, it's sometimes difficult to pull tabular data from a *.pdf file and insert it into a spreadsheet. As an example, let's look at the FBI's hate crime data from 1996, which is available on its Web site (see Fig. 10.24).

If we select it all using Adobe's Text Select Tool and paste it into Excel, we get the screen in Fig. 10.25.

There are two options here; use "Data, Text to Columns" with a space delimiter, as shown in Fig. 10.26. But as you'll see, the columns don't exactly match (see Fig. 10.27).

The only way to fix this is to retype the cells with multiple spaces to get the columns to line up properly. For a large database, this can lead to considerable pain and suffering, but it's still somewhat faster than manually entering all the data.

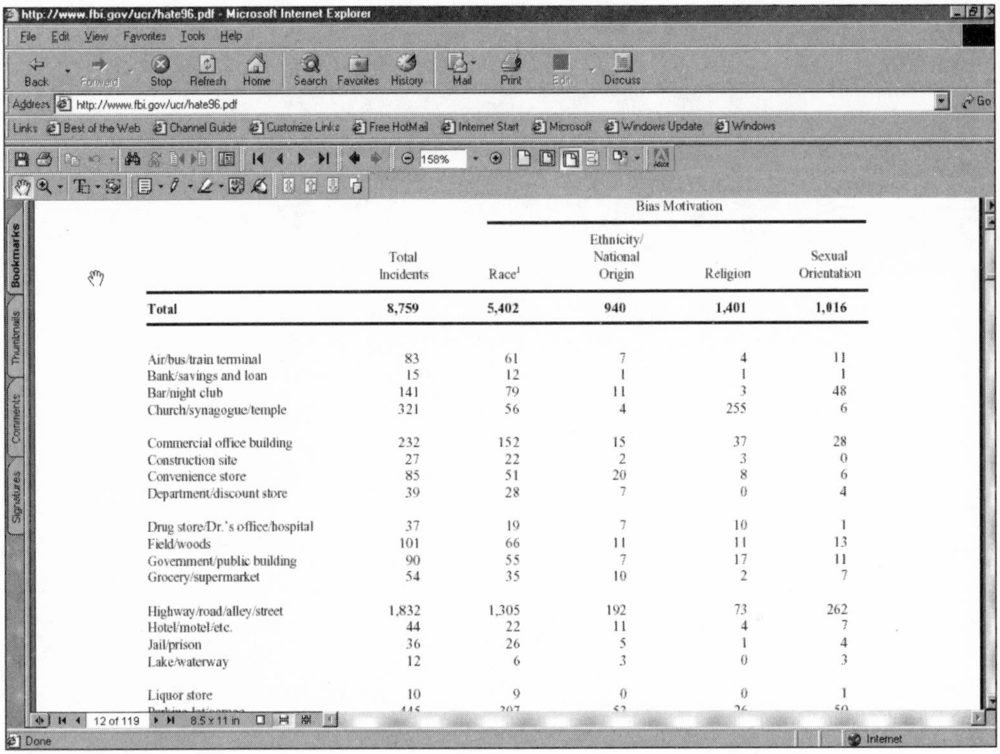

FIGURE 10.24

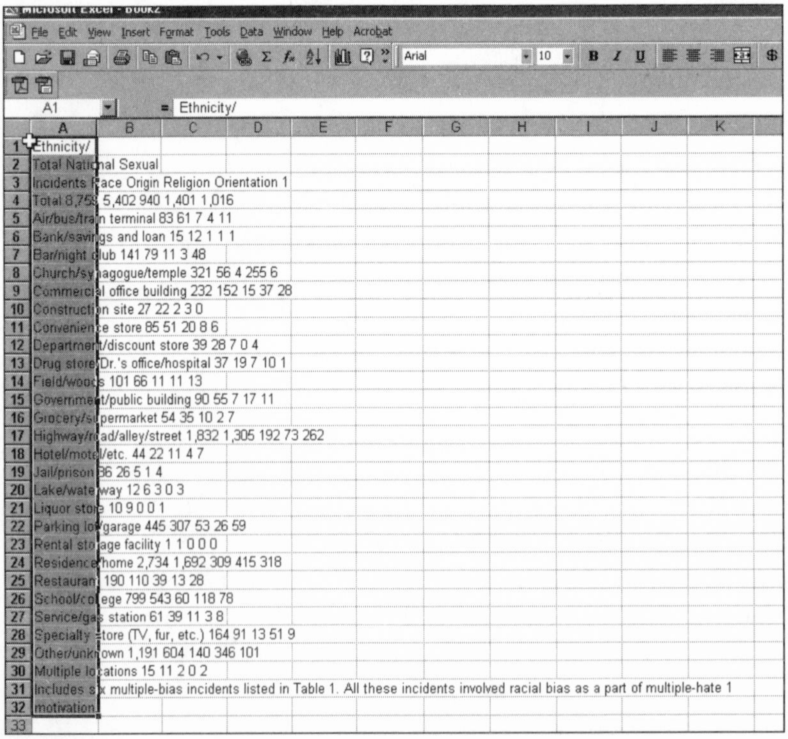

Microsoft Excel - Book2
File Edit View Insert Format Tools Data Window Help Acrobat
Arial 10
A1 = Ethnicity/
A B C D E F G H I J K
1 Ethnicity/
2 Total National Sexual
3 Incidents Race Origin Religion Orientation 1
4 Total 8,759 5,402 940 1,401 1,016
5 Air/bus/train terminal 83 61 7 4 11
6 Bank/savings and loan 15 12 1 1 1
7 Bar/night club 141 79 11 3 48
8 Church/synagogue/temple 321 56 4 255 6
9 Commercial office building 232 152 15 37 28
10 Construction site 27 22 2 3 0
11 Convenience store 85 51 20 8 6
12 Department/discount store 39 28 7 0 4
13 Drug store/Dr.'s office/hospital 37 19 7 10 1
14 Field/woods 101 66 11 11 13
15 Government/public building 90 55 7 17 11
16 Grocery/supermarket 54 35 10 2 7
17 Highway/road/alley/street 1,832 1,305 192 73 262
18 Hotel/motel/etc. 44 22 11 4 7
19 Jail/prison 36 26 5 1 4
20 Lake/waterway 12 6 3 0 3
21 Liquor store 10 9 0 0 1
22 Parking lot/garage 445 307 53 26 59
23 Rental storage facility 1 1 0 0 0
24 Residence/home 2,734 1,692 309 415 318
25 Restaurant 190 110 39 13 28
26 School/college 799 543 60 118 78
27 Service/gas station 61 39 11 3 8
28 Specialty store (TV, fur, etc.) 164 91 13 51 9
29 Other/unknown 1,191 604 140 346 101
30 Multiple locations 15 11 2 0 2
31 Includes six multiple-bias incidents listed in Table 1. All these incidents involved racial bias as a part of multiple-hate 1
32 motivation.
33

FIGURE 10.25

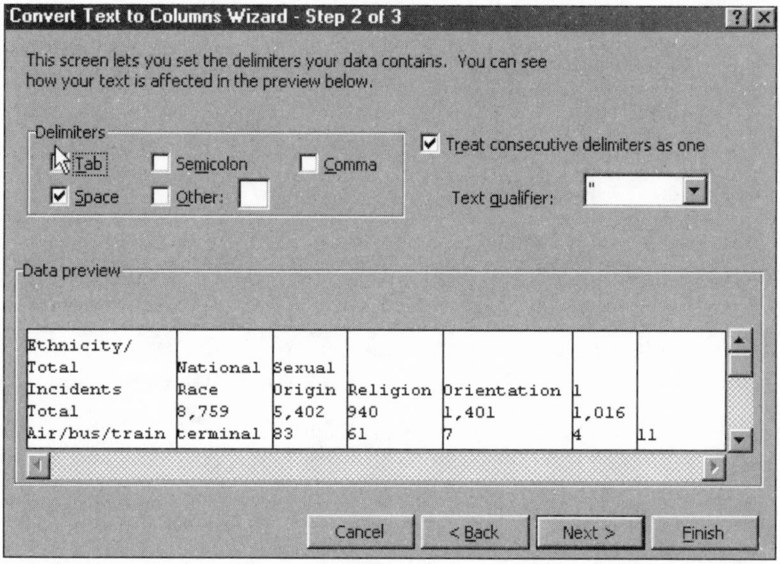

FIGURE 10.26

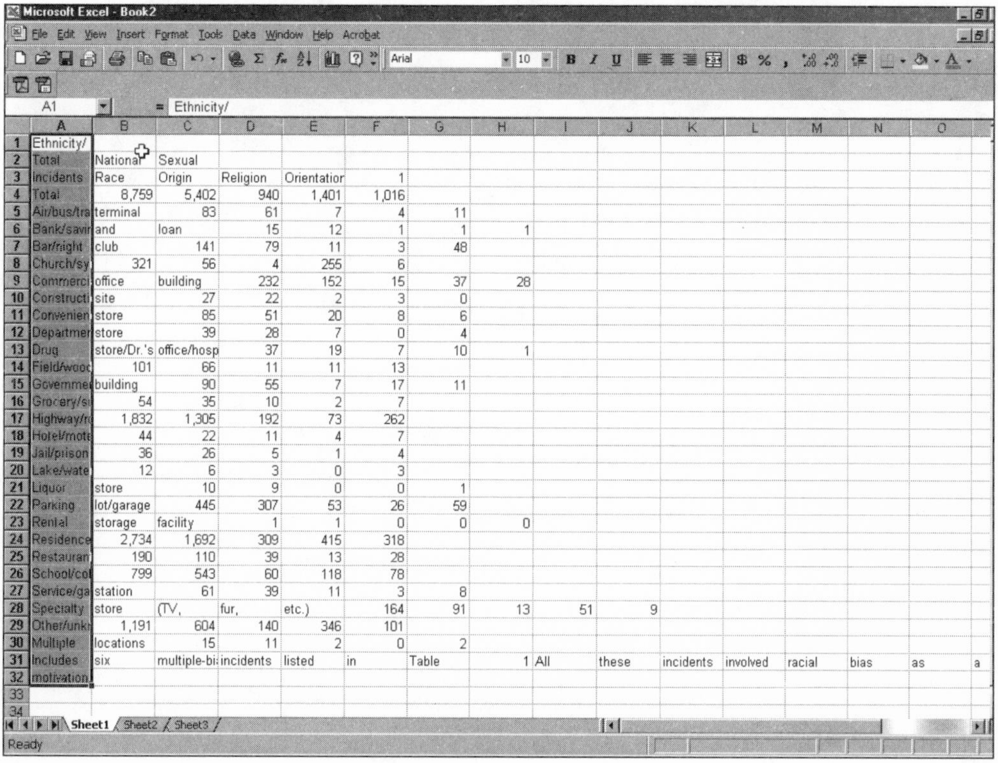

FIGURE 10.27

It's also possible to use Monarch's Redwing software to extract the table directly into Excel. This is a much cleaner, faster solution, although somewhat more expensive; the software costs about $300. Still, for anyone who works regularly with large *.pdf files, it's well worth the investment.

Text Files and Databases

A common problem for reporters who are new to databases involves importing text files. Most database programs, such as Microsoft Access, don't immediately import text files. They require the user to create a new database, then import the text file into it. Fortunately, it's not a very arduous process. First, you need to create a new database (see Fig. 10.28).

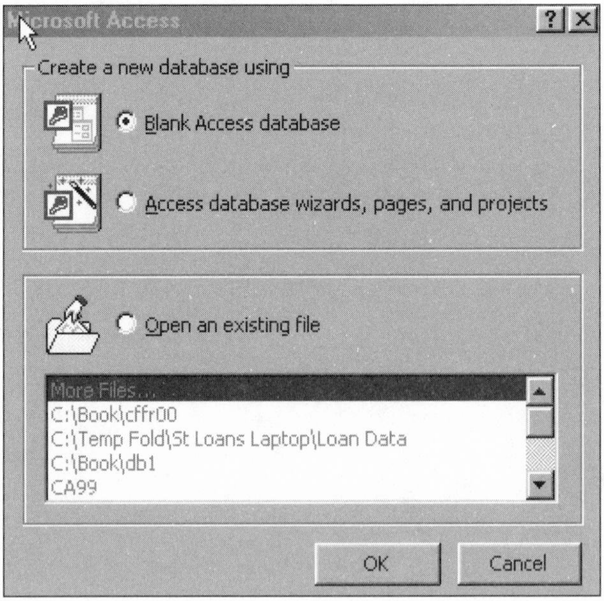

FIGURE 10.28

Give the database an easily remembered name and open it (see Fig. 10.29).

Next, you'll want to go to the "File" menu, followed by "Get External Data" and "Import," as in Fig. 10.30.

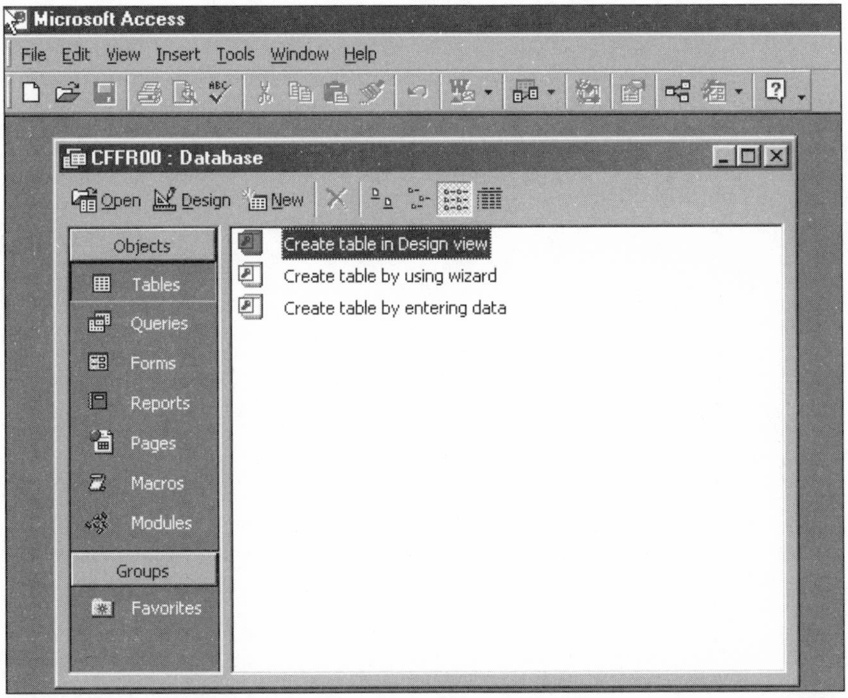

FIGURE 10.29

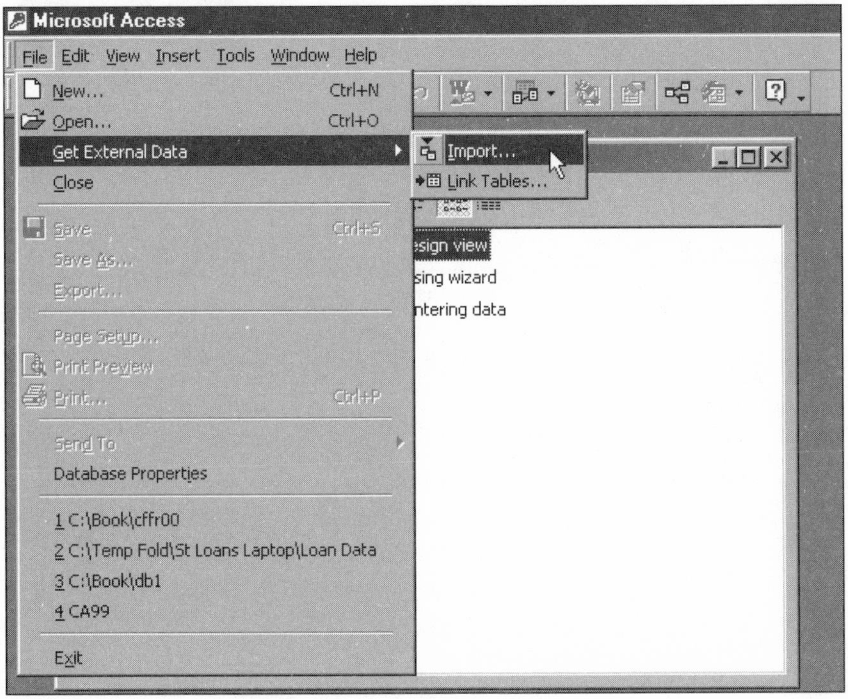

FIGURE 10.30

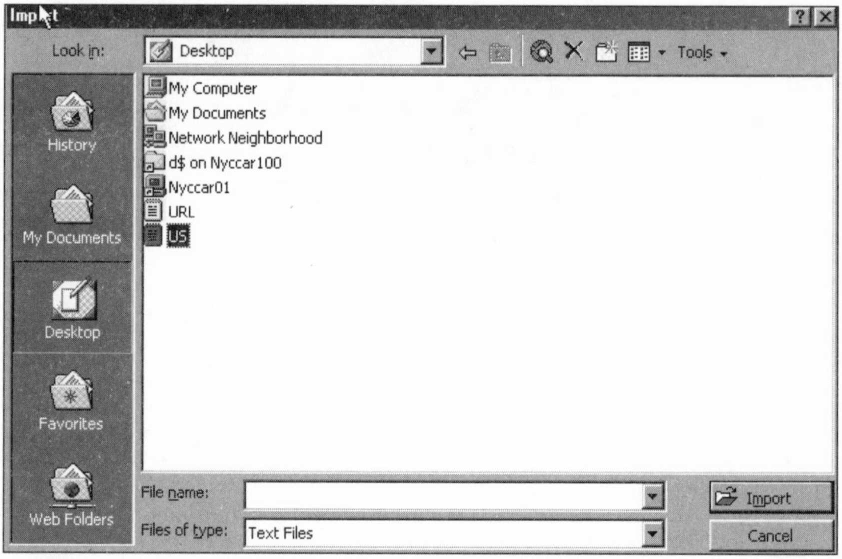

FIGURE 10.31

Browse to your text file, being very sure that "Text Files" is selected in the "Files of type" box at the bottom of the import dialog box (see Fig. 10.31).

When you click on "Import," another import wizard will appear (see Fig. 10.32).

This is a delimited file, so click on "Next" after making sure that the "Delimited" button is selected (see Fig. 10.33).

Be sure that the "First Row Contains Field Names" box is checked and that your delimiter is correct, and click on "Next" (see Fig. 10.34).

Generally, you'll want to store your data in a new table, as shown in Fig. 10.35.

Be sure that your data types are correct. Next, Access will ask if you want a primary key. As a general rule, a primary key isn't a bad thing. It helps Access find records faster. If it annoys you, though, you'll seldom be dealing with databases big enough for it to make too much of a difference, since Access usually slows to a snail's pace on databases larger than one gigabyte. Click on "Next" (see Fig. 10.36).

You can now rename the table (or not) and click "Finish" (see Fig. 10.37).

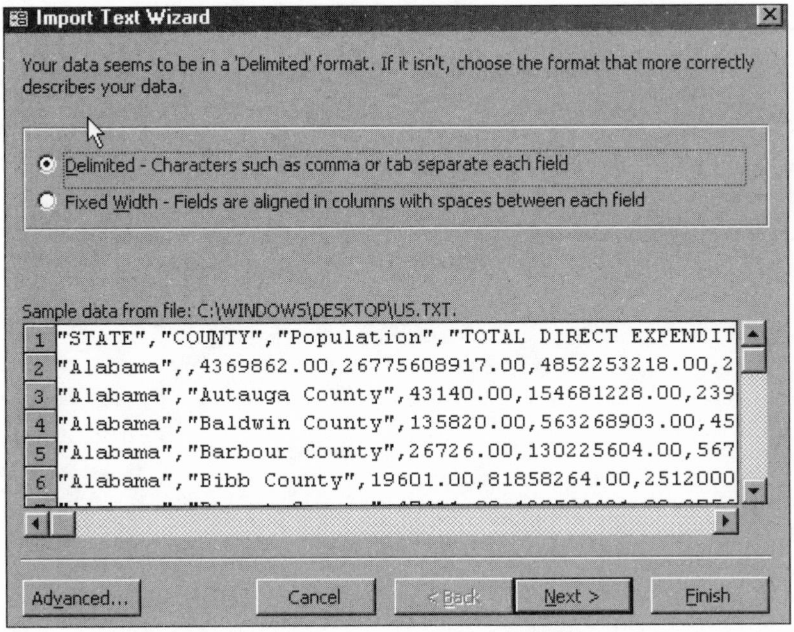

FIGURE 10.32

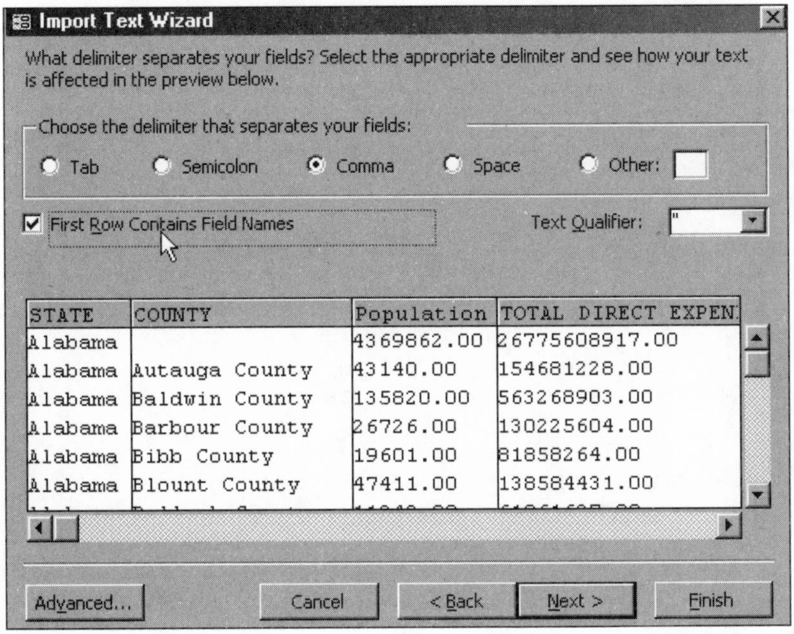

FIGURE 10.33

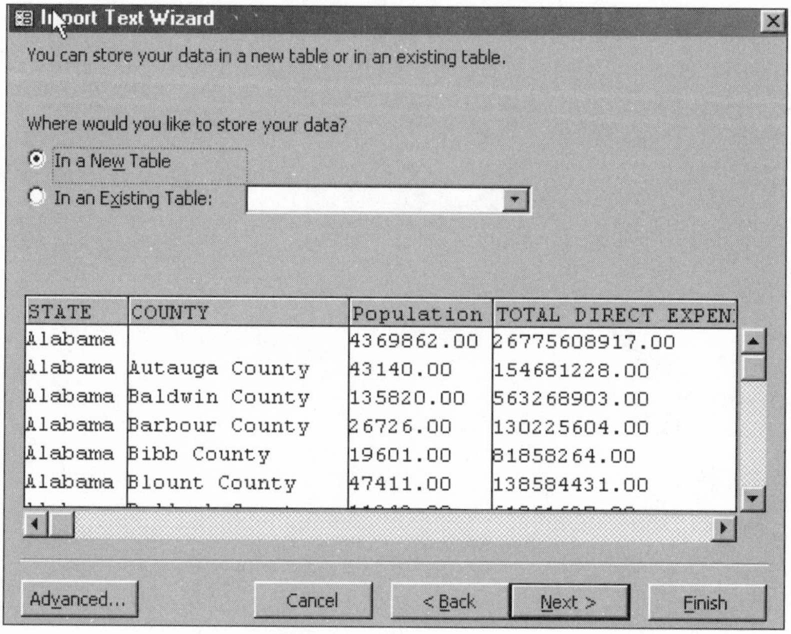

FIGURE 10.34

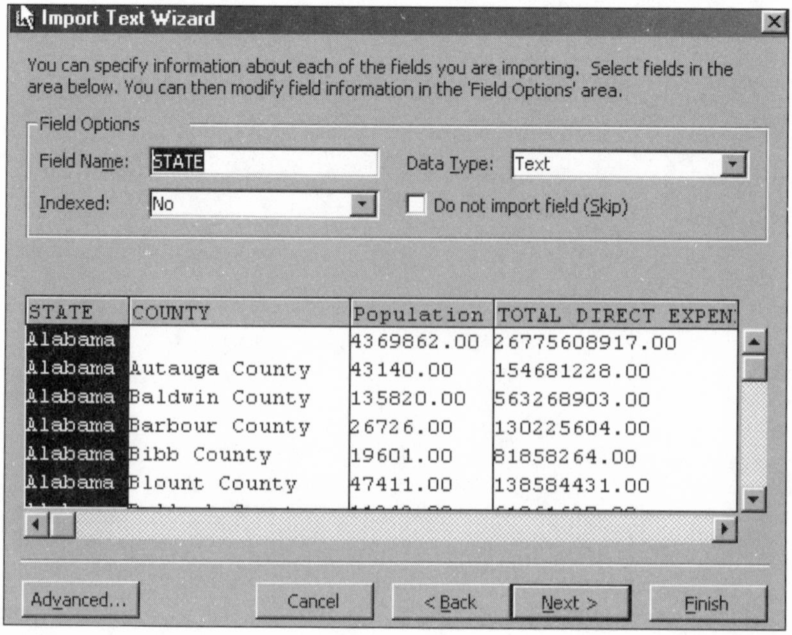

FIGURE 10.35

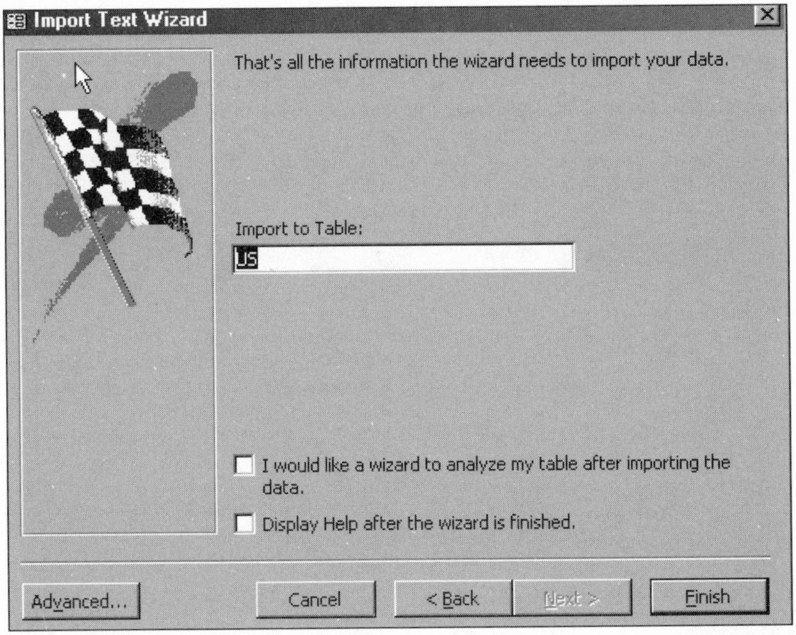

FIGURE 10.36

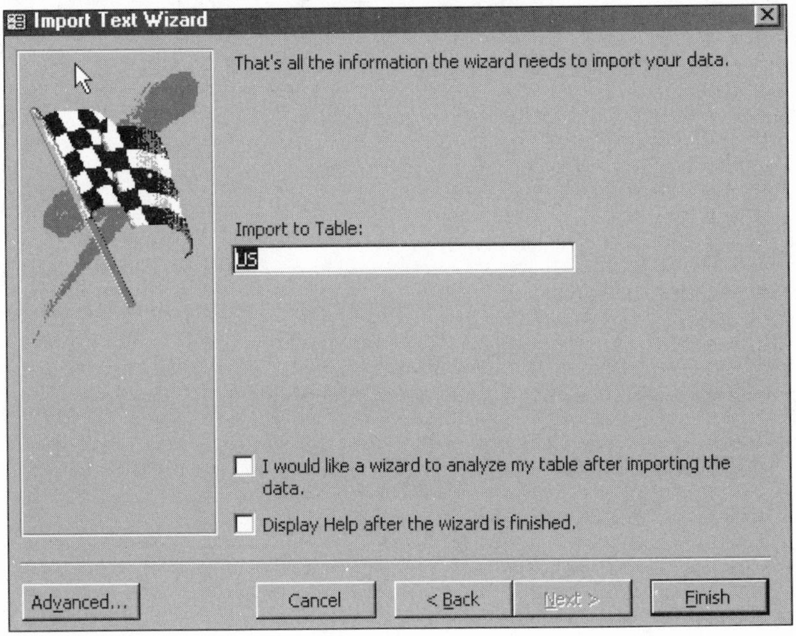

FIGURE 10.37

Generally, it's a good idea to check the design and table views of your database to make sure everything is as you want it. In this case, when we check the table view, as in Fig. 10.38, we see that things look okay.

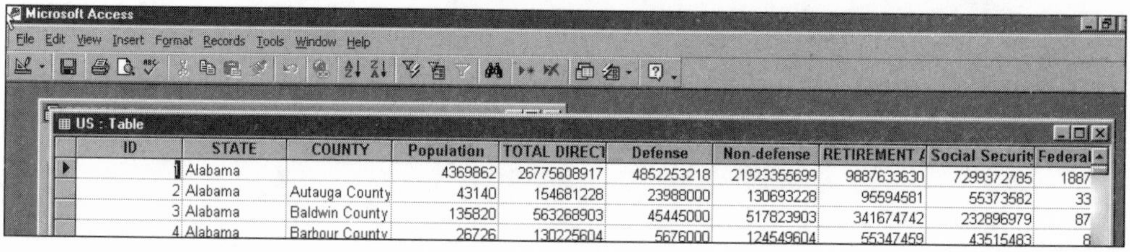

FIGURE 10.38

Now looking at the design view, we see no major problems, either (see Fig. 10.39).

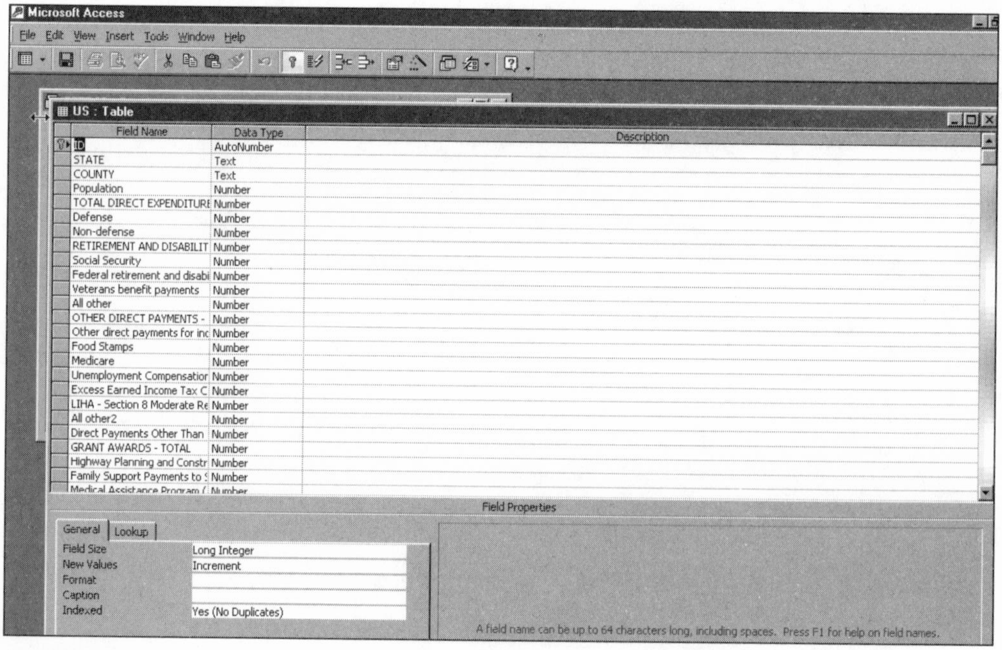

FIGURE 10.39

You can follow the same procedure with different file types in Access, including *dbf, Lotus 1–2–3, Paradox, Excel, and *.html files, among others.

If there are any errors in your import, Access generally will flash a warning message. It will also give you a table that will help you determine the cause of the problem. Open it and read it carefully. Again, importing files may seem a bit arcane. But as more and more agencies put data on the Internet, it's rapidly becoming an essential skill for any reporter who wants to add depth to stories.

CHAPTER ELEVEN

The Paper Chase

So much time and attention have been paid recently to computer databases, the Internet, and online searching that it's sometimes surprising there are still reporters out there who haven't forgotten that good information is available on paper. And while the Internet can be helpful in gaining access to paper documents and printing them out for safekeeping, not everything on a reporter's beat is computerized, and even less is available on the Internet. For most offices, paper reports are still prevalent, and to many reporters and editors, they have a tangible, credible quality that electronic documents will never have.

Here are some beat-by-beat story ideas, both obscure and common, to keep you on the paper trail.

Government and Politics

1. Campaign finance. Not all state and local campaign finance databases are on the Internet, or even on a computer. They're still valuable documents, though, and should be studied. Some reporters have gone so far as to create their own computer databases where computer campaign finance records aren't available. Others with less time or larger amounts of records have created statewide consortiums of news organizations (New York and Virginia, for example) to hire data-entry houses to computerize campaign finance records.

2. Audits. Governments have been auditing themselves for as long as reporters haven't been reading audit reports. Some states have independent agencies with wide-ranging powers to check on government pro-

grams. Others hire outside contractors to check the books. Either way, audits can be a gold mine for journalists.

3. Inspector General reports. On a federal level, all agencies have inspectors general, who evaluate and assess agency programs. More often than not, they're looking at how people and companies that receive federal funds are doing. The offices, which can be reached through the main switchboard of any federal agency, also issue semiannual reports to Congress that summarize their reports. Some states have inspectors general, and their powers and the quality of their reports vary.

4. General Accounting Office reports. The GAO, which is the watchdog agency for Congress, issues hundreds of reports every year on every conceivable category of government activity. While current reports are available on the Web, some older reports are available only on paper. When looking through a new report, it never hurts to look for the name of the GAO investigator who wrote the report; they can be valuable sources. In addition, it's frequently useful to request permission to look through the working documents used to assemble the report. Not every scrap of information goes into a GAO report, and newsworthy items occasionally surface from the working papers. The GAO has a comprehensive Web site at www.gao.gov.

5. Congressional testimony. Various committee and subcommittee hearings can yield reams of valuable information that's not necessarily online. At the very least, consider a congressional testimony roster as a source list. At the very best, some hearings yield reports that can be extremely useful.

6. The Government Printing Office has more than 12,000 publications for sale, ranging from the "Survival Guide for New Teachers" published by the Department of Education to "Code of Federal Regulations, Title 29, Pt 1910" by the National Archives and Records Administration. It also runs 23 bookstores across the nation. The GPO is responsible for printing Census forms, IRS tax forms, and U.S. passports. Online, the GPO operates GPO Access (available at www.access.gpo.gov/su_docs/index.html), which provides access to more than 200,000 individual titles.

7. The U.S. Merit Systems Protection Board can also yield useful information. As a rule, most of their decisions are rather dry and deal with personnel issues rather than government problems. Still, it's a route taken by many whistleblowers who feel they're being punished for pointing out

problems and corruption. Their Web site can be found at www.mspb.gov, and many state and local governments have equivalent agencies.

8. State agencies. Ask for a copy of their annual checkbook. They're seldom available online and you'll need a good database program, but it will always be worth your time. Find out who the biggest contractors are, and compare them with a campaign finance database. Occupational safety and health inspections, which are seldom available online on a state level, can also be useful when investigating businesses.

9. Local governments. Not all investigative reporting centers on federal and state issues. A trove of valuable information can be found at City Hall. Ask for local pollution permits, building permits, and occupational licenses if they're required. Look at budgets and expense accounts. Ask for copies of consultant reports. Look for RFPs (requests for proposals) for big projects. Look at bond agreements. Are the local bond issues always handled by the same law firms? Restaurant, hospital, nursing home, and day-care inspection records should be available. Ask for agendas ahead of time; there's no law that says you have to wait until after the meeting is over to write a good story.

10. Newsletters. If it's a local, state, or federal agency, chances are good that it produces a newsletter or two. Get copies. Even if you can't break news outright that appears in a newsletter before a news release, you can use the newsletters to accumulate sources.

Courts and Cops

1. Review agencies. While cops and courts have the usual assortment of paper that you'd expect—jail logs, dockets, motions, and the like—state organizations, such as sentencing commissions, judicial review panels, and bar associations can help you put things in context.

2. Search warrants. Depending on the state, these can be extremely or somewhat valuable. Some can take up pages and include fine details; others can be one-page, pro forma notes. Regardless, they should always be checked out. For what neighborhoods are cops getting the most search warrants? Why?

3. Grand juries. The most secretive part of the judicial process can also yield some of the biggest stories. Although reporters aren't allowed into a

grand jury room, witness lists can be helpful. Transcripts can also be helpful after the grand jury finishes its work, although not always available.

4. Sentencing files. These aren't always available, although a friendly district attorney will often let you look at one. They're much more likely to allow access after the trial is over. Police investigative files also should be open records after investigations are closed. It's always a good idea to look as much at what wasn't done on a given case as at what was done. In such details and omissions do great stories sometimes lie.

5. Judicial disclosure records. The U.S. Judicial Conference requires federal judges to file reports on their financial holdings. The reports are available and frequently have pointed to glaring conflicts of interest by judges who rule on cases in which they have a financial stake.

Education

1. Teaching licenses. Which school districts have the most teachers who have been licensed under emergency certificates? Why? Which districts have the teachers with the longest tenure? How many teachers are living outside their school districts? State boards of education will often have a lot of information available on teachers that can be used to assess the quality of education in a given district.

2. Test exemptions. With school districts rapidly turning to standardized tests to measure performance, it's no surprise that test scores are rising. But why are they rising? Is it because of better preparation? Overemphasis in the classroom on test material at the neglect of other material? Or are fewer underachieving students taking the tests?

3. Budgets. How are school budgets changing over time? How does a district's budget compare to others, in terms of capital costs, administrative costs, and teacher salaries?

4. Bonds. As school districts expand, they borrow money to build new buildings. An enterprising reporter can get all sorts of information from bond papers. Which firms are handling the deal? How is the financing being arranged? How much money has the district borrowed? How much will it owe over the life of the bonds?

5. School buses. Even if school districts don't have their own transportation system, they'll keep records on their contractors. What's their

safety record? What are their maintenance costs? How much does it cost to send the average child to school?

Transportation

1. A great deal of attention is paid to aviation records. Much of the data can be found at the FAA's Web site (www.faa.gov), but as with most online data, it's only a starting point for a more detailed examination of safety records. Some of the better FAA records to look at are service difficulty reports (SDRs), which describe significant maintenance problems. Generally, reporters covering a crash can get a plane's tail number and check it against the FAA's online database for recurring problems. Reporting isn't consistent, though, and many times it's a lot better to look at recurring problems for the same kind of aircraft rather than focusing on an individual aircraft. The FAA also issues service bulletins, which can address a wide range of problems and suggest repairs. Finally, the FAA issues airworthiness directives, or ADs. Generally, these involve serious aircraft problems, and the FAA will require manufacturers to fix the problem.

2. The National Transportation Safety Board investigates most major accidents. Normally, NTSB investigators will release a report on the accident about a year after it occurs. Reporters can look at most of the NTSB files on an accident. Usually, it's a good idea to look for other accidents that resemble the one you're investigating. Did the NTSB issue recommendations after the other ones? Were they followed?

3. The National Highway Traffic Safety Administration provides information on motor vehicle safety for the general public. The agency keeps information about recall campaigns, technical service bulletins, defect investigations, and consumer complaints. The agency's Web site (www.nhtsa.dot.gov) is a good starting point.

4. The U.S. Department of Transportation's Office of Hazardous Materials Safety is responsible for coordinating the shipping of hazardous materials by air, rail, highway, and water. Some of the more useful files include exemptions from hazardous materials regulations; penalties; incidents; and its Emergency Response Guidebook, which lists potential risks and procedures for accidents.

5. The U.S. Coast Guard (www.uscg.mil) maintains information on

boating accidents and also is responsible for issuing advisories on boating safety. The Coast Guard maintains a detailed database on its Web site at www.uscgboating.org; it's a good starting point.

Environment

1. The U.S. Geological Survey can be a good source of information on pollution. Among other studies, it releases annual reports on water quality for major U.S. watersheds. Since the USGS doesn't have any real regulatory powers, it can be a remarkably unbiased source of information for reporters.

2. The Department of Defense, which is responsible for one of the world's largest environmental cleanup programs (27,000 sites at more than 8,500 military properties), is required to release an annual report to Congress on the progress of its cleanups. A list of related publications is available on the Web at www.dtic.mil/envirodod/brac/publish.html.

3. The EPA, which maintains a vast Web site full of good data, also operates the National Service Center for Environmental Publications, which has more than 7,000 titles. The publications range from the esoteric ["Ambient Water Quality Criteria Recommendations: Information Supporting Development of State and Tribal Nutrient Criteria (Ecoregion III)"] to the useful ("Indoor Air Quality and Student Performance"). Many of these publications are free. For ordering information, look at www.epa.gov/ncepihom/.

4. States are required to file annual reports detailing their water quality to the EPA. The reports, called 305(b) reports, cover a lot of ground. In the 1998 reports, for example, EPA found that more than 291,000 miles of our nation's rivers and streams don't meet established water quality standards. State environmental agencies should have copies of their 305(b) reports.

5. Environmental impact statements. The National Environmental Policy Act of 1969 requires all projects using federal dollars to conduct assessments of their impact on the environment. These statements, which can run into dozens of volumes, frequently require years to complete. Public hearings are held, drafts are circulated, and the project can't proceed until the EIS is completed.

Business

1. Some of the best business news coverage in recent years has looked at nonprofit organizations. Roughly one-third of the 700,000 organizations that are tax-exempt 501(c)3 charities are required to file Form 990 with the IRS. The forms, which are available from either the charity or the IRS Service Center in Ogden, Utah (fax your request on letterhead to 801–773–5194; it helps to have the taxpayer identification number), contain a wealth of data on the charities' spending.

2. Statistical Abstract of the United States. Though most of this information is available on the Internet at the Census Bureau's Web site (www.census.gov), it's sometimes quicker to look up the business statistics in a book. The abstract, which is available at government bookstores, has a huge amount of business-related information at state and local levels.

3. Professional regulatory boards. Whether it's a state medical board or department of funeral home examiners, regulatory agencies can provide useful background or alert attentive reporters to problems. Look at contractor complaints in the wake of hurricanes or lawyer complaints after a major air disaster. Where are the professionals located, and why?

4. Bankruptcy records. Most reporters will focus on two kinds of bankruptcy records found in U.S. Bankruptcy Court. The first, Chapter 7, is simply a liquidation of a failed company's assets. The second, Chapter 11, is the reorganization of a failing company. Chapter 11 bankruptcies generally have more information than Chapter 7 bankruptcies; a Chapter 11 bankruptcy will cite creditors, debtors, and reasons for the company's current problems.

5. Workplace records. The Occupational Safety and Health Administration has a searchable database of inspections of businesses around the country that can be used to get reporters started at www.osha.gov. State labor departments also frequently maintain inspection reports that can be useful.

6. State franchise tax records. These forms, which are usually kept at a Secretary of State's office, will give reporters a look at a company's income both within and outside of a given state, its compensation for officers and directors (as well as their names and titles), and any information about the company's subsidiaries or parent companies.

7. Uniform Commercial Code (UCC) filings. These forms are filed at county and state levels and cite collateral used to secure loans. It's a good place to look for disgruntled creditors if the company gets into financial trouble.

8. Insurance data. Look for market conduct reports that study whether insurance companies are following state laws. State insurance departments also generally keep track of complaints against insurers, as well as quarterly financial data for insurance companies. Finally, look at FAIR plan data, which provide insurance to people who don't qualify for conventional home insurance.

Health Care

1. A good starting point for health care data are 911 records. Police departments keep these, and courts have generally ruled them to be open public records. Look for patterns. Are people from certain neighborhoods being sent directly to county hospitals? How fast are the response times? What are the most common calls?

2. Health licensing agencies. When hospitals expand or build, they're usually required to file certificates of need with state health departments. Why are they expanding? Where are they expanding? How full are their existing facilities? A certificate of need application can tell reporters a lot about the current state of a hospital.

3. Nursing home inspections. Nursing homes that get federal funds are supposed to be inspected roughly once every year. The inspections are done by state agencies and the reports sent to the Health Care Financing Administration (HCFA), which also issues a one-page "Survey Activity Report" that can serve as a rough report card for each nursing home. The safety and management of nursing homes has become a growing issue with the graying of the American population.

4. The Joint Commission on Accreditation of Healthcare Organizations evaluates and accredits nearly 19,000 U.S. health care organizations, including hospitals, laboratories, nursing homes, and home care businesses. Though the commission hasn't always been good about providing detailed information to reporters, it's slowly modifying its release policy to make

its reports somewhat useful. Copies of performance reports for organizations are available by calling 630–792–5800.

5. Organizations that receive Medicare dollars are required to file annual cost reports. Look for two parts, in particular: Worksheet G, which covers the financial issues, and Worksheet S, which covers market share statistics. As a general rule, reporters have to obtain these reports from the local Medicare office.

CHAPTER TWELVE

Copyright on the Internet

by George Galt

The growing use of the Internet has raised the awareness of intellectual property rights among the public and has many believing that the Internet has somehow changed the nature of intellectual property rights in general, and copyright rights in particular.

However, many of the intellectual property issues that people view as new and somehow tied to the Internet are really simply the standard old copyright issues with a new, high-tech face. Most of these problems can be handled under the existing Copyright Act. As a general proposition, if one understands copyright rights in the real world, one understands copyright rights in cyberspace.

Material placed on the Internet is not free for use by anyone. It is governed by the same laws that govern its offline use. For example, if it is illegal for one to photocopy a book, it is illegal to digitize the book and make the copy available on the Internet. If it is illegal to broadcast music over the airwaves without a license, it is illegal to broadcast it without a license through audio streaming technology. If it is illegal to copy a movie from one VCR tape to another, it doesn't make it legal if one copies the movie off the Internet onto a VCR tape.

Much of the debate around copyright and the Internet has been couched in hype from both sides—"information wants to be free" and "the Internet will ruin modern intellectual property based industries unless we control it." Part of this hype arises because many people are encountering copyright issues for the first time—issues that have long been part of the fabric of copyright law. Some of the hype is due to the fact that there are a handful of new issues, or new ways of encountering old issues, that may require a fresh look at old rules. But as is the case with most hype, the truth about copyright and the Internet lies somewhere between the extremes.

Introduction

This chapter is designed to help readers understand copyright law and how copyright law is applied to activity on the Internet. Copyright law is the general term applied to the body of law that protects the expression of ideas in a tangible medium. Copyright law protects the writings of authors, the work of sculptors, the paintings and photographs of artists, the choreography of dancers, and the music of composers, among other things. It also applies to the computer code of programmers, the images of graphic designers, the plans of architects, the photos of photojournalists, the video of camera crews, and the news articles of journalists. What copyright law does not do is protect the ideas and facts expressed in those works—though they may be protected by some other law.

Other Laws

Before delving into copyright law, it should be made clear that copyright law protects only one type of intellectual property—there are other types of intellectual property and just because one's actions do not violate copyright laws does not mean that these actions do not violate other laws. A full explanation of these other laws is beyond the scope of this chapter, but two legal concepts that bear mentioning are (i) the tort of misappropriation of "hot news" and (ii) trademark law.

Trademark law protects the association that consumers make between brands (words, pictures, sounds, smells, colors, etc.) and goods. Because many trademarks include images, and these images may be subject to copyright protection, there can be some confusion between copyright and trademark law. For example, the copyright in Andy Warhol's painting of Campbell's soup cans would be held by Andy Warhol's estate, but the estate could not use (or license others to use) the copyrighted image to sell (non-Campbell's) soup because this use would violate the association consumers have between the Campbell's soup trademarked can and the soup with which the can was associated. As we will see below, activity that may raise copyright issues may also raise trademark issues. So simply being sure that the copyright portion of one's activity is cleared may not fully address the potential liability one faces.

The tort of misappropriation of "hot news" prevents others from using the facts contained in a news story during a short "hot news" window. Copyright law does not protect the facts contained in a copyrighted work. So if one finds a news story on the Internet and writes a new news story based on the facts contained in the original news story, one may not have violated the copyright in the original news story, but one may have violated the rights in the "hot news" contained in that story.

Copyright Basics

What Can Be Copyrighted?

Copyright law protects a number of different kinds of works in forms now known or later developed, including literary works; musical works; dramatic works; pantomimes and choreographic works; pictorial, graphic, and sculptural works; motion pictures and other audiovisual works; sound recordings; and architectural works. This list is generally read quite broadly by courts. Thus a computer program is often considered a type of literary work. However, some of these types of works can be confusing. A "musical work" is not the sounds that you hear on the radio, but is the words and musical notations that are used by the performers to produce the sounds you hear. The sounds you hear are the "sound recording."

Copyright law, then, protects the expression of ideas in a tangible medium, but what does this mean? Copyright law protects the individual way in which an idea (or a fact) is expressed by an author. This attribute of copyright law means that multiple people can write a story about the same event without trampling on each other's copyright rights. For example, The Associated Press, the *New York Times*, and MSNBC can all write separate stories about the latest Middle East peace initiative without interfering with each other's copyright. The ideas and facts of the peace initiative are not protected by copyright (though it is possible that the facts collected by a single news organization may be protected under the hot news doctrine discussed above). The journalists and editors from each company will express the ideas and facts slightly differently and each will have a copyright in their own way of expressing the facts. Anyone who takes the expression of one of these companies (e.g., cuts and pastes the article, or portions of the article) will violate the copyright of the company whose expression they copied, but not the copyright of the other companies.

The legal intent behind protecting expression but not ideas is to help generate and disseminate ideas by providing an incentive to produce works that embody those ideas, and thus to allow free use of the ideas by future authors. This intent is furthered by the requirement that the expression be fixed in a tangible medium of expression from which the expression can be reproduced. If the expression cannot be seen or otherwise reproduced, it cannot be disseminated to the public.

The Copyright Act requires that the work must be "fixed in any tangible medium of expression, now known or later developed, from which they can be perceived, reproduced, or otherwise communicated, either directly or with the aid of a machine or device." Early copyright cases held that if a particular copy required a machine to interpret it, it was not a copy for copyright purposes. For example, courts held that player piano rolls were not "copies" of the musical works embodied in the rolls and therefore did not violate the copyright of the musical works. The court reasoned that because the player piano rolls were not directly perceivable by humans, they were not copies. The Copyright Act overturned this reasoning when it was revised in 1976 and now allows works that must be translated through a machine to be subject to copyright. Thus, the courts have held that a copy stored in the random access memory of a computer is a copy for copyright purposes, even though the copy will disappear if the power to the computer is removed.

The expression protected by copyright law is distinct from the object in which it is fixed. For example, a literary work may be "fixed" in a book, but the book itself is not copyrighted, only the literary work fixed in that book. There can be multiple copies of the book, but only one literary work.

In order to be protected, a work must be "original" to the author. Originality does not mean that the work must be "novel" (e.g., completely different from all works that came before it), but simply that the work is original to the author (e.g., not copied from some other source). Courts have stated, in fact, that two identical works that were both created separately could both be copyrighted. As one of the preeminent jurists of the early twentieth century stated, "If by some magic a man who had never known it were to compose anew Keats' 'Ode On a Grecian Urn,' he would be an 'author,' and, if he copyrighted it, others might not copy that poem, though they might of course copy Keats."

Originality does not mean that the work must be artistic, though there must be a minimum level of creativity. Courts have specifically stated that judges should not "judge" the artistic merit of a work in determining whether or not it is copyrightable. However, there are instances in which the courts have determined that a work was lacking sufficient creativity to support a copyright in the work (e.g., a telephone directory of individual names, addresses, and phone numbers, arranged alphabetically).

Virtually any expression in a tangible medium can be copyrighted. Examples of items containing copyrightable expression include a table lamp, a car hubcap, a circus poster, a computer program, a map, an electronic database of the 100 best baseball cards, and this document.

What Protection Does Copyright Give?

Copyright gives the author of the copyrighted work several rights, which the author can sell or license individually or collectively. In legal circles, this is known as the copyright "bundle of rights." Because the author has these rights, he or she can prohibit anyone who has not received a license or otherwise purchased rights from engaging in a number of activities. The rights granted by copyright law extend for a limited time. Once the time period is over, the work is in the "public domain," meaning that anyone can exercise the rights formerly owned by the author. Finally, copyright law gives the author certain incentives to register a copyrighted work with the United States Copyright Office. These incentives can be very helpful if an author is faced with a copyright infringement.

The Bundle of Rights. Copyright law gives the author a number of rights that the author can retain, sell, or license individually or together. Thus an author can license (or sell the right to) one person to create copies of his or her book, another to create a film based on the book, and another to perform a dramatic reading of the book to the public. In addition, because the author could license or sell either exclusive or nonexclusive rights, more than one person could have the same rights in the book (e.g., two people could both be licensed to produce copies of the book). Finally, because each right is distinct, a licensee cannot use rights not granted by the copyright holder (e.g., someone who can copy the book cannot make a translation of the book into another language and copy the translated version). It should be emphasized that copyright law is a strict liability statute. In other words, one will be guilty of a copyright infringement if one violates any of the exclusive rights considered below, whether or not one was aware that one's activities violated those rights. This is important to remember, in part because so few areas of American law contain a strict liability provision.

The following sections present brief discussions of each of the rights that a copyright owner has in the copyrighted work.

Reproduction The reproduction right is the right most people think of when discussing copyright rights and copyright violations. It is the right to make copies of a copyrighted work or to prohibit others from making copies of a work. Although many people believe violations of the reproduction right to be limited to verbatim copying, the reality of copyright violations is not that simple. When determining if someone has violated the rights of a copyright holder, courts look to see if the supposedly copied work is "substantially similar" to the copyrighted work. As the name implies, the test does not require that one work be identical to the other, only that they be substantially similar. For example, a court found that the George Harrison song "My Sweet Lord" was substantially similar to (and infringed) the earlier recorded Chiffons' song "He's So Fine." Copying also is not limited by copying to the same medium as the original. For example, making a sketch from a photograph may violate the copyright in the photograph. Copying a copy of a work can still violate the copyright in the original work if the intermediate work is itself an illegal copy. Additionally, if one copies a work, but does not sell or distribute the work, one is still guilty of violating the reproduction right. The violation occurs when the copy is made, even if it remains unused.

Distribution One of the exclusive copyright rights is the right to distribute the copyrighted work. Often, the right to produce copies is accompanied by the right to distribute copies. This right allows the author control over the disposition of a copy of a copyrighted work, and to prohibit certain types of distribution. For example, a court found that the authors' distribution right was violated when an illegally obtained copy of a homemade sex video of Bret Michaels and Pamela Anderson Lee was going to be distributed over the Internet. The court enjoined the distribution of the video tape.

The distribution right of the copyright owner is balanced by something called the "first sale doctrine." Once the copyright owner has sold a copy of his or her work (the first sale), the copyright owner has no power over further sales of that copy of the work. For example, if you purchase a book from the bookstore, then a future sale of that copy of the book from you to another is beyond the control of the copyright owner. It is the "first sale doctrine" that allows libraries to lend out books and for used bookstores to be able to sell their wares.

There are some limits to the first sale doctrine, however. The most important for the Internet is whether or not a copy was distributed to the end user. It is possible that what was transmitted to the end user was a "public performance" (described below) rather than a copy. If this is the case, since there was no distribution of a copy, there is no first sale from which one could resell one's copy—even if the end user's browser made a temporary copy on the end user's machine. In addition, there are certain types of works that are "saved" from certain portions of the first sale doctrine. For example, sound recordings and computer software cannot be rented for profit.

Public Performance The Copyright Act allows the copyright owner to license the public performance of his or her work. The public performance right is not as straightforward as some of the other rights, in part because it does not apply to all copyrighted works equally, and because it requires that the performance be a "public" one.

To "perform" a work means to recite, render, play, dance, or act it, either directly or by means of any device or process. The public performance right extends to literary, musical, dramatic, and choreographic works, pantomimes, and motion pictures and other audiovisual works. This means that there is a public performance right in the musical work (the words and musical notations) that is used to create a song that is played on the radio, but there is not public performance right in the sound recording (the artist's rendition of the words and music into something you can hear)—at least not on the radio.

To determine what the public performance right and the public display right license, requires an understanding of what is meant by the word "public" and what is not. During the early part of the twentieth century, the courts determined that "public" meant anything open to the general public, but did not include performances at large gatherings of "members-only" clubs. This interpretation allowed many private clubs to engage in the use of copyrighted works without having to compensate copyright owners. The redrafting of the Copyright Act in 1976 dispensed with this understanding of "public" and substituted a definition of "public" as a place "open to the public or at any place where a substantial number of persons outside of a normal circle of a family and its social acquaintances is gathered." Thus a performance, such as showing a video tape, to your family and a few friends is not a "public" performance, but showing the video tape at a college dormitory or in a public space is.

A further wrinkle to the "public" definition is that the "public" does not have to be gathered in one place. If the performance is available to a substantial number of persons outside of a normal circle of a family, then the performance is a public one. So when a radio station plays music that is heard by a large number of people, each of whom may be in their own home or car, but not gathered in a single place, the performance is a "public" performance.

Similarly, even if the "public" audience viewing or listening to the performance hears or sees the performance at different times, the performance may still be a "public" one. This fact has special implications for the Internet, where multiple individuals may listen to a streaming audio signal at different times.

Public Display The public display right is the right to "show a copy of it, either directly or by means of a film, slide, television image, or any other device or process" publicly. Like the public performance right, the public display right is limited to certain types of copyrightable works—literary, musical, dramatic, and choreographic works, pantomimes, and pictorial, graphic, or sculptural works, including the individual images of a motion picture or other audiovisual work. Traditionally, the public display right has been equated to hanging a picture in a window for the world to see, or showing a movie in a movie theater. However, it can apply to images, text, or other covered works transmitted to end users via the Internet. As noted earlier, since "public" can mean the availability to individual people in different places and at different times, a public display right is part of including an image or text (or other covered work) in a Web page.

Derivative Works The Copyright Act defines a "derivative work" as "a work based upon one or more preexisting works, such as a translation, musical arrangement, dramatization, fictionalization, motion picture version, sound recording, art reproduction, abridgment, condensation, or any other form in which a work may be recast, transformed, or adapted. A work consisting of editorial revisions, annotations, elaborations, or other modifications, which, as a whole, represent an original work of authorship, is a 'derivative work.'" An example of a derivative work is a news story written by a reporter that is based in part on the news from the AP wire service.

Derivative works are important because it is often a derivative work that is created when one licenses content to create other content (e.g., the AP wire service). If one does not have the right to create a derivative work of the content that has been licensed, then one cannot create works based on that material.

Duration. The duration of copyright is, oddly, one of the most confusing areas of copyright law. The only works one can say for sure are no longer protected by copyright law are works published more than 95 years ago from today. For example, if today is February 5, 2002, then works published prior to February 5, 1907, are in the public domain. This rule should hold (mostly) true, absent Congressional modification, until December 31, 2072, when the rule discussed below should cover all works.

For works created after January 1, 1978, copyright lasts for the life of the author plus 70 years. In the case of anonymous works, pseudonymous works (where the real author adopts a fictitious name), and works-made-for-hire (works created while the employee of a company, within the scope of one's employment), the copyright survives for 95 years from the date on which the work was first published, or 120 years from the date of creation, whichever is shorter. If the real identity of an anonymous or pseudonymous author is discovered prior to the end of the work's protection, then the work reverts to the "life of the author plus 70 years" rule.

For works created prior to January 1, 1978, duration is quite difficult to calculate exactly. Suffice it to say that if you need to know the precise duration of a copyright for a pre–January 1, 1978, work, you should discuss it with an attorney who is familiar with the Copyright Act.

Registration and Notice. Throughout most of the existence of the United States, authors were required to register their works with the United States Copyright Office prior to publication, and to place a copyright notice (e.g., "Copyright The Associated Press 2001, All Rights Reserved") on all copies of the work. If the author did not do so, he or she risked placing the work in the public domain. This legal requirement changed with the Copyright Act of 1976 (the current iteration of the copyright law) and subsequent amendments to the 1976 Act. Registration is now only required prior to filing suit for copyright infringement. And notice, while still a very good idea, simply serves the purpose of defeating a claim by an infringer that they were unaware that the author was claiming copyright rights in a work (since copyright law is a strict liability statute, even innocent infringement of a work will result in a finding of liability, but a court may reduce the penalty if it finds the infringement was "innocent").

The primary reason for registering a work with the Copyright Office is simply that if one registers one's work within three months of publication, one may seek statutory damages from an infringer of $750 to $30,000 per work infringed (the court can raise the upper figure to $150,000 if it finds the infringement was willful or lower it to $200 if it finds the infringement was innocent). Statutory damages mean that a copyright owner does not have to prove how much damage he or she sustained by the infringement. In addition, if registration occurs within three months of publication, the copyright owner may seek attorneys' fees from the infringer, which in many cases may be more than the damages awarded.

The United States Copyright Office maintains an excellent Web site on copyright law and copyright registration at www.loc.gov/copyright/.

Fair Use and the Public Domain. A full discussion of the fair use doctrine and the public domain is beyond the scope of this chapter, but a few points may be helpful in understanding copyright rights and the Internet.

Fair use is an important tool that balances the Copyright Act with the

First Amendment. However, the fair use doctrine is probably one of the most misunderstood portions of the Copyright Act. There are a number of myths surrounding the doctrine (e.g., "It's OK to take seven seconds of audio" and "All news uses are 'fair uses'") that are plainly untrue. Furthermore, fair use is an affirmative defense to an allegation of copyright infringement. This means that one is admitting that the actions one has engaged in constitute a copyright infringement, absent the finding of fair use. Finally, fair use can only be established by a court. Simply asserting that the use of something was a fair use will not prevent a lawsuit.

The actual fair use section of the Copyright Act (17 U.S.C. §107) establishes four factors that must be evaluated by a court in determining whether or not something is a "fair use." These factors are: (i) the purpose and character of the use; (ii) the nature of the copyrighted work; (iii) the amount and substantiality of the portion taken; and (iv) the effect of the use on the potential market for the work. The first and fourth factors tend to be the most important. Many courts used to hold the opinion that any commercial use was per se not a fair use. The United States Supreme Court corrected this view in the mid-1990s, but it is still true that commercial use weighs heavily against a finding of fair use. Similarly, any use that substitutes in the marketplace for the original work is unlikely to be found a fair use.

In order to place a copyrighted work into the public domain, the copyright owner must take some affirmative step. Examples of such steps include placing a notice on the work stating that the work has been contributed to the public domain, or otherwise providing a statement that certain works owned by the copyright owner are in the public domain.

Placing items on the Internet does not place them automatically in the public domain. Though the publisher of a Web site may expect individuals to visit his or her Web site for individual/private use, that does not mean that the Web site publisher has licensed commercial use or placed the content on the Web site in the public domain. For example, if a reporter is sitting at home using his or her computer and comes across a news story or photo on the Internet, like any individual, that reporter may, for their personal use, read the story and view the photo, and possibly print out the story and photo. However, that same reporter, sitting in the newsroom, may not be able to engage in the same activities if the purpose is to gather news for his or her job.

One area of public domain works is the United States government. Under the Copyright Act, works created by the United States government are automatically in the public domain. However, if the United States government purchases or is given a copyrighted work, it may maintain that copyright.

Copyright and the Internet

Why Does the Internet Cause Such Concern?

The Internet has been described as one big photocopying machine and it can be used to seriously harm the interests of copyright owners. Early on in the popularization of the Internet, a student used the Internet to allow others to freely distribute copies of commercial software. Such distribution held the potential for great harm to the companies whose software was being distributed. In that particular case, because the student was not engaging in the distribution himself, and because the law as it existed at the time required that the person running the distribution system be doing so for profit in order to have criminal liability attached, the student went unpunished. Congress stepped in and changed the law to allow the prosecution of someone running a similar system.

The advent of the Internet can be seen as a lowering of the barrier to entry of becoming a large-scale copyright infringer. Before the Internet, it required lots of expensive machinery to seriously impact a copyright owner's ability to get revenue from a copyrighted work. For example, to produce sufficient copies of the most recent best-selling novel to harm its legitimate publisher required printing presses and other duplicating technology, as well as reams of paper. Now, a single teenager with access to an unencrypted electronic copy of a novel can send it via the Internet to thousands, if not millions of individuals with the push of a single button (or, more likely, a single click of a mouse).

Are There Any Differences for Copyright on the Internet?

The current Copyright Act is capable of encompassing most uses of copyrighted works on the Internet. However, a number of changes were recently made to the Copyright Act to accommodate certain issues raised by the Internet. The vast majority of these changes concern the liability of Internet service providers over whose systems possible infringements would flow. However, there are a few changes to rights that are worth noting.

Probably the biggest change to the rights available to copyright owners has been the creation of a public performance right for certain digital sound recordings. As noted earlier, the public performance right formerly applied to only musical works (the written words and music), but not to the sound recordings (the actual sounds recorded by an artist). Congress has now created a public performance right for digital sound recordings contained in certain transmissions. A court recently found that a streaming audio signal carried over the Internet containing the music played by a radio station in its over-the-air signal was a public performance of the sound recording for the purposes of the Copyright Act. This decision fell like an unexpected bombshell on the radio industry because although it did not have to pay a public performance royalty for the sound recordings transmitted over its over-the-air broadcast (only for the musical works contained in those sound recordings), it now had to pay a royalty for the public performance over the Internet of both the musical work and the sound recording that contained the musical work.

Another major change has been the introduction of a law that prohibits the circumvention of technological protections for copyrighted works. This new provision means that if an author protects his or her work with some technological scheme (e.g., encryption of DVDs), then the mere act of circumventing the protection scheme is a violation of the author's copyright, possibly even if the circumvention was done to exercise some right that the person circumventing the protection was allowed to exercise. This particular protection is only now being tested in court, and it remains to be seen if the courts will read into the provision some of the rights that users of copyrighted works formerly enjoyed (e.g., fair use).

Finally, in conjunction with the anticircumvention provision, a new portion of the Copyright Act prohibits the changing, removal, or falsification of "copyright management information." It is unclear what exactly is encompassed by "copyright management information" (or "CMI"), but it is possible that it may include the venerable copyright notice discussed earlier. If this is the case, removal, modification, or falsification of this notice could result in liability. However, it is more likely that this provision applies to items such as digital watermarks in image or sound files. Only time and court challenges will tell.

Conclusion

The advent and wide use of the Internet has not significantly changed copyright law, though it has certainly added a few kinks. Generally, if something is a copyright violation in the real world, then it is a copyright violation in cyberspace.

However, there are a handful of issues that remain to be resolved regarding copyrighted works and the Internet. Individuals working on or with the Internet should be familiar with these issues and exercise caution.

INDEX

Locators in boldface indicate pages with figures.